CROSSING ARIZONA

CROSSING ARIZONA

A SOLO HIKE THROUGH THE SKY ISLANDS AND DESERTS OF THE ARIZONA TRAIL

CHRIS TOWNSEND

THE COUNTRYMAN PRESS

WOODSTOCK, VERMONT

Library of Congress Cataloging-in-Publication Data
Townsend, Chris, 1949–
    Crossing Arizona : a solo hike through the sky islands and
deserts of the Arizona Trail / Chris Townsend.—1st ed.
        p. cm.
    Includes bibliographical references.
    ISBN 0-88150-507-2 (alk. paper)
    1. Townsend, Chris, 1949– 2. Hiking—Arizona—Arizona Trail.
I. Title.
GV199.42.A72 A758 2002
917.904'54—dc21   2001042201

Maps by Paul Woodward © 2002 The Countryman Press
Interior and cover photographs by Chris Townsend
Interior and cover design by Deborah Fillion

Published by The Countryman Press
P.O. Box 748, Woodstock, Vermont 05091

Distributed by W. W. Norton & Company, Inc.
500 Fifth Avenue, New York, NY 10110

Printed in the United States of America

10 9 8 7 6 5 4 3 2 1

TO DENISE

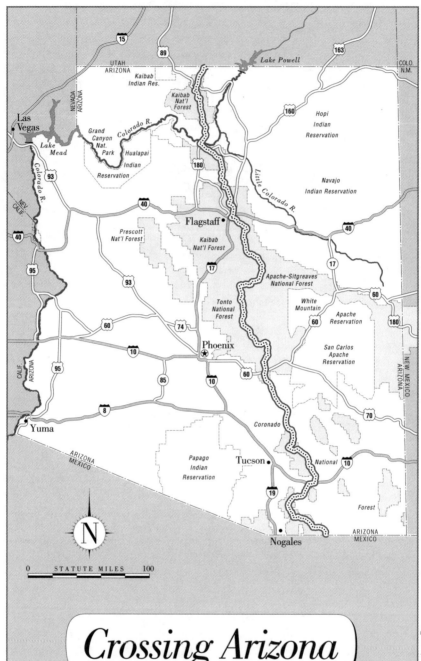

Crossing Arizona

A Solo Hike through the Sky Islands and Deserts of the Arizona Trail

CONTENTS

Acknowledgments   9

1   Inspiration and Organization   *11*

2   Initiation   *21*

3   Sky Islands and Desert Canyons   *37*

4   Across the Sonoran Desert   *71*

5   Superstitions and Mazatzals   *99*

6   Forests and Lakes:
    Across the Mogollon Plateau   *131*

7   In and Out of the Wilderness   *155*

8   The Canyon   *187*

9   Winding Down   *215*

    Afterword   *231*

    Trail Notes   *235*

    Selected Reading   *245*

    Index   *247*

ACKNOWLEDGMENTS

Without the support and help of many people the walk would not have been possible. In particular I'd like to thank the following:

First, Denise Thorn for her love, support, and understanding. It can't be easy having a partner who likes to disappear into the wilderness for months at a time. Denise also read the draft copy of this book and made many corrections and useful suggestions.

My stepdaughter Hazel, who also has to cope with my absences.

Our friends Jane and Andy Smith who provided child care so that Denise could continue to work while I was away.

Karen Berger, Larry Snead, Jim Martin, Bill Watson, and Steve Saway, who provided me with much useful information before the walk. Jim also drove me around so I could place water caches in the Sonoran Desert. Bill provided much welcome support at various places along the way, loaned me his GPS for sections where the trail wasn't built, and gave me somewhere to stay in Phoenix after the walk was over.

All those members of the Arizona Trail Association who have worked so hard to build the trail.

Jake Schas for his companionship when we hiked together.

Paul Leech for his assistance in Oracle and Superior.

Brad, Mark, and Karen Buckhout for returning my first aid kit, not an easy task when they had to trace me via Scotland.

All those friendly people I met along the way—rangers, hikers, store-keepers, motel staff, and many others—who left me with a wonderful impression of Arizona.

David Lynch of Bluedome, who put together web pages on the walk and added my digital photographs to them.

Chris Brasher and Robert Perkins of the Brasher Boot Company for their enthusiastic support and sponsorship and for making the best long distance hiking boots in the world.

Steve Laycock and Perseverance Mills, makers of Pertex, for their support and sponsorship and their excellent fabrics.

Ricoh for supplying their outstanding lightweight cameras.

Craghoppers for their superb shirt, which suffered far more than any shirt deserves to.

Optimus for their exceptional Nova stove.

Kathmandu Trekking for the excellent Basha-Tent.

Kermit Hummel and Ann Kraybill of the Countryman Press for believing in this book and seeing it through to publication.

1

Inspiration and Organization

Rain. Streaming past the windows as the big jet lumbered down toward the runway, pouring out of the dull gray swirling clouds, spreading out across the dull gray concrete of the airport in thin rivulets and lifeless pools. Rain and grayness. A monochrome world bereft of color and warmth. This was not how I had imagined my arrival in Arizona. Phoenix was meant to be hot, sunny, Southwestern. A city shimmering with heat.

The rain had a strange effect on me; a very strange effect given that one reason I was here was for the sun, for a contrast to the wet climate of home. I felt very happy. No—that's too mild. I felt deliriously happy, ecstatic, bursting with joy. I blessed the rain. I thanked the storm gods. As I entered the blasting warmth and noise of the terminal and joined the lines to show my passport, collect my luggage, and explain I didn't have fresh food or any other illegal items, my mind was away in the storm clouds, willing the downpour to continue, hoping for it to become heavier, more torrential, for the rain to fill up the creeks and pools in the wilds beyond the city, for the storm to dump snow in the mountains. Days of tension melted away. The feeling of relief was immense. I needed this rain.

"It has been very dry in Arizona this past six months. Most all of the springs and water catchments are dry."

In the weeks leading up to my departure for Phoenix a stream of e-mails warned that the weather was unusually warm and dry even for Arizona. This information was initially no more than a little worrying, but as the start of my walk came closer and the situation didn't change the reality loomed larger and larger. I was coming from wet and cool Scotland to hike through the deserts and mountains of Arizona. I'd chosen spring for my journey because it shouldn't be too hot and there should be some water available, plus snow in the mountains. But this year neither had arrived. Larry Snead, executive director of the Arizona Trail Association, who was the source of the e-mails, suggested I rent a truck and cache water along my route. I knew without even considering it that I really didn't want to. Seeing much of the country I would be hiking through in advance, even from a pickup, would take away some of the excitement, some of the feelings of discovery from my walk. But as my departure date drew nearer and Arizona remained dry I knew I might have no choice. In the only account I had found of a hike similar to the one I was planning the author described using his pickup to cache water and supplies. Maybe that would be the only way.

For several months before starting out I followed Arizona weather on the Internet. Storm track after storm track passed to the north. The forecast was always dry and hot. Then, just a few days before my departure, as I was wondering just how long it would take to put out caches by truck and how much it would cost, the forecasters spotted a big storm moving in toward Arizona. There was excitement on the Arizona weather web sites, hardly surprising after six months without anything happening and with a severe drought in progress, and excitement in Scotland too, at least for one person. Everyone else was hoping our very wet winter would soon come to an end. I was possibly the only person in the whole country thinking about Arizona, let alone more interested in the weather there than in Scotland.

The storm broke just before I arrived in Arizona. Truly perfect timing. Escaping from Phoenix by shuttle bus I stared at the wet roads, the wet desert, the wet cacti as we sped down Interstate 10 to Tucson, spray flying up all around. Out to the east the clouds covered all but the feet of the various mountain ranges. I was happy not to see them. The rain and snow falling from those clouds would keep me alive for at least the first few weeks of my walk. They meant I could forget about trucks, water caches, backbreaking loads.

In Tucson, the city nearest to the start of the trail and my base for a couple of days of hectic planning, I spent a day walking around in the rain collecting supplies—maps, food for the first week, other bits and pieces—and doing last-minute chores. The roads were sheets of water, the sidewalks awash. There was an incredible roar of falling water. It took me a short while to place the noise. Then I realized it was caused by water pouring in great sheets off the flat-roofed buildings. No rain gutters here. It was the only time on the entire trip that I wore my rain jacket all day.

Why Arizona though? Why the heat, the lack of water, the desert? And why travel on foot?

To start with the last, because walking is my passion. Because I find walking the ideal way to discover a place, to explore it and learn a little about what is there and how it works, to become absorbed in it, to feel it, be part of it, know it beyond the superficialities of facts and figures. I especially love long distance walks, ones long enough to become my life, to become what I do. Walking day after day, week after week, and camping out at night is, in my view, the way to really experience nature in all its aspects.

I am also passionate about wild places, about wilderness, about nature, whether mountain or desert, forest or tundra. My desire to go for a long walk in the desert Southwest had been growing for many years. In part that longing had been inspired by the works of Colin Fletcher and Edward Abbey, two of the writers who have influenced me most. I wanted to explore the landscapes that inspired them. Their words, their shadowy presence, would be with me many times in the weeks to come. I wanted to experience the desert and try to come to some understanding of its nature, to feel what life was like there. Not that I was a desert novice. I'd hiked for weeks through desert and semidesert lands in southern California on the Pacific Crest Trail and in New Mexico on the Continental Divide Trail. But these had been small parts of much bigger walks, and I felt that though I'd walked through the desert I hadn't connected with it, hadn't felt any sort of rapport or closeness. A two-week hike in the Grand Canyon had revealed something about desert canyons, but the time was too short for more than a brief glimpse. The desert remained an alien place, a place I didn't understand or even know how to understand. Maybe I never would, but I felt that a walk with the desert at its heart was the most likely way to learn something.

After the Grand Canyon trip I knew I wanted to spend much more time in the Southwest and go for a much longer walk. I planned several, with no idea how feasible they were or what would be involved. One idea kept coming back. Standing on the North Rim of the Grand Canyon I had stared south across a vast dark forest to distant mountains, the San Francisco Peaks. What would it be like to walk to those summits from the Canyon?

I did no more than ask questions, think vague thoughts, and make vague plans until I discovered the existence of the Arizona Trail. When complete, this trail will run for around eight hundred miles, from the Mexican border to Utah, linking the San Francisco Peaks and the Grand Canyon en route. The existence of a trail along a large part of the route (it was around 70 percent complete at the time of my walk) would make planning, and probably hiking, much easier. At the same time, because it was a new trail, incomplete in places, often unsigned, and without the infrastructure that comes with popularity, hiking would still be an adventure, would still involve an element of exploration and discovery. The more I learned the more excited I felt. It seemed to exactly fit my aims and wishes.

Arizona, as everyone knows (always a dangerous phrase), is a desert state, so I expected the trail would be mostly in desert country. (Actual estimates as to how much of the state is desert range from 40 to 65 percent.) As I don't like knowing too much about new places I'm going to walk through, I didn't do much research into the nature of the terrain. I prefer to learn when I'm there, entering with an open mind rather than preconceived views, so although I read a little about the lands the Arizona Trail traverses and somewhat more about the logistics of the walk, I started the trail without that much knowledge of what lay ahead. Despite my intentions I did have one fixed idea, an idea reinforced by the little I'd read, and that was that traveling the Arizona Trail is basically a walk in the desert. I was to discover that it is much more.

Since 1994 the Arizona Trail has had its own organization, the Arizona Trail Association (ATA), a dedicated group of people who have put great effort into planning the trail and ensuring that it is built and maintained. The first thoughts of a statewide trail began many years earlier, however, the inspiration of one man, Dale Shewalter, a teacher in Flagstaff. He came up with the idea in the 1970s, then started to work out a route in 1985 when he hiked from Nogales, on the Mexican border, to Utah. The resulting trail, developed over the years since Shewalter's exploratory walk, runs through a corridor of mostly federal land (around 70 percent managed by the Forest Service, the rest by the National Park Service and Bureau of Land Management) that runs down the center of Arizona, leaving only small areas of private land for which access permission had to be obtained.

Planning my hike was fairly straightforward, as the ATA publishes planning sheets for completed sections (called passages) of the trail; a trail guide to the same sections was published in 1998. There were long sections where all I had were maps and a rough idea of the proposed route, but this just added interest. Working out where I could resupply with food and how far it was between these points were all the logistics I needed or wanted. Rigid itineraries, ones in which you know how far you'll walk every day, where you'll be every night, and just what to expect along the way are not for me.

The big unknown was, of course, water. The whereabouts of creeks and pools and how much water I would have to carry couldn't be planned in advance, as water availability is dependent on how much precipitation there has been in the immediate past. Few sources are always reliable. ATA members Bill Watson and Steve Saway provided lists of possible sources, but I knew that I couldn't assume there would be water in many of them. As Larry Snead told me, water could be there one day and gone the next. Being prepared to carry several gallons of water and collecting what up-to-date information I could was all the planning that was possible. Perhaps the most important advice came from long distance hiker and backpacking writer Karen Berger, who had hiked the trail in two sections and written a feature on it for the May 1997 issue of *Backpacker* magazine. "Always be thinking about water," Karen e-mailed. She also told me that she and her husband had found more than they expected, which was reassuring, especially as she had hiked part of the trail in May and June, when it is generally hotter and drier than earlier in the spring, when I would be on the trail. I was starting in early March and planned to finish by early May, before the heat really began to build up.

In Tucson it was hard not to think about water as the rain crashed down all around. Even in this sprawling city walking was interesting. Among the concrete and the freeways there were still some old Spanish-style buildings. By exploring much of the city on foot I also discovered places that I would probably have missed in a vehicle, like a good natural-food store where I bought most of my food for the first week and an Audubon Society bookstore where I bought a natural history guide to the Southwest that I carried for the whole walk, it was so useful. Tucson was too big to walk everywhere I needed to go, however. A taxi was required and here my hotel came up with a gem in Donna's Transportation, a one-woman taxi company. Donna had been driving taxis in Tucson for many years and knew where everything was, taking me to outdoor sporting goods stores and map shops, and providing masses of information about the city. "I used to drive for Yellow Taxis," she told me, "but I got to dislike taking drunks home late at night. Now that I work for myself I only work in daylight." Startled when I revealed my plans, Donna warned me about illegal immigrants from Mexico. "You don't want to walk alone near the border," she said.

This was a warning I was to hear from others. It wasn't new. I'd been told the same when setting out on the Pacific Crest Trail in California eighteen years earlier. After two days I left Tucson on a shuttle for the start of the walk. Angel Transport only charged $45, which seemed a bargain. I don't think they realized exactly where I was going, a remote spot on an unpaved road far from any town. The driver was late and turned up looking somewhat tired. She warned me about the dangerous "illegals." "I wouldn't hike down there." I was more worried about her fast, somewhat erratic driving on the busy interstate. Large quantities of coffee kept her awake. I was relieved when the route left I-10 and another driver met us to take me the rest of the way. Mike from Sierra Vista was fully awake and much more relaxed. He was retired but said he'd taken up shuttle and taxi driving "because I was getting bored." He didn't think I'd have any trouble with migrants. "They don't go up into the mountains and they don't want to be seen," he said, "and you're starting out in a national monument where there are rangers." Mike didn't think the migrants were dangerous anyway and said he thought the vast amounts of money and time spent on trying to stop them crossing the border were a waste. "I'd let them come in, we need their labor anyway," he said.

Mike had spent years in Africa and Europe. He told me stories of the African savanna, of close encounters with lions and other wildlife while I stared out at the desert terrain, as strange to me as Africa had been to him.

The storm had cleared now and as we drove south I could see snow high on the sides of forested mountains. Below the mountains undulating desert stretched out, pale and hazy. Mike pointed out a large, tethered, silver, torpedo-shaped balloon high in the sky on the edge of the mountains. That's for watching for migrants, he told me. I was more interested in the mountains it hung above, mountains I'd be hiking through in only a few hours. The snow didn't look too deep from down here, just a dusting. Enough, I hoped, to provide water for a while but not so much that walking was difficult.

A dusty dirt road led the last miles to the Coronado National Memorial Visitor Center, a low, red-roofed building set in a mix of big trees and yuccas with the rocky slopes of the Huachuca Mountains rising behind it. I heaved my pack out of the van. From now on I would be walking. This wasn't quite the nearest road access to the trail, but a phone call with a ranger the day before had produced the information that the road over Montezuma Pass, which the trail crossed, was closed because of snow and ice. This was hard to believe, as here it was hot and sunny. The pass is 1,400 feet higher than the visitors center, however, and the road to it is steep. Even so, when I reached the pass later in the day there were cars and little sign of snow. It waited higher up, as I would discover. The visitors center was, anyway, a fine, scenic spot to start the walk.

Before starting out I wandered inside to find out a little about who Coronado was and why this area was named after him. His full name was Francisco Vasquez de Coronado and he'd come to Mexico from Spain in 1535, just sixteen years after Cortez conquered Mexico and forty-three

The start at the Mexican border.

years after Columbus reached America. Fame came in 1540 when he led an expedition into the Northern Mystery, as the Spanish evocatively called the unknown lands beyond Mexico, in search of the legendary (and illusory) Seven Cities of Cibola, reputedly full of riches. With a huge entourage—three hundred Spaniards, more than a thousand Native Americans, and fifteen hundred stock animals—Coronado headed into what is now Arizona and then on north and east as far as Kansas. However, instead of the wealthy cities he had hoped for all he found were villages with inhabitants who were often hostile. After two years he returned to Mexico disappointed, without the fortune he had set out to find. It was a major venture and an amazing journey though, and opened up the Southwest for further exploration.

The Coronado National Memorial lies in the Huachuca Mountains, which rise to more than 9,000 feet, but Coronado wouldn't have come this way. Why march over a small but steep mountain range when he could go around it? That sort of lunacy is left to modern-day hikers. Coronado probably traveled up the San Pedro River Valley just to the east of the Huachucas. My route ran along the mountain crests in the Miller Peak Wilderness. But first, I wanted to walk the few miles south to the Mexican border.

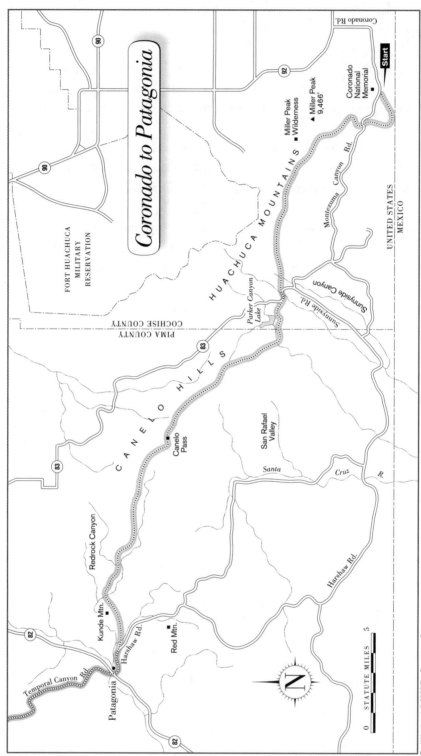

Coronado to Patagonia

Start

Coronado Rd.

90

92

Miller Peak
Wilderness

▲ Miller Peak
9,466'

■ Coronado
National
Memorial

90

Montezuma Canyon Rd.

FORT HUACHUCA
MILITARY
RESERVATION

H U A C H U C A   M O U N T A I N S

UNITED STATES
MEXICO

COCHISE COUNTY
PIMA COUNTY

Parker Canyon
Lake

Sunnyside Canyon

Sunnyside Rd.

83

C A N E L O   H I L L S

San Rafael
Valley

■ Canelo
Pass

Santa   Cruz   R.

83

Redrock Canyon

Harshaw Rd.

Kunde Mtn. ■

Harshaw Rd.

■ Red Mtn.

82

Temporal Canyon Rd.

Patagonia

82

N

0   STATUTE MILES   5

Paul Woodward, © 2002 The Countryman Press

2
Initiation

CORONADO TO PATAGONIA

58 miles

Shouldering my pack, heavy with a gallon of water as well as all my gear, I turned away from the cool of the buildings and strode out into the hot sunshine and on to a narrow path signed JOE'S CANYON TRAIL. It was almost midday. Widely spaced small trees, scrubby bushes, and spiky yucca plants dotted the red and gold stony slopes that rose to peaks of shattered rocks on either side. Soon the road and the buildings vanished and I was alone in the desert. The walk had begun. I felt excited but also a little unreal. The break from urban life, from planes, freeways, hotels, cities, shuttles, communications, was too sudden. Although I knew this was the start of a long journey, that I would now be living in the wilds for weeks, it didn't mean anything; I didn't feel it inside me. It would take several days before I shrugged off the constraints and limitations of "normal" life and started to live in the present, to relax. I knew too that it would take time to slip into the simple rhythm of walking and camping and shrug off the worries and concerns about life outside the wilds. It would happen though; I knew that from previous long walks. For now it was enough to have begun.

Joe's Canyon Trail led up a shallow canyon to Yaqui Ridge, a long spur of rocky desert stretching down from the Huachuca Mountains into Mexico. Here I joined the Arizona Trail as it wound around a hillside and down the ridge to the barbed wire fence and the concrete pillar, Monument 102, that marked the border. To the south Mexico stretched out, vast desert flatlands dotted with isolated mountains, the pyramid of San José Peak being the most prominent. There was a sense of space and lightness, a sharpness and clarity in the views, a cleanliness to the air and the ground that I was soon to learn were typical of the desert.

Looking south into Mexico from Yaqui Ridge near the start of the trail.

Turning away from Mexico I headed northward back up the trail. Day hikers were wandering down from Montezuma Pass, the last people I would see for two days. Soon after crossing the road at the pass, where a large, ornate signboard showed the route of the Arizona Trail, I entered the Miller Peak Wilderness and headed up the southern ridge of Miller Peak itself on the Crest Trail. From the Mexican border the trail climbs steadily for more than six miles, one of the most grueling starts to a long distance trail I've done. The open desert gave way to the thickets of small bushes known as chaparral and then to small trees—piñon pine, juniper, and oak—and finally to large conifers. The first snow appeared, just small patches at first but soon a covering up to a foot deep. Plodding upward through this was difficult and slow, and day soon began to vanish into dusk. Big pines and tall blocks of pale rock loomed on either side. There was a fine red sunset over Mexico, but I was not in the mood to appreciate it. The first water on the trail lay on the crest of the mountains a mile and a half beyond the top of the climb. That had been my goal, but with snow all around I didn't need water. However, the narrow ridge meant there was nowhere to camp. Nowhere I could see in the growing darkness anyway, so I had to keep going.

The line of snow that was the trail would have been hard to follow except that someone had been here before. The half filled-in indentations of boot prints marked the route, just enough of them remaining for me to follow. In the dark the snow still stood out but everything else was a solid black. I needed a light to identify objects and, in places, search for the trail when it changed direction. Not having planned on hiking in the dark my small headlamp was buried deep in my pack. I didn't want to lose time by taking the pack off and searching for it so I used a tiny LED flashlight I carry as a backup that happened to be in a pants pocket. It shone only when the switch was pressed and gave a weak blue light. It was just enough though to check the line of the trail and illuminate the occasional black spot to tell whether it was a rock or tree stump. Mostly I could see well enough without it.

The climb finally over I followed the trail along an invisible ridge past the high point of the Huachucas, 9,466-foot Miller Peak. Hiking in the dark on an unknown trail is strangely hypnotic. Nothing seems to change as you put one foot in front of the other again and again. I was in quite a dreamlike state when I suddenly saw an old bathtub sitting on the snow in front of me. It was quite surreal even though I was expecting it, as this was the first water on the trail, Bathtub Spring. The tub was full and frozen with just a trickle of water coming out of the spout that fed it.

I pushed on, more interested in a campsite than water, to stop on a broad wooded saddle not far away. A gusty cold wind swept over the ridge, and as soon as I stopped I started to shiver and became aware that my boots and pant legs were soaked. I quickly stamped out a platform in the soft snow, pitched my large, square nylon tarp, and heaped snow around the edges to keep the wind out. Once under cover I stripped off my sodden socks and boots, pulled on dry socks, and stuck my cold legs into my sleeping bag. A fleece pullover and down vest went on my top half. I fired up the stove, its roar shattering the quiet of the forest but welcome nonetheless, and started to melt snow. Soon I had hot drink and food inside me and was feeling warm and comfortable even if somewhat surprised. This was not how I had expected the first day to end. Even though I knew that snow had fallen in the mountains, I hadn't thought about the effect this would have on hiking and camping as well as water supply. I'd been so concerned about heat and lack of water in the buildup to the walk that I hadn't managed to shake this off and adjust to the new situation.

At 8,800 feet this first camp was to be one of the highest on the walk. It was also the only time I camped on snow. I fell asleep just after midnight. The day had been hard. I'd hiked eleven miles and ascended 4,880 feet in nine hours, too much for the first day out with a heavy pack, especially as I wasn't fully trail fit and wouldn't be for a week or more. Despite all my plans I hadn't managed to do quite as much hiking in the months preceding the walk as I'd hoped. Work, phone calls, e-mails, and a million loose ends had, as always, taken more time than expected.

I felt quite empty as I lay in my sleeping bag. I should, I thought, be glad to be here, but all I felt was relief that I'd stopped hiking. Also, where was here? Any views had disappeared hours before I made camp so all I had was a vague impression of big trees around me and open space beyond.

Dawn changed everything. I was awoken by the sun shining on my face through the open end of the tarp. Birds were singing loudly all around. A woodpecker drummed nearby. The snow sparkled, the sky was deep blue, the trees—ponderosa pines—glowed in the sunshine, their deeply furrowed bark red-gold, their bunches of long needles brilliant green. Just a few steps away from my camp the mountainside fell away,

Morning at the first camp in the Miller Peak Wilderness.

the wooded slopes dropping steeply to the pale gold desert that stretched away to the horizon. By chance I had found a beautiful and spectacular campsite.

Staring out over the desert I had my first understanding of the term "sky islands" that is so often used for the small but very steep mountain ranges that rise abruptly out of the southern Arizona desert. Standing here on the crest of the Huachucas did feel very like being on an island of green in a desert sea. Sky islands are typical of basin and range country, which consists of low, flat desert valleys and steep, narrow, long, straight mountain ranges, and which covers most of southern Arizona.

According to many writers, climbing from the desert to the mountain summits in Arizona means passing through so many habitats that it's equivalent to traveling from Mexico to Canada. What this means is that the type of environment found at low elevations in Canada occurs at high elevations in Arizona. And that environment is a conifer forest.

From my camp high on the crest of the Huachucas I could see the succession of habitats. Far below and far away was the hot, arid Sonoran Desert, which rises to 3,500–4,000 feet. Next, up to 5,000 feet, came semi-desert grasslands dotted with cacti and small shrubs followed by semi-desert woods of piñon-juniper-oak forest to 7,000 feet. Finally there was subalpine forest with tall pines and firs, which is where I was. (Above 11,000 feet alpine tundra is found, but only one small mountain range in the north of the state, the San Francisco Peaks, reaches this height.) The elevations are only approximate, of course, and the different habitats merge gradually into one another. Location matters, too. In shaded, north-facing canyons big pines and firs grow at quite low elevations while on sunny, exposed slopes yuccas and cacti grow high in the mountains. I was to become used to seeing cacti and firs growing within yards of each other.

The higher the elevation, the cooler the weather and the more rain and snow, resulting in more and bigger trees. The largest forests in southern Arizona are on the tops of the mountains. As you ascend the vegetation becomes thicker and taller and there are fewer views, the reverse of what is usual in other mountain regions. In Arizona the most open landscapes and widespread views lie at the feet of the mountains, not on their summits.

From contemplating the nature of the environment I went to considering the state of my boots. They were frozen solid. A short time in the sun thawed them enough for me to force my feet inside. This felt most unpleasant and my feet were soon very cold. The weather was hot and sunny though, and later in the day I expected to be below the snowline where my boots could begin to dry. Until then I would just have to put up with this unexpected discomfort.

My digital camera didn't like the cold either and refused to work, so it too sat in the sun with the batteries removed and placed on the black camera case so they could absorb the heat. This would become a morning ritual.

Before breaking camp I hiked down to Bathtub Spring, surprised at how steep the slope was and how deep the snow, to collect some water and take some photographs. Three quarts would be enough, I decided, as the rain and snow should means creeks would be flowing lower down while up here there was snow to melt.

The first part of the day's walk was a mixture of pain and pleasure. For more than an hour I followed the crest of the mountains. Magnificent ponderosas and Douglas fir lined the trail while agaves, looking strange with their thick, fleshy bayonet-shaped leaves covered with snow, grew in open areas. Granite blocks and pillars rose out of the forest. Beyond the mountains the desert shone. Ravens soared overhead. I was to see these birds almost every day of the walk. I watched them wheel effortlessly across the rich blue sky. How wonderful to travel so easily. My progress was slow and arduous, a cumbersome slog through the deep snow. The trail was narrow and on very steep slopes in places, making me glad of my hiking poles and the dense vegetation, which would break a slip, though I hoped it wouldn't be the sharp pointed leaves of a yucca that I slid into. My feet were cold and wet and my legs ached with the effort of lifting them high out of the snow at each step, a method of locomotion known appropriately as postholing. At the same time my shirt was soaked with sweat and I felt very hot from the waist up.

After several hours I reached a trail junction and left the aptly named Crest Trail for a welcome descent into Sunnyside Canyon, welcome because it would take me out of the snow. Out to the west lay the open wooded Canelo Hills with the dark splash of artificial Parker Canyon Lake among them.

Steep switchbacks, awkward in the snow, led rapidly downward. Soon the snow thinned and faded away and I was walking on dry ground. My boots steamed in the hot sun. Sunnyside Creek wasn't flowing but there were many large pools in the creek bed. I drank deeply from one of these as I had a headache and my urine was dark yellow. These signs of dehydration within twenty-four hours of starting the walk were an early warning that I would have to drink much more than I was used to.

Leaving the Miller Peak Wilderness and the subalpine forest I entered parkland-like open woodlands of piñon pine, oak, and juniper. I was down in the foothills, having crossed the Huachucas in a day and a half. Red-barked madrone and manzanita bushes dotted the grasslands. A flock of pale mourning doves flitted from tree to tree. Across a dirt road and a large parking area with corrals beside it lay Scotia Canyon, a relaxing, pleasant valley shaded by large sycamores, oaks, and junipers. Again, the creek bed was full of pools. As I descended into the canyon I noticed something moving in the bushes nearby. Two dark, humpbacked, hairy piglike animals appeared snorting and snuffling. Collared peccaries or javelinas, said my field guide, adding that "families with young may charge aggressive humans," which was hardly surprising. I didn't feel aggressive, though I had when postholing through the snow. I was just pleased and excited to have a close-up view of these animals, which live in the desert and semidesert grasslands.

Camp was under a big alligator juniper in Scotia Canyon. Setting it up consisted of throwing down my foam pad and then my sleeping bag. My pack leaned against the tree for a good backrest. As the day ended the stars slowly appeared and a bright, fat crescent moon rose into the black sky. Two javelinas snuffled past, dark bulky shadows against the pale, moonlit ground. The contrast with the previous night was huge, both in the situation and in my mood. No snow or wind here, just a quiet wooded valley. No feelings of emptiness either. This was a night to enjoy.

The next two days were spent ambling for thirty miles through the gentle, rolling Canelo Hills. After the hard trekking in the Huachucas it really did feel easy. The trail wound through hills, down canyons, and across open, savanna-like meadows. Back to the east the Huachucas rose, their slopes a mix of green and white, forest and snow. As I passed below Parker Canyon Lake, built by the Forest Service for fishing and boating, and began the descent into Parker Canyon I met a tall, clean-shaven man dressed in cloth boots, blue jeans, camouflage sweatshirt, camouflage hat, and check shirt. Water bottles hung on his belt, large binoculars were slung around his neck, a tiny daypack rested on his back, and the butt of a gun protruded from a hip pocket. "Hi, how far are you hiking?"

Semidesert grasslands and pinyon pine–juniper woodland in the Canelo Hills, March 12.

"I'm hoping to hike the whole Arizona Trail," I said, feeling that even to hope it was a little presumptuous on my second day out. Jeff was hiking the trail too, only in a series of day hikes whenever he had a free day from his job as a policeman in Tucson. He reckoned it would take five years. Today he was going to the next road crossing at Canelo Pass where his wife would meet him. "If you need water there's five gallons in the truck. Just come on over when you get there."

Much of the walking in the Canelo Hills was pleasant but undramatic, just open woodland and undulating grassy hills. When the views did open up, however, they were tremendous and exciting. To the south lay Mexico, stretching palely to the horizon, to the west the grasslands of the San Rafael Valley. The Huachucas stretched out in a long line behind me. Ahead rose the Santa Rita Mountains with the snow-capped cone of Mount Wrightson dominant. I would be there in a few days. Other more distant sky islands, long strips of jagged gray, rose out of the desert, the Dragon Mountains, the Whetstones, and more.

Much closer by a small flock of blue-colored jays, probably western scrub jays, sped noisily across the trail and vanished into the trees. Beautiful orange sulfur butterflies floated through the meadows. A bird of prey soared high overhead—most likely a red-tailed hawk. Small cacti grew in sunny places, and I had my first experience of how painful their spines could be when I put my hand on some fallen ones at a rest stop below a small cliff. Looking up I could see a desiccated prickly pear cactus hanging over the cliff's top. My hand looked like a pincushion. I plucked the tiny spines out with the tweezers on my Swiss Army knife and made a mental note to be more careful where I put my hands and where I sat—pulling spines out of my backside wouldn't be so easy.

In places the route followed old dirt roads. I was climbing up one of these, a very rutted, long-abandoned-looking road when a pickup appeared, descending precariously. I quickly stepped off the trail and stood well back in the bushes. The engine noise slowed. I waited then stepped back on to the road. The pickup eased forward. The driver leaned out. "We only caught a glimpse of your pack," he said. "We thought it was a horse's tail!"

As I'd expected there was water in just about every canyon, so when I came upon my first dirt tank I didn't have to take water from it. Dirt tanks are depressions in the ground, often in the bed of a dry creek or a low meadow. Some are natural, some natural but enhanced by being dug out and walled with earth, while others are manmade, built to provide water for livestock and wildlife. I was glad I could pass this one by as it was pretty murky and the earthen shore had been trampled by numerous cows. In fact, because I didn't know how much water lay ahead I carried too much most of the time, at one point hauling a gallon over a high saddle only to find a pool of clear water on the far side.

Another night was spent under an alligator juniper, its bark split deeply into squares, hence the name. I woke to frost on my sleeping bag and a temperature of twenty-four degrees Fahrenheit. Tiny bridled titmice darted through the bushes around camp, calling harshly. With their little crests and dull plumage they reminded me of the crested tits of home.

By early afternoon it was eight-two degrees in the shade. For me, used to the cool climate of the Scottish Highlands, this was exhaustingly hot. I would need time to acclimatize to such temperatures. My feet, soft and sore after the soakings of the previous two days, felt hot and swollen in my boots so I hiked in sandals. I was now in the West Canelo Hills, which were drier, dustier, and more desertlike than the East Canelo Hills the other side of Canelo Pass. That meant less shelter and less water so the heat was much more noticeable. There were fewer trees and more cacti, including the first cholla, an attractive, soft-looking, almost fluffy, treelike cacti. The appearance is deceptive. The fluff is in fact a dense mass of sharp barbed spines. The joints covered with these spines break off very easily and attach themselves to passing animals or hikers. They also fall and lie on the ground, waiting to catch your shoes, socks, and pants. I quickly learned to be especially careful in cholla country when wearing sandals and shorts. There were also plenty of prickly pear cacti, with their flat pancakelike joints. I'd already learned to avoid these.

Cacti aren't the only spiky plants in desert and semidesert areas, they're just the most noticeable, along with agaves and yuccas, most of which have sharp points on their leaves and often along the sides too, though these are easily avoided. Much more insidious are thorn bushes of various sorts, as it's easy to miss seeing the thorns and brush against them. They form dense thickets, unlike the cacti. Avoiding contact with any plant unless absolutely necessary soon became an automatic habit. In the desert assuming that a plant can probably draw blood is wise. Here in the West Canelo Hills I came across whitethorn, which has curved, hooklike thorns, and soon learned why it's called the wait-a-minute bush. Also present were mesquite bushes, less clinging but still sharp and spiky.

This is cattle country, and although there was some water in dirt tanks and creek beds it looked distinctly unappetizing and I passed it by. At Cott Tank Enclosure, Redrock Canyon was fenced in to protect the riparian environment from grazing, trampling, and cow dung so I took a little water from there. Further down the canyon I reached a full stock tank at Red Bank Well. Large, sickly white, bloated frogs floated dead in the water, which was slimy with green algae. But it was probably the last source for twelve miles. Neither Steve Saway or Bill Watson, whose lists of possible water sources I was carrying with me, mentioned any other water, and the map didn't show any likely places either. A float bobbed at one end of the tank. I pressed it and was delighted when fresh cool water poured out of the inlet pipe. Given the hot sun, lack of shade, and distance to the next water source I filled up a gallon. I'd already learned just how fast dehydration could begin in this hot, dry climate.

A windmill stood near the stock tank by some large oak trees. Across the valley rose the vivid cliff of red rock that gives the canyon and the well their names. It would have been an attractive spot but for the ground, which was hard-baked dirt, grazed bare by cattle and covered with dung. Small puffs of dirty dust marked every footfall. There were several large corrals, and cow paths radiated in every direction, making trail-finding difficult. A sticker on a wooden post called for the removal of cows from public lands.

Beyond Red Bank Well the trail traversed rocky slopes above protected, environmentally sensitive Gate Spring. Three mountain bikers, carrying their bikes, appeared coming toward me. They were heading for Canelo Pass and then, possibly, returning the same way. They confirmed there was no water between here and the town of Patagonia, where I hoped to be that evening, making me glad I was carrying so much in spite of its weight.

As I neared the western edge of the Canelo Hills they became more rugged and mountainous with distinctive, steep-sided peaks—North Saddle, Native American Head, and Kunde Mountains—rather different from the rounded bumps found farther east. Most of the terrain was open and dry with scattered mesquite trees and cacti. Huge patches of bright yellow lichen decorated the rocks in places. The broad north face of North Saddle Mountain was covered by a thick forest, however, which stood out dark and green against the pale brown slopes all around.There is gold, silver, copper, and lead in these hills and many old mines, some named on the map—Sansimon, Santa Cruz, Elevation, Aztec, and the unusual Christmas Gift.

The rocky trail was hard on my now-tender, snow-softened feet as I descended steeply to gravel Harshaw Road but the three miles of road walking that followed were even worse. It led through a scattering of houses and into the little town of Patagonia, situated at 4,044 feet in the Sonoita Valley, and my first supply point. I'd only walked fifty-eight miles, but the first section of my journey was complete and I felt I had truly begun. My feet certainly knew they had and were in need of a rest. I checked into a hotel, the only accommodation near the center I could find, for two nights.

My first port of call after dumping my pack in my room was the post office. Here I collected the running supply box that I had mailed from Tucson. It contained maps, film, repair items, spare food, and other bits and pieces, plus a set of clean clothes and some toiletry items. During the walk the box went on ahead to the next post office, its contents slowly dwindling as maps and other items were removed for the next section and then sent home when no longer needed. Back at the hotel I showered and changed into clean clothes. I was now fit to go out and eat.

Examining my feet in the shower I discovered a blister in the soft puckered skin. Immediately afterward I discovered I'd lost my first aid kit. As I hadn't used it yet this was a puzzle. I was sure I'd packed it. All I could do was assemble another one from what I could find in local stores. I didn't expect ever to find out what had happened to my original kit, let alone see it again, yet this was to happen much later in the walk. And not because it was lurking at the bottom of my pack or hidden in a pocket somewhere.

Patagonia is a pleasant little town with, purely from my point of view, one great attraction. All the facilities I needed—post office, grocery stores, bookstore, restaurants, laundry, library—were within easy walking distance of each other. At the time I didn't realize that this was quite unusual. In retrospect Patagonia was to seem an even better trail town. It is quite small, with a population of under one thousand, but has some interesting stores, including neat little Mariposa Books, where I managed to keep my purchases down to just a few volumes despite great temptation, and a natural-food store where I stocked up on couscous, mac'n'cheese, muesli, fruit leathers, trail mix, cookies, Bear Valley Meal Pack bars (my favorite snack and lunch food), Clif Bars, and even some very tasty non-meat jerky.

Patagonia used to be a railroad town, situated on the line that was built in 1882 between Benson and Nogales; it closed in 1962. The depot is now the town hall and the old railroad yard a park, complete with butterfly garden. The name comes from the Patagonia Silver Mine, which opened in 1858, though the town wasn't founded until forty years later. Mining ended long before the railroad but ranching has lasted and is a major business.

Unlike many small towns Patagonia has retained an identity and charm of its own; the newer buildings were built in a style that fits with the older ones. There are few of the soulless boxes so common elsewhere. There's a dearth of the all-too-familiar large, glaringly bright logos advertising generic businesses. Overall, the feeling was one of relaxation and slowness, a bit of a backwater away from the hustle and noise of a more driven world. This fitted well with the wild country on either side. I liked Patagonia.

My rest day was spent doing the usual chores—eating, laundry (it's surprising how dirty clothes can get in four days of hot, sweaty hiking), shopping, eating, writing letters and journal, phone calls, eating, planning the next section of the walk, eating. Four days wasn't quite enough to have built up a really big appetite, but I still welcomed fresh food rather than dried rations and based myself in a restaurant, snacking throughout the day with meals in between.

I was delighted to discover I could send and receive e-mails at the library, a facility I'd never had on previous long walks and which made communication with home and the outside world (or at least that part of it that had my portable e-mail address) much easier. Being able to send trail reports back to a magazine in the U.K. that was covering the walk and answer e-mails from friends and family made the world seem small, yet just two days before I had felt quite isolated up in the Huachuca Mountains in the snow. Even though I could now phone or e-mail all over the world, up there I had been alone. No one else had even known where I was. Awareness of that and that it would take several hours or more to descend made the Huachucas seem large, never mind the world. I knew I could have had a phone up in the mountains and e-mail access, too, if I'd wanted either and been prepared to carry the gear. I'd have still been alone though. Having others know where I was, or being able to talk to them would not, could not, protect against the cold and the wind, make for a comfortable camp, make the walking in the snow easier, ensure I wouldn't slip, or change any of the other aspects of the physical reality of being in the mountains.

Phone calls produced a date for the weeks ahead and the promise of an umbrella. The date was with Jim Martin in the town of Oracle in eleven days' time. Jim was a member of the Arizona Trail Association with responsibility for the section north of Oracle, the lowest in elevation on the whole trail and therefore the hottest and driest. Before the walk Jim had e-mailed to say there wasn't any water in this area and had offered to drive me around to leave water caches. Now I knew when I could take him up on his offer. This was the one place where I accepted that I would need water caches. Oracle was about 160 miles away on the far side of the

Santa Rita, Rincon, and Santa Catalina Mountains. By coincidence, I usually average sixteen miles a day on long walks, so I felt fairly sure I could make the rendezvous. Knowing that if I didn't the next section would be a real problem was a big incentive to keep moving.

The umbrella should have been with me in Tucson but for reasons that never became clear it hadn't arrived. It was a special lightweight and durable hiking umbrella, made by a new company called GoLite, that I wanted for shade in the desert. It was being sent to Benson, my next supply point.

In Patagonia I saw the first backpackers of the trip. Or rather I saw their packs, two large ones outside the post office. Later, I saw a hiker holding sections of the Arizona Trail guidebook. I was hesitant about speaking to him. Maybe he was hiking south? He ignored me, dressed as I was in my town clothes and clean and fresh from a shower. I didn't look like a hiker. Before I'd decided whether to speak or not he'd gone. If he was heading north I would probably meet him somewhere.

3

Sky Islands and Desert Canyons

PATAGONIA TO ORACLE

157 miles

The problem with towns is roads. Not the ones in the towns, the ones that lead in and out. At least they are often a problem for long distance hikers like me who don't like walking on them. I imagine the towns' residents find them useful. I'd rather have foot trails but few towns have these. However, as I do like the amenities found in towns and, indeed, need some of them—food for example—road walking is sometimes a necessity.

Six miles of gently rising gravel road led out of Patagonia up Gringo Gulch toward the tantalizing, beckoning pyramid of Mount Wrightson. As I plodded upward, the pack heavy with food and water, a red-tailed hawk soared down a side canyon just below me, a wonderful sight and a welcome back to the wilds. Soon afterward I left the road for a more preferable jeep trail, preferable because the less there is between you and nature the more you see and the more contact you feel. Or so it is for me. A road holds you away. The bigger it is the farther away you are, the more you become an observer looking in from the outside. Go cross-country and you really feel nature, quite often literally and sometimes painfully. Getting scratched and impeded is a salutary lesson. In areas

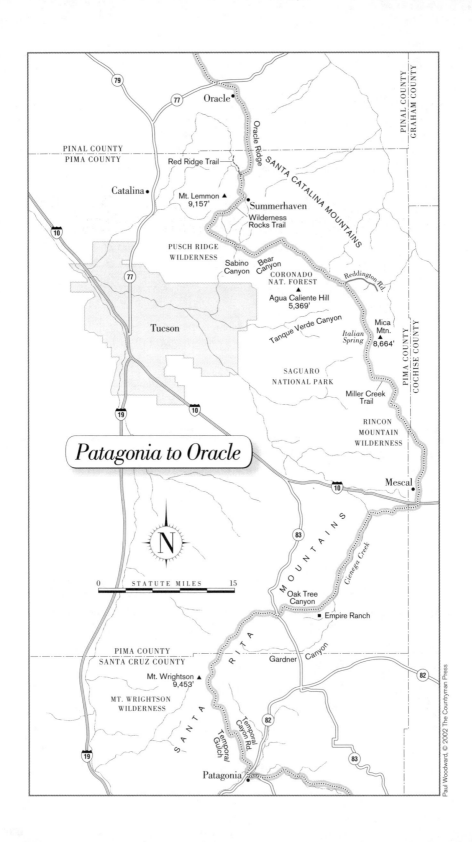

Patagonia to Oracle

79

77   Oracle

PINAL COUNTY
PIMA COUNTY

Red Ridge Trail

Oracle Ridge

SANTA CATALINA MOUNTAINS

PINAL COUNTY
GRAHAM COUNTY

Catalina

10

77

Mt. Lemmon ▲
9,157'

Summerhaven

Wilderness
Rocks Trail

PUSCH RIDGE
WILDERNESS

Sabino
Canyon

Bear
Canyon

CORONADO
NAT. FOREST

Reddington Rd.

Agua Caliente Hill
5,369'

Tucson

Tanque Verde Canyon

Italian
Spring

Mica
Mtn.
▲
8,664'

PIMA COUNTY
COCHISE COUNTY

SAGUARO
NATIONAL PARK

Miller Creek
Trail

19

10

RINCON
MOUNTAIN
WILDERNESS

Mescal

10

83

Cienega Creek

M
O
U
N
T
A
I
N
S

Oak Tree
Canyon

Empire Ranch

PIMA COUNTY
SANTA CRUZ COUNTY

Gardner   Canyon

82

Mt. Wrightson ▲
9,453'

S
A
N
T
A

R
I
T
A

82

MT. WRIGHTSON
WILDERNESS

19

Temporal
Canyon Rd.

Temporal
Gulch

82

83

Patagonia

0   STATUTE MILES   15

N

Paul Woodward, © 2002 The Countryman Press

where the vegetation is just too dense and spiky foot trails are perhaps the best compromise—thin ribbons of ground that allow easy walking while leaving you close to the land. Roads are for vehicles, trails are for feet. As I prefer traveling on foot I prefer trails. If I have to walk anything wider than a foot trail, I prefer first a rutted jeep trail, followed by a primitive dirt road.

The jeep trail led up Temporal Gulch, past a series of pools of water shaded by some huge and magnificent Arizona sycamores and ashes, bright with the fresh green leaves of spring. A scattering of snapped-off branches below some smaller, and presumably weaker, oak trees must have been a result of the previous week's storm.

The day's rest had been worthwhile, especially for my feet, but a day had been enough and I was glad to be hiking again. I felt different now, no longer a beginner, separated by that town stop from the start of my walk. Despite having a deadline—the meeting with Jim Martin in Oracle—I felt more relaxed than I had before Patagonia. More deeply connected to my surroundings, I was less concerned with the external matters that had to some extent dominated the first four days—worries about water, mileage, finding campsites, coping with the heat. In the future I would deal with problems when they occurred. What was really happening was that I was losing more general fears about the walk as a whole, fears about the enormity of it, about whether it was possible for me to do it, general fears that expressed themselves as specific concerns. This was a process I was familiar with from other long walks. I knew it took time to fully accept what I was doing and not hold the walk at a distance while my mind jumped ahead to worry about things that hadn't happened yet and probably wouldn't. Now that I was settling into the walk I could concentrate on the immediate—the next few hours, the next day. What would happen next week was too far away to think about now. I was living at walking pace. The end of the walk didn't exist and wouldn't for many weeks. Settling in to the walk was made easier by the abundance of water, as that had been my main concern. The snow I could see on the mountaintops was a constant reassurance that there would be water.

I was also pleased to be heading north at last. The fifty-eight miles to

Patagonia had mostly been in a westerly direction, and I had only progressed eighteen miles from the Mexican border. Now I really was heading toward distant Utah.

The long, slow, unrelenting climb into the Santa Rita Mountains became hard work, especially as it was very hot. The forecast had said it would be ten degrees above normal with eighty-two degrees forecast for Tucson. That would be a heat wave in August in Scotland. The trees up ahead drew me on. It would be cooler and shadier the higher I climbed. I paused to watch an acorn woodpecker with a bright red head prospecting a tree trunk. Tall pines and firs appeared as I entered large Walker Basin. The air below them was dark and cool. I rested under the dark branches and dressed another blister on my foot, which had appeared even though I was wearing sandals. As I patched it I chewed a piece of fruit leather. Suddenly I felt a crunch, bit on something hard, and spat out the best part of a front tooth, broken into three large pieces. I cursed. I'd had a checkup only a few weeks earlier. All I could do now was hope it would stay pain free until I could get to a dentist. In fact it never did hurt and I got used to it, waiting until I was home to have it seen to. How other people took my now gap-toothed smile I don't know, but no one seemed too startled.

Beyond Walker Basin the jeep track became a foot trail that climbed steeply to a high, 6,560-foot saddle. I was deep in the mountains now. Patagonia already seemed distant. It was. It was down there in the flatlands, and that was another world. It's surprising what a difference a few thousand feet of elevation make to one's outlook. The narrow rocky trail traversed steep slopes with good views of the now close rocky summit of Mount Wrightson. Not far below the top a plume of thick white smoke rose into the sky. Someone's campfire I guessed. Pinnacles of rock rose out of the forest, showing that under the green skin this was a rough and rugged place. I was now in the Mount Wrightson Wilderness. There were bicycle tracks on the trail even though bikes aren't allowed in wilderness areas.

A sign indicated water, Bear Springs, down a side trail. The creeks were flowing so I passed it by and continued down into Big Casa Blanca

Canyon. Here I found a rippling creek and a large, well-used campsite with a huge fire ring and the signs of many horses. It wasn't a hundred yards from the creek, let alone the quarter mile recommended so as not to keep wildlife from scarce water sources, but it was the only flat ground around so I camped there. I think it's best anyway to use established campsites where they exist rather than make new ones and create more impact. I prefer to camp where no one else has, leaving no trace when I leave, but when a site like this appears at the end of a long day, I use it. I set up camp under a big juniper. It was the first time I would fall asleep to the faint sound, just at the edge of hearing, of running water.

The harsh, quarrelsome cries of jays woke me. Sunshine was slanting down through the trees. I was up quickly, feeling a strong urge to move on, to see what was around the next corner. I hadn't felt quite so keen on previous mornings. It was another sign that I was coming to terms with the walk, of not just accepting that for now this was what I did but actually reveling in it.

Although wild now, in the late nineteenth century the eastern slopes of the Santa Rita Mountains were scoured by hundreds of miners following the discovery of gold in 1874. It turned out to be the biggest deposit in southern Arizona. Mining was hampered, however, by the lack of flowing water. This was placer gold, gold that had been washed down streams to settle in sand and gravel beds—the term is from the Spanish *placel*, "sandbank." Water is required to wash away the lighter sand and gravel, leaving behind the heavier gold, but in the Santa Ritas water was very scarce; most creeks are dry much of the year. The miners carried water up to their claims on burros or carted sacks of gravel down to what little running water there was. It was hard work and only worth doing for the richest deposits, which were worked out by 1886.

In 1902 James Stetson, a mining engineer from California, came up with a way to make mining in the Santa Ritas much easier. He planned to use runoff from the spring snowmelt to fill a reservoir with enough water to run a placer mine. To this end he set up the Santa Rita Water and Mining Company in 1904 and began construction. I came upon the first signs of this scheme soon after leaving camp. The trail ran beside an old aqueduct built to transport water to the reservoir. This section of trail is known as the Chinaman Trail because of a story that both it and the aqueduct were built by Chinese workers.

The aqueduct and other relics of the mining era are historical artifacts now. When they were in use this area would not have had the wilderness feel it does today, not with hundreds of miners and their camps, fires, diggings, and trails. Much of the forest would have been stripped away to provide wood for heating and cooking. The exploited wilderness has recovered, the forest reclaiming the damaged land, nature restoring itself. The few remnants of the mining era are interesting and curious, reminders of long-gone industry. This process, by which environmental damage and destruction becomes acceptable, protected even, long after the event, has fascinated me for many years. Time plays a major role, as does nature. As the mining happened a long time ago objecting to it is fairly pointless. More important, the return of the forest and the aging of the artifacts gives them a more natural look. Faded and overgrown, they seem part of the landscape in a way that a new intrusion doesn't. Once this aqueduct was a freshly dug ditch with clean sides and bare earth piled up all around. Many, probably most, of the surrounding trees would have been cut down or had branches removed. It wouldn't have looked attractive. Now the aqueduct has been absorbed into the landscape, its edges softened and rounded. Plants grow on the once-bare banks, trees encroach on them.

Walking along beside the ditch and thinking of the miners of a hundred years ago and more reminded me of a previous long walk, when I followed in the footsteps of the Klondike gold rush in the Yukon far away to the north. The Chilkoot Trail in southeast Alaska that thousands of gold seekers took to reach the Yukon is now a quiet, forested, wilderness path. In 1897 it was a crowded thoroughfare lined with shantytowns and busy with people and horses, the trees cut down for buildings and firewood. John Muir described the scene at the trailhead as a "nest of ants taken into a strange country and stirred up by a stick." The speed with which nature returned and healed the damage is heartening. Of course the stuff left by the gold seekers in both the Santa Ritas and along the Chilkoot

Trail was mostly made of wood, leather, cotton, wool—natural materials that rotted fairly quickly. Iron implements rust and decay, too. Even our modern chemical, metal, and plastic goods would disappear back into nature in most places given time, though they might still be there in the undergrowth.

I first discovered the ambivalence of our attitude toward historical relics in the wilds at Inscription Rock on a walk through New Mexico. Generations of travelers, starting with the first Spanish explorers in the 1500s, carved names and messages into the soft sandstone of this cliff. And long before the Europeans, Native Americans cut hand- and footholds into the rock so they could climb down from their village on the top to the pool of water at the base. Inscription Rock is now the centerpiece of El Morro National Monument, and carving your name or climbing on it is strictly forbidden. It's vandalism. You might damage the rock, which of course is protected because people have carved their names and climbed on it.

The trail and aqueduct contoured around the slopes of Ditch Mountain. Above rose the bare snow and rock summit of Mount Wrightson while out to the east and south ran the long lines of the Whetstone and Huachuca Mountains, the latter still very snowy. Below me rugged cliffs rose out of the forest in Big Casa Blanca Canyon. Tunnel Spring was dry but there were pools of water in Gardner Canyon. A pickup with a horse trailer was here too, at the end of a dirt road. I'd met three day hikers a short while earlier and was to meet two more, with a baby, soon afterward. Fresh horse tracks could be seen on the trail, overlaying the bike-tire marks. Although it seemed remote, this small mountain range lies quite close to Tucson and is easily accessible.

There was much wildlife in the Santa Ritas. Three red-tailed hawks dived and soared above Gardner Canyon, coming so close I could hear the rush of wind through their feathers. More of a shock was a snake, the first I'd seen, as it was only a few feet away when I spotted it. It wasn't a rattlesnake, though, but a nonpoisonous striped whipsnake, long and thin with black-and-white striped sides. It shot away into the grass, living up to its name. I glimpsed many birds—quail, jays, swallows, woodpeckers—but not for long enough to be sure of the exact species. A white-tailed deer ran across a meadow, its eponymous tail held erect. Cumulatively, the effect of all these brief encounters, some lasting only seconds, was to create a feeling of intense anticipation and expectation, an increase in alertness and awareness as I watched and listened for the next bird or animal. The forest felt alive, a complex tangle of interwoven life.

After miles of curling around the eastern slopes of the Santa Ritas the trail descended rapidly into Fish Canyon. Soon afterward adobe buildings began to appear. This was Kentucky Camp, built in 1904 as the headquarters of the Santa Rita Water and Mining Company. The company was not a success due to personal tragedies unconnected with mining. Founder James Stetson died in 1905, killed in a fall from a Tucson hotel window, and there were financial problems after the company's main backer, George McAneny, became entangled in an expensive divorce. Soon after McAneny died in 1909 the company closed. Kentucky Camp was sold and used as a ranch until the 1960s. Now it's in the Coronado National Forest and the site is being restored. There are complete buildings, such as the fine main house with information displays inside, as well as low ruins.

As I was wandering around the camp the caretaker appeared. There was no water here he said, he had to haul his in, but he could give me a gallon, which I needed, as it was many miles to the next creek. He went on to tell me that two other Arizona Trail hikers, Jim and Jake, had camped near here the previous night. I guessed one of them was the hiker I'd seen in Patagonia. My pack now noticeably heavier I wandered on through a complex of dirt roads, jeep trails, and foot trails that ran up and down little hills and along little canyons. Mount Wrightson now looked far enough behind for me to feel I'd made some progress. To the north the next range, the Rincon Mountains, came into view for the first time. Much closer were two steep outliers of the Santa Ritas, Weigles and Harts Butte. Somewhere between two big canyons called Box and Oak Tree I made camp among grassland and scattered oaks in a shallow valley. A three-quarter moon rose and hung above my camp.

Dawn came calm and clear. The sun was soon high and hot. I was now on my way out of the Santa Rita Mountains and heading for the desert grasslands of the Empire-Cienaga area, where the Arizona Trail had not yet been built but where there was a network of dirt roads. I just had to find the ones going my way. In particular I had to find Cienaga Creek, as this held probably the only water for the next thirty-two miles and I had just two quarts left.

Soon after leaving camp I was surprised to see a party of eighteen day hikers silhouetted on a ridge behind me, by far the largest number I was to see until I reached the Grand Canyon. Oak Tree Canyon was indeed full of oaks, many of them impressive, massive trees with huge spreading branches. A paved highway cut across the canyon; the trail running under it through a large culvert. On the far side was a plastic gallon jug of water. On one side of the jug the words "Hiker Chris from England," [sic] were written in thick black ink. On another side, "Jim, Jake, Hiker Going to Utah arrv. kc 17:15 Bert Waddell." The Kentucky Camp caretaker had told me he was going to cache water for the other hikers. This must be it. Or some of it. I didn't think it was meant for me but the others must have thought it was and left it. Having departed Kentucky Camp the previous morning they had to be up ahead. As I loaded the heavy jug into my pack I hoped there had been enough water for them. I later discovered that the water was indeed for me, Bert having kindly put out three gallons rather than the two the others had requested.

Oak Tree Canyon faded into high desert grassland sparsely dotted with small, straggly juniper and mesquite bushes along with yucca and cacti. There was a sense of enormous space and freedom as the grasslands stretched away to far-off mountain ranges. The Arizona Trail markers came to an end as I left National Forest for Bureau of Land Management (BLM) land. Soon I could see roofs among some greenery off to the south. This was Empire Ranch, built in 1876 and now owned by the BLM, which still runs cattle here. I headed away from the ranch, north along a dirt road. A pickup, a large trailer, and a horse stood beside the road. As I approached several barking dogs dashed out from under the trailer. A man appeared and greeted me. He was looking after the trailer for a party of professional dog trainers who were away in the backcountry with dogs and horses. Good weather for hiking, he said. The sky was cloudless and deep blue, the sun hot. I walked on up the road. To my right a thin line of bright green slowly converged with the straight brown line of the road. As the two came together I saw the dusty road turn wet and black. Startled, I realized this was water, running water, Cienaga Creek in fact. The bright green strip was revealed as the new spring leaves of the tall cottonwood trees that lined the banks. The shade of the trees was welcome and I dozed under one for half an hour, my feet up, my hat over my face. The rest was surprisingly refreshing.

Cienaga Creek, a sudden burst of green in the desert.

For the most part the greenery extended only a few yards either side of the creek, though in some places there were extensive, reed-filled marshes with the road running along an embankment above them. Beyond the strip of watered ground lay the high desert. Prickly pears, yuccas, and thorny bushes dotted the gentle rolling terrain. There were ocotillos too, strange plants consisting of bunches of long, thin, sticklike gray stems covered with spines, looking a bit like briars. A huge fat barrel cactus loomed up at one point. A vast beast about six feet tall, three feet around, and covered with long curved spines, it looked as though it might waddle away at any minute. Another barrel cactus, this one a bit smaller, had a noselike protuberance on one side. It resembled a hunched, misshapen troll out of Norse mythology even though this desert was a long, long way from the cool, wet mountains of Norway.

The road forded the ankle-deep creek several times, which was very refreshing to my hot, sandal-clad feet. A roadrunner, one of those strange members of the cuckoo family that eat rattlesnakes and have been made famous in cartoons, raced across the road in front of me. The liquid descending call of a canyon wren rang out, and I watched the little white-throated brown bird with its long, curved bill as it flew low over the rocky ground. A red-tailed hawk and a raven flew out of a thicket of trees. Something dead in there, I reckoned. I didn't go and look.

The creek grew wider and deeper, and the vegetation on the banks grew thicker. As the road turned through the trees to another ford I was astonished to see a white pickup in the middle of the creek, the water lapping the tops of the wheels. It was pretty new and had been driven deep into the creek bed. Even if it had made it through the creek, beyond the water there was a low but steep bank that looked insurmountable. I wondered what had happened to the driver and any passengers. It was a good eight-mile walk to the nearest highway, most of it across hot, exposed desert. I splashed through the shin-deep water beside the pickup and continued on to a section of the creek known as The Narrows. This was a beautiful spot shaded by huge cottonwood, ash, and walnut trees. But sadly and sickeningly the ground all around was soiled with garbage from picnics and parties. There were feces and used toilet paper lying on the ground near the creek as well. I had intended to camp here, but the trash was too off-putting and depressing, making me feel tense and angry, so I forded the creek and clambered up onto a shelf on the far side where I found a space just big enough for my sleeping bag among a thicket of whitethorn and mesquite. The trickle of the creek sounded from below, a relaxing sound. However, I could also hear the less soothing rumble of traffic on Interstate 10, about six miles away in a straight line, and the occasional train on the Southern Pacific railroad, which ran near the interstate.

Cienaga Creek is part of the Empire-Cienaga Resource Conservation Area. It flows for about ten miles before disappearing into the ground and is home to rare wildlife. South of The Narrows it's on BLM land, to the north state trust land for which hikers are supposed to have a recreation permit. I wrote for details but received no reply so I hiked anyway. I wondered if any of the parties who drove in and trashed the place bothered with permits. If the creek is really to be protected then something needs to be done to educate the people who visit it. A few rangers would probably help too. The problem lies in part, in large part, in ease of access. Being able to drive to an area too often brings people who have no respect for nature and who would never make the effort to get there otherwise. They treat the area like a city park and expect someone else to clean up after them. (Not that people should litter in city parks.) Most probably never feel any closeness to the land or any sense of responsibility. Walking brings you closer to nature and makes appreciation and respect easier and more likely. Not that all walkers never leave litter, far from it, but I have found that the farther I get from roads and trailheads the less garbage I usually find.

A purple glow suffused the sky above low pale green and gray hills when I woke. The subtlety of the dawn soon vanished as the sun rose, harsh and hot, hammering down from a cloudless blue sky. I continued along beside the creek, fording it frequently. A prairie falcon flashed past close by, a pale brown raptor with pointed wings and a long tail. A beautiful pipevine swallowtail butterfly with iridescent blue and black wings flitted over a sandbank. Creatures of the desert and the creek, at home here and unconcerned by the brief presence of a visitor.

A bit over a mile from The Narrows at Bootlegger Well the water became intermittent. Soon afterward Cienaga Creek became just another dry, stony desert wash. It had been magical while it lasted though, a compelling demonstration of the life-giving power of water in nature.

The jeep trail wound on up the dusty valley. Discarded beer cans stood at intervals beside the trail. I wondered idly who'd put them there. Maybe the people from the stuck pickup as they walked out.

At Alfalfa Well a locked gate with a private notice on it blocked the road. I was expecting something here as a small block of private land was shown on my Forest Service map. What I didn't know was what to do if there was no access. The gate suggested that continuing on the road might not be advisable, especially as buildings were marked on the map not far down the road. I had no desire for a run-in with a possibly angry, probably armed rancher. The Forest Service map didn't show any other roads or trails. The USGS quad did, though, and there it was on the ground, a jeep trail running up the side of the valley to the west. I took this and was rewarded with a fine high-desert walk through ocotillo and yucca with far-reaching views west to the Empire Mountains and east to the Whetstones.

After a couple of miles the jeep trail dropped back into a shallow valley close to some ranch buildings. The proposed route of the Arizona Trail headed northwest along Cienaga Creek for another three or so miles to I-10. I needed to reach the town of Benson to resupply, however, and that lay some fifteen miles to the east. The USGS map showed power lines leading to the little town of Mescal on I-10 some six and a half miles from Benson. Knowing that a maintenance track normally runs below power lines I headed in that direction along a dirt road. Sure enough the track was there and I took it to Mescal. The power lines ran parallel to I-10, and I could see the steady stream of vehicles rushing along the freeway. This wide desert gap between the Santa Rita and Rincon Mountain ranges has been an important overland route since 1858, when the Butterfield Overland Stage came through here en route from Missouri to California, a distance of more than twenty-eight hundred miles that was covered in around twenty-six days. The twice-weekly Butterfield Stage was the first reliable link between the eastern and western United States and carried passengers, mail, and freight. In the three years that founder John Butterfield ran it before being taken over by Wells Fargo it was late only three times.

In Mescal I crossed I-10 on an interchange bridge. The noise and smell were overpoweringly unpleasant. I looked down at the traffic roaring below my feet. Hiking in and out of Benson along I-10 seemed an extremely unattractive idea. I wanted to get there before the post office closed too, so I called a taxi that whisked me at what seemed an astonishing and alarming speed along the busy interstate, taking me first to the post office and then to a motel.

My supply box had arrived, along with the umbrella, but of real interest was a letter from my partner, Denise. In the five years we'd been together this was the first time I'd been away for so long. I'd done an even longer walk four years previously but that had been in Scotland and Denise had come to meet me regularly. I'd even spent a few nights at home during the walk. Now we wouldn't see each other for two months. I missed her but I was doing something I passionately wanted to do. I knew it might be hard for her, left at home with Hazel, her daughter and my stepdaughter. Denise had to go to work and run a house without me there to help. We live in a remote area, and it was a seventy-mile round trip to her workplace. I also knew, as she did, that I would become miserable and curmudgeonly if I didn't go on a long walk occasionally. We'd known each for twenty-three years and Denise had seen me off on my first-ever long distance walk twenty-two years previously, so she knew well what I was like.

The letter had been written the day I arrived in Arizona. "I have not got used to your being away," she wrote, saying my absence was "too disturbing to contemplate all at once" so she would take it one day at a time. I had phoned her in Patagonia but had not picked up any unhappiness then. Perhaps I'd been too wrapped up in myself and the walk. I went out to find a phone. Denise assured me she was fine and used now to my not being there. Hearing her voice I wondered why I was away. But I only had to think of the desert and the mountains. I needed this walk, this long, close contact with the wilderness. Over the years spending weeks and months in the wilds had become one of the most significant parts of my life, the most significant in fact. Hiking was what I did, it defined who I was. But for most of those years I had lived alone. Now Denise and Hazel were equally important. Compared with other long walks I'd done this one was relatively short, two months rather than six. They were the reason. Before there had been no one to come home to and therefore no reason to want or need to be home.

Benson was a functional overnight town stop. Since I needed to be in Oracle in six days I had no time to linger. The motel was basic, the restaurant dinner adequate, the café breakfast, after too little sleep due to the noise of traffic and trains, nondescript. This wasn't Patagonia. Not that Benson had a chance to make much of an impression. I wasn't there long enough. I never went into the town center at all. The evening I arrived I raced around a supermarket buying supplies for the next six days then sat in the motel room discarding all the excess packaging. Before leaving I did have time to talk to the sad-looking woman who ran the motel. She'd been all over North America she said, but she couldn't do it now because of a bad back and a fiancé in a wheelchair. She talked as though she were old and looking back to a golden past, but she appeared to be in her midthirties. She liked living in Benson; the people were friendly. Phoenix she was not keen on—New Year's Eve they all go out and fire guns, she said. They do that at home, I thought—but that's out in the country not in a big city.

The same taxi collected me from the motel and took me back to the post office where they wouldn't accept the bundle of maps I wanted to send home as they had no rates for overseas mail. The taxi driver offered to mail them from another post office so I left them along with a few dollars. They were home in a couple of weeks. Then it was back along I-10 to Mescal, less than twenty-four hours after I'd arrived. En route we passed a hiker slogging along the edge of the freeway. The pack looked familiar. One of those I'd seen in Patagonia, I thought. Was this Jim or Jake? And would we ever meet and if so where? Very soon perhaps. He would only be a few miles behind me.

From Mescal a gravel road ran sixteen miles into the foothills of the Rincon Mountains. That would be my day's walk. I wasn't looking forward to it but was looking forward to reaching my third sky island. As I left Mescal a large black bird with long broad wings held in a slight V soared lazily overhead. A turkey vulture. I watched it glide silently away. Edward Abbey always said he wanted to come back as a vulture. He had spent the last years of his life in Oracle, not that far away now, certainly not for a vulture. I was to see many of these birds in the weeks to come. With each sighting I thought of Abbey and wondered. I doubt reincarnation is true in the physical sense. But by putting the thought into his writing Abbey ensured that the sight of a vulture would remind people of him. It is appropriate that if his spirit is anywhere it is flying free above the desert he loved. I couldn't get used to calling them buzzards as Abbey and others did. Buzzards were the big hawks I saw at home, close relatives of red-tailed hawks. They symbolized the Scottish Highlands. Here vultures would come to symbolize the desert.

The railroad tracks crossed the road just outside Mescal. I waited as a long, slow freight train passed by. It took ages. I wondered where it was going and whether there were any hobos on board. Was jumping trains still possible? It reminded me of Jack Kerouac, hopping freights in *On The Road,* and the songs of Woody Guthrie. Edward Abbey first arrived in Arizona on a freight train too. There is an excitement, an air of adventure about trains that cars just don't have. I love long train journeys. I love waking after a night on a sleeper and looking out on a different world. The thing I like least about the States is that I can't get there by train. Jumbo jets are soulless sardine cans, bulk carriers to transport people from place to place without any awareness of what lies between.

It being Saturday a steady stream of pickups and cars bumped up and down the road. Beer cans littered its edges. Many had been stood upright, like those on the Cienaga Creek jeep trail. Again I wondered who'd done it and why, but didn't give it any serious thought.

As the mountains grew nearer the cactus and yucca desert gave way to piñon-juniper-oak woodland. A solitary giant saguaro cactus, that distinctive emblem of Arizona, stood next to the road, the first one I'd seen in the wild, though there'd been plenty of ornamental ones in Phoenix and Tucson. This one was rather dilapidated and tatty, with drooping arms.

The road ran alongside Ash Creek, which had pools of water in it. On one side rose the dark green, forested Rincons, steep, rugged mountains split by deep canyons and with much rock visible among the trees. On the other side were the lower desert mountains of the Little Rincons, a tortuous mass of contorted, bare rock.

The loud crack of a gun sounded ahead of me. In a clearing a man wearing ear protectors was aiming a rifle at a target on a tree. He was firing parallel to the road, only about twenty yards away. Another man watched. Both were big and heavy with beer guts hanging over their jeans. I hesitated. A woman noticed me. "There's a guy," she called out. The man lowered his rifle and waved. I waved back and walked on. No more shots. Others rang out from high in the hills though. I didn't mind guns, as long as they weren't pointed at me, but I did worry about walking past a rifle being fired so close to the road. How good a shot was he? What about ricochets? I was glad when I was well out of sight and, I hoped, out of range.

Big cottonwoods rose beside dry creek beds. Beyond them dusty land stretched away to the mountains. Then, suddenly and surprisingly, fields of green grass dotted with huge oaks with massive low, sweeping branches appeared. It could have been southern England except for the backdrop of mountains and desert. This was Miller Ranch, right on the edge of the Rincon Mountain Wilderness. A few people were camped at the trailhead, one guy asleep in a hammock slung between two trees.

There was no water at the trailhead, where I had thought the creek might be flowing, and I had only a quart left when I headed up Miller Creek Trail. As soon as I found some I would camp. The creek remained dry except for some damp patches of sand. I pushed on rapidly as darkness fell. I could see from the map that the trail would soon start to climb steeply. I was just thinking I'd have to turn back and go on to the next trailhead, where there was supposed to be water, when I spotted a tiny pool in the creek bed. When I scrambled down I found several more little pools. It was enough. I camped several hundred yards away in a small glade surrounded by oak trees on a shelf above the valley bottom. Steep ridges rose up on three sides; at only 4,200 feet I felt I was back in the mountains again. It also felt very remote even though I knew that the road and the other campers were only about a mile away. The climb into the Rincons would be long and steep, but I was looking forward to it, excited by the rugged terrain.

The excitement was justified. In camp the next evening I wrote in my journal "a long, hard, tiring, and magnificent day." It began before dawn when I woke feeling chilly. The temperature was thirty degrees and the very slight up-slope breeze, just strong enough to move the grasses by my camp, felt surprisingly cold. I closed the hood of the sleeping bag and dozed until it was light. When I did get up I donned my down vest for the first time in a week. There was ice in the water bottles.

Most of the Rincon Mountains lie inside Saguaro National Park. Camping is restricted to designated sites and a permit is required. Back in Tucson, way back it now seemed, somewhere in the distant past before the walk that had now taken over my life, I had gone out to the park head-quarters and obtained a permit to camp at Manning Camp high in the mountains. My guess as to when I would get there was almost right. The permit was for the previous night. Looking at the map I thought I should be able to cross the park in a day and camp outside it. There was a 4,000-foot climb at the start, but I'd done that much on Miller Peak on my first day. This was my eleventh, and I was much more trail fit now.

Dappled brown northern flickers with white rumps and red under-wings and bright-blue-tailed Mexican jays darted through the trees call-ing noisily as I started up the long climb. I soon reached the boundary of the national park and a trail register. I noticed that one Jake Schas had signed in the day before. Shortly afterward I spoke to two descending backpackers. They'd camped with an Arizona Trail hiker called Jake at Happy Valley the previous night and thought that I might be his com-panion. I must be between the two hikers now. Surely I would meet one of them soon.

The trail wound up an incredibly rough, rocky, and steep mountain-side of boulders, trees, and shrubs. I could see why it was signed FOOT

TRAIL ONLY at the start. I couldn't imagine horses climbing or descending this. The effort of the ascent almost went unnoticed though as interesting rocks and canyons appeared at every turn. Tremendous views opened up too, east to the rough Little Rincons with other ranges beyond them, south to the cone of Rincon Peak itself, the final bare rocks just poking above the trees, and north to the bulky mass of forest that makes up the other end of the Rincon Mountain chain. As I climbed the vegetation slowly changed from small piñon pines and oaks to larger ponderosa pines. Three more backpackers passed me from the other direction. They returned my greetings but seemed to resent my presence, one commenting loudly that there was "a lot of traffic on this trail." Another noted how much quieter the Turkey Creek Trail was. I saw no one else all day.

Finally I reached Heartbreak Ridge, the main crest of the Rincons. A long, undulating walk along this ridge led to the complex northern end of the range around Mica Mountain. In the forest I came to Manning Camp, where an old park service log cabin is set in dense forest, along with corrals, campsites, and pit toilets. Shaded by large conifers the empty camp was dark and gloomy. It seemed strangely eerie with no one about. I was quite glad not to be camping there. Just beyond the camp a creek tumbled down an attractive waterfall. I filled up with two quarts of water.

A tangled network of trails spreads out from Manning Camp. Even with two maps and pages from the trail guide I took a wrong turn at one point and then missed the trail for Italian Spring, unsigned and hidden by a tree, and had to backtrack. Sometimes following trails can be more confusing than going cross-country.

A steep descent led to Italian Spring, a small, shaded pool beside the trail. I loaded up with another two and a half quarts of water in case I made camp before reaching the next water source, a wise precaution it turned out as the descent that followed was steep and difficult, taking far longer than I had expected. This was due to a recent forest fire that had burned a huge area. The trail switchbacked down through the dead trees, many of which had fallen across the trail. Clambering over them was arduous, slow, and frustrating. Gradually the pines and firs gave way to piñon-oak forest and the walking became easier. I crossed the park boundary and descended a series of very steep, loose, eroded gravel washes with manzanita growing all around. To the east lay a ridge of bulky, shattered rock towers and pinnacles that turned gold then red then pink in the setting sun. The evening light was glorious. Brilliant, shining mountain ranges faded into the distance. To the north the snow-capped Santa Catalina Mountains, the next sky island to cross, glowed. A fine end to a fine day.

I reached the first flat area with just enough time to make camp before the last of the daylight went. A gusty wind blew over the stony ground, but I was too tired to pitch the tarp, let alone look for a more sheltered site. After 5,050 feet of climbing and sixteen miles I didn't think the wind

Evening light on rock pinnacles in the Rincon Mountains.

would keep me awake. I was wrong. At midnight much stronger gusts woke me up. The edge of my foam pad was lifting off the ground, and the fabric of the sleeping bag rippled and rustled.

After a short while I realized I wouldn't sleep until I could get out of the wind. Reluctantly I crawled out of the sleeping bag and pitched the tarp, being careful not to tear it or my legs on the small, sharp-leafed yuccas known as shin dagger that grew all around. The moon was full and the light bright, which was useful as my headlamp batteries failed. It took half an hour to get the tarp so it didn't flap. At least it wasn't cold. The fifty-four-degree low was the highest of the walk so far. Before going back to sleep I measured the windspeed with my tiny anemometer. It was gusting to twenty-one miles per hour, enough to rattle the tarp. Later in the night stronger gusts woke me several times. At dawn my altimeter showed a slight drop in pressure. A forecast I had heard in Benson had predicted a big storm north of here for this night that might include showers over the Rincons. I guessed I was catching the edge of it. The sky to the north and west was slowly clouding over, but nothing appeared to be coming this way. I was wrong again.

The water from Italian Spring turned out to be full of silt. I'd brought a foldable coffee filter and some filter papers to deal with dirty water but hadn't tried it before. My delight when it worked well felt a little excessive. In the backcountry it's surprising how satisfying something simple can be.

The mountains were going by quickly. Having the Rincons behind me felt wrong. It was only yesterday I'd started up into them. But behind me they were. Ahead lay the high desert of Redington Pass with the Santa Catalina Mountains rising beyond. Ten minutes after leaving camp I reached the water I had been aiming for the previous evening, a lovely spot with a deep pool shaded by trees and a rippling creek. It was still windy, with gusts to twenty-eight miles per hour, so it would have been no more sheltered than where I had camped.

The descent continued through rolling piñon-juniper and chaparral country to graded dirt Redington Pass Road. Two miles west was the trailhead for the next completed section of the Arizona Trail. Those miles were two of the most unpleasant of the whole walk. I was heading straight into the wind, which was strong enough to make walking difficult. It whipped up the dust too, sending choking, stinging clouds of it blasting into my face. The trailhead wasn't marked, the signs described in the trail guide having vanished, and I went past, took a wrong turn, and then returned when I realized my mistake.

Once I'd left Redington Pass Road the day changed from tedious to marvelous, in spite of the increasingly dark skies. The terrain became more and more wild and rugged with far more cacti than I'd seen before—a rich profusion of prickly pear, cholla, and barrel cacti plus a few saguaro spread out all around, an impressive sight, covering the stony desert hills that rose on either side, somber under the gray clouds.

A pool called The Lake was a disappointment. The trail guide talked of a "beautiful pond . . . complete with waterfowl and white sandy shores . . . this lush area is an oasis." All I found was a small, dirty pool surrounded by dried mud crisscrossed with off-road vehicle tracks. Agua Caliente Wash was delightful and refreshing, however, with big, new-leafed cottonwoods and small pools of water. There were other signs of spring too. The ocotillos I'd seen so far were just dry sticks. Here they were covered with tiny green leaves that made them look furry from a distance. Some of the mesquite bushes sported their first new leaves, and I saw the first wildflowers of the trip: the white and yellow daisylike fleabane and some sort of tiny purple geranium.

The day finished with a steep climb up a switchbacking path to a saddle that provided great views back to the Rincons, the summits now hidden in thick cloud. Ahead rock walls and pinnacles rose out of Molino Basin at the foot of the Santa Catalina Mountains, another spectacular view. I didn't linger though. The first spots of rain had fallen as I approached the saddle. Just as I reached it they turned to a more solid rain. I made a rapid descent down the steep trail to the Catalina Highway and Molino Basin Campground. By the time I arrived the rain had turned to hail. I hadn't intended to camp here, but the storm made stopping seem a good idea, especially since I was wet and cold from the descent. Not thinking the rain would last long I hadn't bothered to put

A bulging barrel cactus near Redington Pass.

on rain gear. How quickly I had come to assume the weather would be dry and warm.

The campground had no water, but the host kindly filled my bottles from his private supply. For the first time I was paying to camp on an official site with picnic tables, fire pits, and toilets. I donned my rain jacket and pitched the tarp as the hail turned to snow. I was at only 4,300 feet, but this felt like winter. Once under the tarp I donned all my warm clothing and fired up the stove. The temperature was thirty-seven degrees.

The first day of spring dawned with a covering of snow. During the night I'd been woken by campers arriving and then other campers packing up and leaving, making a lot of noise as they revved engines and shouted at each other. I gathered they weren't prepared for the storm and were wet, cold, and fed up. I heard a voice call out "leave the trash," and sure enough, in the morning I could see a raven tearing up pieces of cardboard at a nearby site. Cans, bottles, and foam cartons were strewn everywhere. A man from a nearby tent was walking about in the cold air looking forlorn despite his ridiculous hat with yellow Mickey Mouse ears. The air was gray and dull, the land and trees a soft white. Soon the sun rose, returning color to the world. Its heat loosened the snow on the trees so it cascaded gently downward, making it seem as though it was snowing.

The campground host said that the next water was seventeen miles away, but the map showed a spring and reservoir after about four miles as well as many creeks that I expected would have water after the storm. As the day would involve much ascent as I climbed into the Santa Catalinas, I took the risk and left with just two quart bottles.

The Santa Catalinas are Tucson's mountains, lying right on the edge of the city, their ridges and rock towers dominating the eastern horizon. Some trails into the Santa Catalinas start within the city boundaries. From Tucson the Catalina Highway winds up to the little town of Summerhaven and the highest peak in the range, 9,157-foot Mount Lemmon, location of the most southerly ski resort in the United States. It had not been a good season. I had watched pictures of skiers and snowboarders on the television in Tucson, taking advantage of the snow brought by the storm in which I had arrived. It was the first of the season. Too little, too late, said the resort manager.

From the touch of civilization of the highway and campground I quickly returned to wilder places. The trail wound through chaparral, paralleling the road for a mile, then climbed to a saddle and the boundary of the Pusch Ridge Wilderness. Ahead lay the rugged, rocky peaks and canyons of this wilderness area with wooded Mount Lemmon rising above them. From the saddle the splendid Sycamore Reservoir Trail traversed steeply down across a stony mountainside through manzanita, oak, various yuccas, and beargrass. This last I thought of as the "friendly agave" as it has soft fronds rather than the spiny leaves of other agaves and yuccas. It was one of the few plants I could push through without fear of being scratched. The descent ended at small Sycamore Canyon Reservoir, hidden behind a dense screen of trees. To the south the ground dropped away abruptly into narrow and dramatic rock-walled Bear Canyon, a tremendous view.

As I'd hoped, carrying much water wasn't necessary. The creek was flowing in upper Sycamore Canyon. Another climb led to another saddle and another fine vista, this time down to broad Sabino Basin and then up the West Fork of Sabino Creek to Romero Pass. The trail descended steeply into the basin on a narrow trail with big drops below it in places. The basin was dotted with huge saguaros and rugged hills. I described it in my journal as "desert mountain scenery at its finest." Two day hikers were sitting in the shade. Remote and wild though this place seemed it was only five or six miles down the canyon to the edge of Tucson.

Farther up the West Fork the canyon narrowed and a huge, impressive, water-filled slot backed by high cliffs came into view. This was Hutch's Pool, a popular destination for Tucson hikers. A tent was pitched near the water, the first other wild camp I'd seen. A man sunbathed on the rocks in front of it. The permanent water attracts birds, too. A beautiful black-headed, red-breasted, painted redstart darted across the rocks by the water while a little gray American dipper bobbed on a stone, reminding me of the dippers of home, frequently seen in wild Highland burns where they swim underwater.

Beyond Hutch's Pool I crossed the flowing creek a few times then began a steep climb to Romero Pass. Ten rather tired-looking teenage backpackers were descending. I stood aside to let them go by. We exchanged cursory greetings. "Anyone at Hutch's Pool?" "A man and a tent." "Good. He should be waiting for us." With that they tramped off down the trail.

As I climbed, the now-distant Rincon Mountains came into view and beyond them the faint outline of the Santa Ritas while just above rose the pinnacled ridge of Cathedral Rock. Pausing to look at these views was a welcome excuse to rest. From the pass an even steeper climb led up a rough, rocky, narrow ridge through piñon-oak woods and into ponderosa pines. To either side the slopes fell away into deep canyons. To make the climbs easier I broke them into sections—to 5,000 feet, to the pass, to 6,000 feet, and so on. As I climbed I checked my progress on my wrist altimeter. At the end of each section I paused briefly. I did 1,000-foot sections until the last 1,000 feet when I dropped to 100 feet at a time due to the steepness of the trail and growing tiredness. During the day I climbed 4,850 feet.

At a trail junction I abandoned the Arizona Trail, which runs to the summit of Mount Lemmon. I often make side trips to summits, yet here I was making a side trip to avoid a summit. The reason was the ski resort. I don't like ski resorts. They destroy any wilderness feel, bringing the mass tourism of holiday beaches and fun parks into the mountains. If people want to play in such places they should build artificial mountains, put a dome over them, and spray them with fake snow. And do this well away from real mountains. You can't experience or appreciate mountains or wilderness among the crowds and industrial machinery of a ski resort. I feel particularly strongly about this because great damage is being done in my home mountains, the Cairngorms, by the construction in a ski resort of a funicular railway that will reach almost to the summit of Cairn Gorm itself. This piece of vandalism is justified because it will "bring jobs," a mantra that seems to justify any developments, however crass and destructive. It's not usually true either. Bah! A curse on all such tourist junk that degrades nature. If people want organized mass activities let them be where the masses live, in the cities. There are many abandoned factories, warehouses, train stations, and the like that could be converted into ski resorts. They're full of ugly metal trash already so adding a bit more won't make much difference.

Knowing that seeing the ski resort on Mount Lemmon would fill my head with such thoughts and the anger that went with them I turned off onto a trail into an area known as the Wilderness of Rocks. This used to be the Arizona Trail and is still signed as such. A gentle descent led into a huge, strange basin with pale, broken rock pinnacles, towers, slabs, and

The Wilderness of Rocks in the Santa Catalina Mountains.

walls rising out of the forest all around. The climb into the Santa Catalinas had felt familiar, just like those into the Huachucas, Santa Ritas, and Rincons. It wasn't just the succession of plant zones that was the same; it was the very nature of the mountains. The sky islands were all giant heaps of shattered rocks, their roughness partially covered by a skin of green forest. Here though the rocks were bigger, piercing the skin more frequently and forcefully.

Up here at more than 7,000 feet there were large patches of snow under the trees and plenty of pools and running creeks. The sky had gradually clouded over during the afternoon. Thinking of storms, I pitched the tarp on a flat area of gravel that I reckoned would catch the early-morning sun.

The night was cold with a low of twenty-eight degrees. I had to get up twice for a pee for the first time on the walk. For once I must have drunk more than I needed the previous day. Yet I knew I hadn't drunk nearly as much as on other days. The difference was the heat. The afternoon clouds had kept the temperature down. My feet benefited from the cooler temperatures, too. For once they hadn't ached or felt sore.

Dawn came with a weak sun shining through thin clouds. There was no heat in it. The temperature had barely crawled above freezing when I set off. A beautiful western bluebird, its bright feathers a colorful spot in the dull gray and green of the rocks and forest, flitted around the camp.

An undulating, twisting trail led through the Wilderness of Rocks. Contorted, shattered pillars of pale stone appeared at every turn. Rocks balanced on rocks at impossible angles. The eroded soft sandstone brought memories of a darker rock, the gritstone of the Peak District in England. There, on the bleak peat moorlands of Kinder Scout and Bleaklow, the rocks also formed strange towers and pinnacles. Today's gray weather was more suited to England than Arizona. Only the trees were different, the magnificent trees—tall bulky ponderosas—and I thought, as I had thought on every trip to the wild country of North America, how much we had lost in Britain, how the forests gave a completeness to the mountains, how important they are and how valuable to the health of the land.

Patches of snow lay in shady areas, creeks were flowing, and there were many beautiful pools reflecting the rough texture of the rocks. Icicles hung from boulders. The sun strengthened but the day never got very warm. All sense of the desert was gone. The forest thickened as I walked alongside Lemmon Creek. The trail climbed steeply toward Marshall Saddle and vanished into a snow patch. Larger patches followed and keeping to the trail became difficult. I was aided by a large number of footprints going the other way, probably those of the youth party I'd met the previous day. The trail was slick and slippery where they'd walked, and I edged around their tracks. They'd lost the trail a few times. I did, too, sometimes by following their route, at other times all by myself.

Kicking my boots into the hard, refrozen surface of the snow and carefully pushing down on my poles for balance I tried to pick a route up this gloomy, forest-shrouded, snow-covered mountainside to ensure that if I slipped I wouldn't slide too far before a tree or bush stopped me. I had to concentrate and check each foothold carefully. Thoughts of anything outside this slope vanished. The snow changed everything. The mountainside wasn't very steep; without the snow it would have been an easy walk. I wouldn't have fallen far if I had lost my footing, but with a heavy pack even a short slide into a big, hard tree could have caused injuries.

From the saddle I descended through a thick Douglas fir forest to a shaded trailhead. With steep slopes to the west and big trees all around the sun didn't penetrate here this early in the year. A breeze blew and it felt very cold. I walked briskly down the snow-spattered road into Summerhaven, a secretive little town mostly hidden in the woods and consisting mainly, as far as I could see, of a series of Swiss-style chalets. I'd sent my box here, though I wasn't sure why as I hadn't planned on a rest day, as it was only 10 miles to Oracle, where I needed a day off in order to put out water caches. I retrieved the maps for the next section and mailed the box ahead, paying for an express service so it wouldn't arrive too long after me. My café lunch was passable; it would have been nice if the food and drink had been hot rather than lukewarm, especially given the cold outside.

I left Summerhaven in a snow flurry, bundled up in fleece sweater, windshirt, warm hat, and gloves. An unpleasant half mile was spent edging along the curving Catalina Highway, unpleasant because, although it wasn't busy, cars would appear without warning, their sound muffled by the trees, and then streak past close to me. With relief I reached the trailhead for the trail down Red Ridge, a long arm of forest reaching out to the north. As I descended the sun finally came out and shone on the jagged spine of the Reef of Rocks, the next ridge to the west. In the distance the desert lay, pale and shimmering, with the distant gray silhouettes of mountains rising out of it. At the bottom of the ridge a creek flowed, as I'd hoped. I had planned on camping here. Indeed, that was why I'd come this way instead of Oracle Ridge, which led in a long straight line from the crest of the Santa Catalinas right into Oracle, but where there'd be no water and probably nowhere to camp. However, it was still early and I felt too full of energy to stop. I studied the map. There might be space to camp at Dan Saddle on Oracle Ridge. I filled up with a gallon and a half of water and began the long climb. Beyond the old cabins called Catalina Camp the trail became a steep, rutted jeep trail. I wasn't so full of energy when I reached the saddle. There I found I needn't have hauled the water up, as there were large patches of snow on the shaded, east side.

The ridge was fairly broad at the saddle with plenty of space between two large ponderosas among a scattering of oak, juniper, and prickly pear for a comfortable camp. A large fire ring showed that others had thought so too. A strong, cold wind whipped across the ridge, so I pitched the tarp. At 6,880 feet this was the highest camp I would have for a while. In fact I would hike 180 miles before I went above 6,000 feet again. Ahead lay the lowest sections of the route, across the hot Sonoran Desert and the Superstition and Mazatzal Mountain ranges. The sky island section of the walk was almost over. I'd walked two hundred miles, roughly a quarter of the way to Utah. The journey was truly underway now with a life of its own, a rhythm both like and unlike that of other long walks. I was beginning to feel a connection with the land and an understanding of the connections within it. I could see how it worked, superficially at least, as I watched the different aspects merging into one another.

The stars came out but there was no moon and it was very dark when I fell asleep. The sun came early, slanting golden light through the trees. My camp was too shaded to get much warmth, and I wore warm clothing while I packed up. The wind had eased, though I could hear it in the treetops. The storm that began as I entered the Santa Catalinas was ending as I was leaving them. The sky was a clear blue, and the barometric pressure was rising. My appetite was rising, too, and I was looking forward to reaching Oracle. For the first time on the walk I felt really hungry. I'd have to carry more food from now on. This wasn't a surprise. I'd been out two weeks, and I knew from previous walks that this was when my appetite made itself felt.

By the time I set out the wind had dropped completely. There was total silence except for the occasional birdcall. The undulating ridge slowly descended through pine forest to piñon-oak scrub to semidesert grassland. The numbers of yucca and cacti increased as the elevation decreased. There were occasional views back to flat-topped Mount Lemmon, green and white with trees and snow, the sharp spines of the Reef of Rocks and Red Ridge running down from the summit ridge. Ahead smaller, browner desert hills rose beyond a flat desert plain. As they had done on and off for a week bits of Tucson popped in and out of sight. The city was now behind me and slowly fading from view. The scattering of white houses that was Oracle appeared at the foot of the ridge, tiny white boxes dropped seemingly at random onto the desert.

Jeep trails ran along the ridge in places, though I spent most of the time on a narrow foot trail that was sometimes almost hidden in the vegetation. In places it was steep, loose, and slippery, requiring concentration, in others it was a gentle woodland stroll. The Arizona Trail branches off from the ridge to circle around Oracle. If I followed it I would have to walk the highway into town, so I continued on down the ridge, passing a day hiker sitting on a rock just as I came close to the first houses.

I was in Oracle by midafternoon. Plenty of time, I thought, to find a room, dump my pack, and collect my box and any other mail. However, although small, Oracle is spread out over three miles, the buildings interspersed with areas of desert. A Circle K gas station marked each end of town. I spent three frustrating hours marching up and down the very long main street. At first I was in search of a motel. When I found one, having been redirected after choosing the wrong way from the only two options, it was closed. A note on the door gave a number to ring. Off I went in search of a phone. Once found I dialed the number. "We'll be back from Tucson in an hour and a half." I did some window shopping—not that there are many shop windows in Oracle—and browsed the shelves in the grocery store for food I would buy later. I didn't want to carry it now. I was not impressed with what I found. That's one of the risks of resupplying as you go along. You have to accept what's available. Finally the motel owner turned up, and I rented one of a row of small A-frame cabins. Tall, thin, dark green Lombardy poplars separated the cabins to create a very formal, structured, yet surreal effect that seemed completely out of place in this desert town.

Since I started planning the walk I had thought of Oracle as Edward Abbey's town, the place he made his last home. Reflecting on my hot tramp up and down its main street and how frustrated and bad tempered it had made me, I decided this was an appropriate welcome. Abbey liked things to be challenging, awkward, cussed, demanding. But, some readers may be asking, who was Edward Abbey? This is not an easy question. One answer is that he was a writer who lived and wrote about the Southwest and who was a passionate advocate for wilderness and against development. But that is too simple. Abbey was an iconoclast, a rebel, an anarchist, an individualist, a desert philosopher, and that's just for starters. He liked questioning, he wanted to make people think, to be individuals and not part of the mass. Offending people was fine as long as it jerked minds into action. His views can't be corralled into a system or captured by a convenient label. I doubt there's anyone who's read much of his work who's agreed with everything he said. Most people, I expect, would strongly disagree with at least some of his ideas. I think some of them stink. But others I find amazing, uplifting, stimulating.

Abbey viewed himself as a novelist but is at least as well known for essays that cover a huge range of subjects, all in his inimitable style. At the heart of his writing is the idea that wilderness matters and is the true home for the individual. The desert was his special passion, and he railed long and loud against those who would despoil it. His words have reached so many ears, influenced so many minds that in a sense he is part of the desert now. Once you've read Abbey it's impossible to consider the desert without his words coloring your thoughts. He was one of the reasons I was here.

But I can't tell you anything about Abbey he can't say better himself. Go read some of his books, if you haven't already. I'd suggest starting with *Desert Solitaire, The Monkey Wrench Gang,* and *The Journey Home.* And get out into the desert, on foot, with a pack on your back, and see what he was talking about.

In the shade of the motel room I lay on the bed in a hot daze thinking about Abbey before going back out to the phone. Denise wasn't in so I left a message on the answering machine saying where I was. This was my check-in system for the walk—soon after arriving at a supply point I would ring home. I also rang Jim Martin, who arranged to pick me up early the next morning on his way to an Arizona Trail Association meeting at Oracle State Park just outside the town. Would Abbey have liked the Arizona Trail, liked a trail that required an association? I don't know, but in his wonderful essay, "The Great American Desert," he wrote: "I welcome the prospect of an army of lug-soled hiker's boots on the desert trails." Why? "To save what wilderness is left in the American Southwest—and in the American Southwest only the wilderness is worth saving—we are going to need all the recruits we can get." The Arizona Trail, I think, is part of that effort.

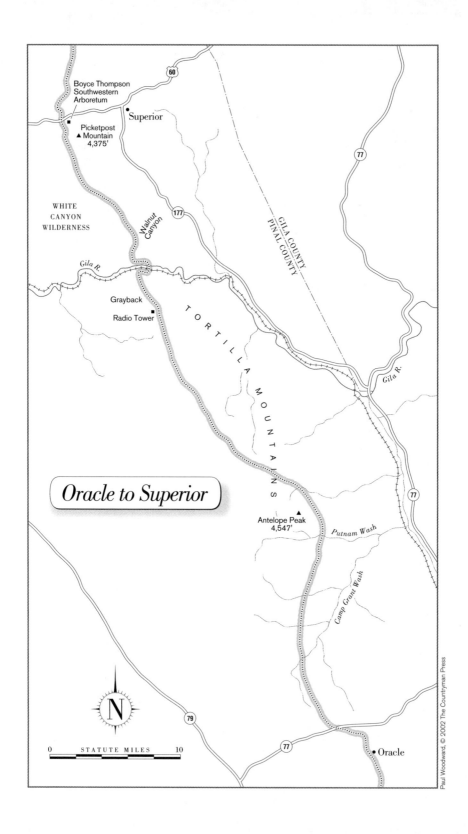

Boyce Thompson
Southwestern
Arboretum

Superior

Picketpost
▲ Mountain
4,375'

WHITE
CANYON
WILDERNESS

Walnut
Canyon

Gila R.

Grayback

Radio Tower

GILA COUNTY
PINAL COUNTY

Gila R.

T O R T I L L A   M O U N T A I N S

Oracle to Superior

Antelope Peak
4,547'

Putnam Wash

Camp Grant Wash

N

0   STATUTE MILES   10

Oracle

4

Across the Sonoran Desert

ORACLE TO SUPERIOR

79 miles

After ten days without a break I needed a rest. I didn't get one in Oracle. It was all traveling and people. Jim Martin turned up at seven in the morning and whisked me off to Oracle State Park for the ATA meeting. The Arizona Trail runs through the park, and this gathering was to discuss organizing trail work for later in the year. We arrived at the park headquarters—a fine old ranch house. It was open, but no one was there. We hung around for a bit then drove back into Oracle. Jim made a phone call. The meeting didn't start until later. That gave us time for breakfast. When we returned to the park Larry Snead showed up and then Frank Hogg, who ran the park. Both had given me advice before the walk so it was good to meet them and thank them in person. More people arrived and talk turned to the day's activities. I wasn't involved in this and had various chores I needed to do, so Jim drove me back to the motel and arranged to pick me up after lunch to place water caches.

These few hours left me feeling overwhelmed and confused. After two weeks alone on the trail with only minor interactions with other people this sudden rush of introductions, ideas, faces, voices felt quite disorienting. I wandered down to the post office and collected my box.

Sitting outside sorting through it felt quite normal. I looked up to see three people approaching, one of them a wild-looking, suntanned character with baggy clothes, a cap on his head, and battered running shoes on his feet. Something told me they were coming to see me, not the post office. I was right. "Hi," they said, "you're Chris Townsend." The wild man was Jake Schas, the hiker I'd been almost meeting since Patagonia. I wondered how I appeared. Two weeks on the trail makes a difference. I recognized one of the others but couldn't initially remember where from. "We had breakfast together five years ago at the annual Gathering of ALDHA-West [the American Long Distance Hiking Association—West]," he reminded me. Paul Leech was an experienced long distance hiker, but today he was here to support Jake. The third person, Kay, was a friend of his. I was glad to meet fellow hikers but, still feeling a little bewildered by the start of the day, I found it hard to relate to them. I was beginning to worry about getting my chores done too.

A mass of information poured over me. Later I sorted it out in my mind and worked out what we'd been talking about. At the time I felt curiously detached, though I tried hard to maintain some semblance of contact. Luckily neither Jake nor Paul were surprised at how I was behaving. Jake later told me that he'd felt a bit the same on meeting Paul and Kay. It turned out that although he lived in Mesa, on the edge of Phoenix, Paul also was renovating a house in Oracle. Jake contacted him before starting his hike and Paul offered him a room. After discovering I was here from people at the post office, they went to the motel, only to learn I'd just left. They returned to the post office. Being in Oracle seemed to involve an awful lot of traveling. Paul was doing even more. He had to go to Tucson later that day. This was useful for me as he offered to buy supplies there. Having seen the poor selection available in Oracle I gratefully accepted the offer and quickly scrawled a list of everything I could think of.

Jim Martin returned early in the afternoon. As the ATA steward for this section he knew it well, having visited it many times and made a through-trip on horseback. Depending on the route it was at least forty miles across the hot, shadeless Sonoran Desert to the Gila River. There were a few cattle tanks that might have water in them, Jim said, but they weren't reliable. Also, delicate negotiations were going on with ranchers about trail access. Jim felt that if hikers were found taking water from the tanks it wouldn't be helpful with these talks.

I hoped to reach the Gila River on the fourth day out from Oracle at the latest. If I cached six gallons of water that ought to be enough. Before starting the walk Jake had already cached some water on a graded dirt road that ran through the area. We talked about hiking this section together, but I didn't like the sound of Jake's route. Hiking the whole way on a graded road sounded tedious. Jim had offered to show me a good route so I hadn't done any detailed planning. We pored over the maps as he pointed out a complicated but interesting-looking route involving foot trails, dirt roads, jeep trails, and cross-country sections. As Jake didn't really like his road walk idea either—it had just seemed the best option— he decided to come with me on Jim's route.

There was also the question of what to do about the Gila River, which lay on the far side of the desert. Unable to find out much about water levels I'd planned to cross it at a road bridge, the same place the Arizona Trail will cross when it is built. This was well to the east of the trail's continuation on the far side of the Gila, however, and the maps showed what looked like very rough, trackless terrain between there and the bridge. This section would be fine once a trail is built, but without one it was likely to be very slow and difficult and involve struggling for miles over rugged terrain. The diversion would add maybe twenty miles. Jake had planned on fording the river. Jim reckoned the river could be only inches deep or it could be a raging torrent, depending on what was happening upstream. If the river was fordable we could stay in the wilds. I agreed to try fording the river. We could always walk to the bridge if necessary.

The route decided, Jim took us on a wild ride around a complex network of rough, sometimes washed-out desert tracks. I was surprised at some of the places a pickup could go as we climbed in and out of dry washes and up and down steep banks on heavily rutted jeep trails. He kept naming places and relating them to our route. Jake and I tried to keep track of where we were on our maps, but I was soon confused. The brown land was fairly flat and dotted with sparse bushes and cacti. From the truck it all looked the same. We put out two caches, nine gallons twenty miles from Oracle, the same again eight miles farther on. I marked both places carefully on my map. We could have cached the second one farther away, but after many hours of being jolted and bumped we wanted to get back to town and unwind. Collecting Jake's original caches, we returned to Oracle feeling tired and shaken. Driving around the desert was much more exhausting than walking across it.

That evening we went out for a pizza with Paul and Kay. Paul was frustrated; he wanted to hike with us. He did have a big trip planned for later in the year, though. He was going to the far north to follow the route of the Klondike gold seekers over the Chilkoot Trail and then by raft down the Yukon River to Dawson City. But that was in the summer. He wanted to come with us *now*. Unable to do so, he was really keen to help and offered to meet us at the trailhead at the end of this section and take us into the nearest town. The supplies he'd bought in Tucson were really useful as neither Jake nor I had had time to do any shopping.

The next morning I dashed around doing final chores, including reading a bundle of e-mails on a computer at the library. While there I logged on to the web site that I was sending pictures to. Although I was using a digital camera I was sending the tiny cards with the images on by snail mail. The first ones, sent from Patagonia, were on the site. I looked at my first camp in the snow and the Canelo Hills. It felt strange. It seemed a long time ago.

By midmorning Jake and I finally managed to leave Oracle with two gallons of water and six days' food apiece plus, in my case, two slices of the pizza that, despite my growing appetite, I hadn't been able to finish the night before. An unpleasant few miles on the highway, which Jake noted was far more dangerous than being in the wilderness, led to the only few miles of the Arizona Trail that have actually been built in this area. The trail was enjoyable, but soon we were on the network of dirt roads we were to follow for much of the next three and a bit days. The walking was easy, the land flat and the vistas wide. The rolling desert spread out to far-off mountain ranges. Low brown hills rose around us. Cacti grew

Jake Schas hiking toward Antelope Peak in the Sonoran Desert
between Oracle and the Gila River.

everywhere. In places there were forests of saguaros. The stop in Oracle had been tiring and busy and I left feeling tense. Only now that I was hiking again did I start to relax. The land looked completely different from the day before, when we'd seen it from the truck. Our hiking speed was so different from even a fairly slow ride in a vehicle. Jim had pointed out a few distinctive landmarks, one of which was pointed Antelope Peak. As the only real hill around it was the main focal point for the first two days out of Oracle. Behind us Mount Lemmon was visible, slowly shrinking as we headed north.

There was also time for us to start to get to know each other. As both of us had spent most of the previous two weeks alone we relished the opportunity to talk at length. Words poured out. People who know me often wonder how I manage alone in the wilderness, as I'm usually very talkative. I've never had a problem with this, but when I do meet some-one I tend to talk even more than usual. Walking along dirt roads in little-changing scenery was the ideal place to do this too. Jake was quite keen to talk too so it wasn't totally one-sided.

Jake told me he worked as a chef, a career he'd chosen because it allowed him to travel. "People always want to eat." And travel he had. For the past few years he'd been working in Antarctica. Now he was free until September. After the Arizona Trail he was going to California to hike the Pacific Crest Trail from Mexico to Canada, a twenty-seven-hundred-mile walk he'd nearly completed a few years before. I was jealous. My two-month, eight-hundred-mile spring suddenly seemed short. I'd hiked the Pacific Crest Trail eighteen years earlier and would love to do it again.

Jake learned that I was on the trail from Bert Waddell, the caretaker at Kentucky Camp, whom he'd met on the road the morning after I'd passed through. He hadn't known my name until Summerhaven, where he'd asked about other hikers at the post office. He was surprised to discover I was ahead of him there, but worked out he should catch up to me in Oracle. I'd seen two hikers in Patagonia, and Bert had written the names Jim and Jake on the water jug he'd left me. Who, and where, was Jim? He wasn't Jim he was Andy, said Jake, and he was only going as far as Oracle. It was Andy I'd seen walking up I-10 from Benson; Jake hadn't gone into the town. Where Andy was now Jake didn't know. He hadn't seen him since the interstate.

Jake also explained the standing beer cans on the Cienaga jeep trail and the road to the Rincons. He'd put them there to amuse himself when bored. He'd even left notes for me in two of them, but I never noticed.

Brought up in Arizona, though he now lived in Oregon, Jake was familiar with the desert wildlife and plants and pointed out aspects of many of them I would otherwise have missed. Had I seen a saguaro skeleton? I hadn't and wasn't even sure what one was. Jake found one, a long section of woody ribs that looked like the remnants of a rotting boat. This stiff core supports the weight of the cactus, enabling it to grow up to fifty feet high. As a saguaro can soak up as much as two hundred gallons of water; a big one can weigh a great deal, up to eight tons. I could relate to this. I knew just how heavy the few gallons I was carrying were.

Jake's hiking style was very different from mine. I like to travel fairly light, and I take into account the weight of every item I carry. Jake, however, was traveling ultralight. Without food and water his pack weighed less than half mine at around twelve pounds. His load consisted of the bare minimum of clothing, a sleeping bag, small tarp, mini foam pad, and a few odds and ends. Each item was made as light as possible by cutting and trimming every extraneous ounce. The zipper had been removed from his sleeping bag, leaving a hooded quilt. He had also removed the frame, lid, and many straps and buckles from his pack. The latter weighed two pounds empty. Mine weighed six and three-quarter pounds, over half the total weight of Jake's gear. Add six days of food and two gallons of water, around thirty pounds in total, and the difference between our loads lessened. I picked up Jake's pack at one point to see how it felt. I'd rather carry the extra weight of mine and have the comfort and useful gear that went with it, I convinced myself. Secretly, though, I would have loved to carry as little as Jake. But how could I manage without my binoculars, natural history guides, cameras, tripod, paperback books, and other items totally unnecessary for hiking and camping but essential to my enjoyment? (And, it must be said, for my work—for the articles and slide shows that would follow the walk, and, of course, for this book.)

Jake hiked in running shoes with the tongues cut out and homemade cotton clothing. He also wore dark glasses and a desert rat cap with an extra long bill and a Foreign Legion–style neck flap that he wrapped around the lower part of his face and referred to as his veil. He had an umbrella too, a bright red-and-white one that he'd lined with reflective silver material. I asked him why he was so covered up. After working in Antarctica for months on end, he said, his skin was pale and would burn easily unless he used sunscreen, which he didn't like as he hated the feel of sunscreen, sweat, and dirt all mixed together on his skin. He also couldn't afford to get sunburned as it could affect his chances of future work in Antarctica. Because of the thinning ozone layer and the resulting danger everyone going there had their skin carefully checked beforehand. I don't much like hot sunshine anyway, he finished. After a winter in Scotland my skin was certainly pale, but I didn't mind using sunscreen and preferred to wear shorts and roll my sleeves up—maybe because I lived where there aren't often opportunities to do this.

I wore my sandals as it was too hot for boots and used my umbrella for the first time. It definitely felt cooler under its canopy, and I could see its usefulness for open desert hiking.

Walking down the middle of the road we reckoned we'd hear or see any traffic long before it reached us. That idea vanished when a pickup came up from behind. It was only a few yards away when we realized it was there. The driver was a wildlife ranger. He gave us his card and said to call him if we saw anything "unusual." I guess he meant poachers.

We were relieved it hadn't been a local rancher. The land here was state trust land for which Jake had a permit but I didn't, never having had a reply to my letter of inquiry. This didn't particularly bother me, however, as I doubted anyone would ask to see a permit. Meeting a rancher was much more likely. The roads we were on, which weren't public ones, ran through some private land and near some ranches. We intended circling around these but didn't really want to have to explain this to any of the owners, nor have one of them suspect us of planning on crossing their land.

As we approached broad, shallow Camp Grant Wash an ultralight

Protection from the sun—Jake Schas at a rest stop in the Sonoran Desert.

aircraft appeared buzzing low over the desert. Was this what the wildlife ranger had meant by "unusual"? It disappeared and silence returned. We guessed it must have landed in the wash. It reappeared, buzzing around a few more times as we made camp in the wash. Later we heard the sound of vehicles driving away.

This was my first camp in the Sonoran Desert and at 3,150 feet the lowest of the walk so far. The night was calm and the sky black and clear with a spectacular display of stars and planets. The huge H of Orion was prominent and Mars, Jupiter, and Saturn could be seen in a straight line. It's a cliché to say that the stars make you feel small, humble, insignificant. The more we learn about the vastness of the cosmos, the knowledge that most of space is empty and where it isn't mainly consists of swirling masses of hot chemicals, the greater the risk that the cliché will seem true. Yet if Earth is unusual, perhaps unique, because of the life on it, it is all the more significant and all the more precious. Looking at the impossibly huge, incomprehensible sky I remembered a passage from *Winter Holiday* by Arthur Ransome, whose children's books about outdoor adventures had inspired me when I was a young boy. Dick, a youngster interested in astronomy, is looking at the stars on a winter's night in the English Lake District. "He felt for a moment less than nothing, and then, suddenly, size did not seem to matter. Distant and huge the stars might be, but he, standing here with chattering teeth on the dark hillside, could see them and name them and even foretell what next they were going to do." And I lying here in the dark desert could do the same. It was a reassuring thought.

While I fired up my stove and began heating water for drinks and a meal Jake simply opened a plastic bag and started eating. He'd made up all his meals for the trip, dehydrating various items and mixing them together. Midafternoon he'd add water to one of his bagged meals so that by the time he camped it had rehydrated. Most were pasta based. "I could cook them," he said, "but they're tasty cold." He did have a tiny, solid-fuel stove, some fuel tablets, and a small pot, but he rarely used them.

Just after dusk a pack of coyotes burst into song, their wild yips, yaps, and howls echoing eerily around the desert. I lit a candle to write my journal by and dozens of small moths flew around it, many immolating themselves in the tiny flame. The coyotes stilled; I fell asleep to wake in the dark to the soft cry of an owl. Soon afterward the coyotes greeted the new day with a short burst of cries. A cactus wren began churring loudly in the bushes. The desert came alive in the reddish dawn. Dry it might be, dead it was not.

Jake, I discovered, didn't eat breakfast until he'd been hiking an hour or so. He started out shortly after waking up. I prefer a more leisurely start with a few hot drinks and a bowl of cereal before stirring from my sleeping bag. Neither of us wanted to change our now well-established routines so we agreed to meet at our first cache, which lay about three miles away in dramatically named Bloodsucker Wash. The walk there, through the usual gently undulating, cacti-spattered, pale brown desert, was uneventful.

From the cache a dirt road led to the first private property. A fence with a PRIVATE sign on it blocked the road. There was no way we could pretend we didn't realize we were trespassing if we went on, so we followed the fence east and then north around the area.

Once we left the road our progress abruptly slowed. From striding along at three to four miles an hour we went to slowly picking our way around spiny plants, up and down stony mounds, and in and out of loose washes. Vegetation was the main problem. Everything that grew bore sharp spines and spikes, drawing blood and tearing clothes at the slightest touch. Thickets of catclaw acacia and mesquite bushes blocked the way, forcing us to make detours. Even worse were the forests of cholla cacti. The furriest, most cuddly looking of these, the teddybear cholla, was particularly nasty. The name seems ironic but is actually appropriate, like a real bear it looks soft and friendly but is actually fierce and savage and will tear you to shreds if you come too close. Skirting around these cacti wasn't enough to avoid getting snared as many small pieces of them were scattered over the ground for yards around. These little bundles of spikes would attach themselves to anything they touched. Catch the edge of one with your foot and it would flip up onto your leg. I was painfully stabbed several times, trickles of blood running from the wounds. I was reminded of something Edward Abbey wrote in *Desert Solitaire:* "When traces of blood begin to mark your trail you'll see something, maybe." I had the blood and, I hoped, something of the vision, too. Everyone knows that cacti have sharp spines. But walking through masses of cholla taught me just what this really meant.

Pain, though, was not what this was about. It's my belief that to really understand, really "see" the desert or the mountains or any other aspect of nature effort and commitment are required. Glancing out of a car window or from a roadside scenic viewpoint, taking a quick snapshot and saying "that's pretty" is superficial and ultimately unsatisfying. There's no connection, no feeling, no understanding. Walk through the desert or up a mountain and you become a part of the landscape, no longer an out-

Hiking through cholla cactus.

side observer. And the farther you walk, the deeper into the wild you go, the more intense the feeling of contact, the greater the appreciation of where you are and the value wilderness has. Staying out overnight heightens this even more. Staying out for many days and nights forges a bond, a closeness, that stays with you for life, however far from wilderness you may be at times.

As they were completely covered with spines I couldn't touch the bits of cholla and had to pluck them off using my trekking poles as giant tweezers. I'd encountered cholla before but only in small numbers that were easily avoided. Here they covered large areas. Wearing sandals didn't help, though I did find that the spines couldn't pierce their thick soles. I didn't want to wear boots in the heat, so telling myself I'd be back on the road soon I tiptoed on, eyes scanning the ground for fuzzy green monsters. A snake was entwined in one cholla, presumably the spines couldn't pierce its skin. It was certainly a safe place to shelter.

Eventually some pink flagging that Jim had told us to look out for appeared dangling from bushes. It marked the route the Arizona Trail will take, and we followed it past Antelope Peak to another dirt road. There was a scuffling in the bushes and several javelinas emerged, some crossing the road, others rooting in the scrub. We saw jackrabbits bounding over the desert on their long, thin legs, massive ears pointing upward. Ravens soared above, and at one point a black vulture. Paloverde bushes grew by the road. These strange plants have smooth green bark with which they can photosynthesize. They also have thorns, of course.

After crossing graded gravel Freeman Road and picking up our second water cache we started along the maintenance road of a buried gas pipeline. Camp was under a mesquite tree in a small wash just off this track. We'd been out nine and a half hours but were only twelve miles closer to the Gila River, though we'd walked much farther than that. The river was twenty to twenty-five miles away and the walk there should mostly be on dirt roads, though there were some ranches to skirt. We had three to four gallons of water apiece, which should be enough to get us there.

I lay in my sleeping bag looking at the stars and the silhouettes of the bushes and cacti around our camp. We were in the heart of this part of the Sonoran Desert now. I'd been through several bits of desert earlier in the walk, but they were just that, bits, strips of desert between forested mountain ranges. Here the desert reached to the summits of the low hills.

As I was finding out the Sonoran Desert is rich in wildlife and plants, the richest of the four types of desert that make up the North American Desert, or, as Edward Abbey called it, the Great American Desert. The Sonoran Desert forms a great sweep across southern Arizona. Rainfall varies from one to twelve inches per year. The ways in which plants, animals, and birds have adapted to this arid terrain are fascinating. I bore the scars from one method—cactus spines. These are a defense against animals eating sections of the plant and taking some of the precious moisture. The spines provide shade and also shelter the plant from drying winds. Cacti have thick, moist flesh, hence the name succulents. This flesh is protected by a waxy outer layer that minimizes evaporation. In some cacti, such as the saguaro, the skin is heavily grooved so that it can easily expand to hold more water when rain falls. Rather than growing leaves, from which much water would be lost, cacti have green limbs. The chlorophyll that gives the green coloring is needed for photosynthesis, the method by which plants use sunlight to turn carbon dioxide and water into carbohydrates. In cacti the pores through which carbon dioxide enters the plant only open at night, thus reducing water loss. Cacti also have shallow root systems that spread out over a wide area just below the surface, ready to take up the slightest rain.

Plants that do have leaves, such as the ocotillo, mesquite, catclaw acacia, and creosote bush, produce only small ones that won't lose much water. On some plants these leaves appear immediately after it rains and disappear soon afterward. On others the leaves appear in spring but are shed before the hottest summer weather. Much of the year these bushes and small trees are leafless bundles of spiky sticks. Small herbaceous flowering plants react to water even more dramatically than do the shrubs and cacti, springing up immediately after rain to create the beautiful desert blooms. This doesn't occur most years, though. The seeds of these plants can lie dormant for many years until enough rain falls.

Many small mammals adapt to the heat and lack of water by coming out only after dark, staying hidden by day—buried in the sand or nestled inside a hole in a saguaro or deep in a clump of bushes. Other animals, including many birds and reptiles, only come out in the morning and evening, staying out of the sun during the hottest hours. Some animals have adapted in strange ways. The jackrabbit's enormous ears radiate heat and help keep it cool. Javelinas eat the moist pads of prickly pear to get water when creeks and pools are dry.

To travel on foot through the desert we humans get by carrying portable shade and water. We can only survive in the desert by using tools and artifacts. We're so good at this that we can build huge cities such as Phoenix in which millions of people can live comfortably right in the middle of the Sonoran Desert.

Dawn at a typical camp in the Sonoran Desert.

Cold air flowed into the wash during the night, and we woke to a chilly thirty-six degrees, which made the sight of sunshine filtering through the upper branches of the mesquite tree most welcome. Low clouds hung along the western horizon, probably the edge of the storm that was meant to arrive about now according to a forecast we'd heard in Oracle. Many birds were singing, drowned out occasionally by brief but noisy bursts of the coyotes' dawn chorus. Soon after I set off one of the coyotes ambled nonchalantly across the road in front of me, not glancing my way even though I'm sure it knew I was there. Javelinas appeared, running and snorting through patches of prickly pear. Overhead black vultures soared. The usual wildlife. Two days in the Sonoran Desert and I expected to see these creatures.

There were insects about too. A common sight was a large black beetle that when approached stuck its rear up into the air so it looked as though it was standing on its head. My field guide told me this was an armored stink beetle, a threatening name for a threatening creature. Apparently it can release a foul-smelling black liquid from its backside. I didn't check. I'm sure the book was right. It was a change from things that stung or pricked anyway.

I caught up with Jake just before the private Tecolote Ranch. The detour around it was shorter and easier than the one the day before, and we were soon back on the road, named the Old Florence Road on my map that, I noted, was dated 1949. Ripsey Ranch followed. It was an old ruin so we kept to the road. To our right lay low, rounded, sun-baked brown hills called the Tortilla Mountains. To our left the desert spread out in a series of gentle waves. Everything was dry and dusty, and it was a shock to come upon a fine big cottonwood in Ripsey Wash. The fourth private parcel, Horse Ranch, we never saw. Just as we were expecting it to appear a large corral full of cattle blocked the road. A jeep trail led around the corral and on past power lines to a graded gravel road. We took it.

Tracking all these roads and trails on the map was sometimes difficult. Occasionally there was an extra track that didn't appear on the map. One power line didn't quite run where it should have. Maybe it hadn't been surveyed correctly. We were now on a quadrangle that said it had been field checked in 1964. Much could have changed in thirty-six years. New roads built, old ones fading back into the desert, new power lines, pipelines, ranches, cattle trails. How would we know? There were a few signs. A radio tower on a small rise and a steep hill called Grayback both stood out. By orienting the map with the terrain we could see that the radio tower was marked on the map. Most of the roads seemed in the right place too. Maybe things didn't change that fast out here.

We passed a good dirt road leading down to the northeast that we reckoned must lead to a ranch called A-Diamond on the banks of the Gila River. Ahead we could see rugged, interesting-looking terrain on the far side of the river, terrain much more mountainous than here. We were almost certain which road we were on when we stopped to camp far enough away that we'd be out of sight of any vehicles. Three days out from Oracle and we were about six miles from the Gila River and hoping to cross it the next day.

During the day the sky had slowly clouded over, and just before we camped there was a very short shower. The wind was picking up, so we pitched tarps. Jake optimistically tied his to some sagebrush with dried yucca stems for poles. A burst of heavier rain and a gusty wind swept over us. The storm didn't last; it was over in less than half an hour. The skies remained gray, though, and it grew chilly.

Having seen no persons or vehicles for two days and feeling as though we were in the heart of the desert, we were surprised when a steady stream of trucks and cars drove along the road during the evening. Out to the west the lights of Phoenix showed we weren't that far from civilization. An owl hooted nearby then flew past close to the camp. We weren't in civilization either. It was just a bit close.

"Hoo, hoo . . . hoo, hoo." The owl called softly as it grew light. Coyotes and birds welcomed the dawn in their very different ways. There were clouds rather than sun, and it had rained again briefly during the night. From under the tarp I could see sagebrush, yucca, juniper, paloverde, and the straight column of a young saguaro, not yet old enough to sprout arms (which happens after they're seventy-five, apparently). I had a house plant too, a sagebrush bush next to my sleeping mat. While

I was contemplating the plant life and feeling happy to be in the desert Jake set off, wearing a fleece sweater and a warm hat as it was quite chilly. I followed an hour later.

Surprisingly, the roads and installations marked on the 1964 map were there on the ground. There were newer ones as well, so care was needed to avoid a wrong turn. A power line and substation appeared as expected, then a jeep trail started down a sandy wash toward the Gila River. Jake had left stone arrows in the sand in places to show which way he had gone. I kicked them apart out of habit. The dirt road was a far bigger scar on the desert.

Across the gash in which the still-hidden river lay the world changed. Instead of a desert plateau with gentle rolling hills there rose a tangle of cliffs and canyons and steep rocky peaks, an exciting and enticing prospect. Clouds shrouded the highest summits. These were mountains and as mountains always do they stirred my blood and stimulated my mind.

I found Jake waiting part way down the descent. We would see the river together. As we reached the valley bottom the Southern Pacific railroad appeared. We crossed the track and started to push through the dense bushes on the far side. I was tense with anticipation. What would we find? Could we cross the river?

A wide, fast, dirty brown, swirling river came into view. We stared at it in disbelief and disappointment. The clear, six-inch-deep, slow stream we'd been told we might find was not in sight. While we had told each other repeatedly that we might have to walk to the bridge we both really believed we would be able to ford the river. Reality was not pleasant. A quick check with a pole showed that the water was two feet deep near the bank and the current pulled at the pole. There was no way across here.

On the far side of the river lay Walnut Canyon, where our route continued. It was only a few hundred yards away but completely out of reach. We felt as though we'd glimpsed the promised land but had been turned back on the very threshold. Here we were at the lowest point on the Arizona Trail, 1,700 feet, the end of the hottest, driest section, and a big river barred our way. The Gila was already far from its source in the Mogollon Mountains in southwest New Mexico where I'd last seen it fifteen years earlier near the end of my hike on the Continental Divide Trail. The Mogollon Mountains had been covered in snow then. I guessed they were now and that it was the melt from that snow that surged in front of us.

We looked at the maps. Six miles or so to the east the railroad crossed the river. Maybe we could sneak across with it. If not, it was a couple more miles to the road bridge. We set off next to the rails. Although it seemed unlikely we still hoped to find a ford and every so often clambered through the vegetation for a look at the river. After about a mile we came to a wash with a jeep trail that dropped down the bank. A colorful jeep appeared with two Mexicans in it, the back full of tools. They stopped

Jake Schas fording the Gila River, the only difficult river crossing on the walk and the lowest point at 1,700 feet.

on seeing us and sat there looking, probably in disbelief. Jake went over to them but they spoke only Spanish, which neither of us knew, so although he showed them his map they couldn't really help. As they drove off, no doubt wondering what these madmen on foot were doing, Jake said that the driver had produced a 9mm pistol and placed it on his lap. Given Jake's dark glasses and the flap of his cap drawn up over his lower face they probably wondered if they were being robbed. "I took my map out of my shirt very slowly," said Jake.

At the bottom of the wash the river was wide and fast. We split up to see if we could find a ford. After staring at the water for a bit I reckoned a diagonal line could be made across the widest section if it wasn't too deep. I went off in search of Jake. He'd found a narrow section with a small island in the middle. He thought we could maybe use logs to make a bridge to the island and then use the same logs to reach the far bank. On looking at my line he reckoned it was worth trying first. An experienced angler who'd worked as a fishing guide, he was used to wading out into rivers and thought it looked good. He went first while I changed my boots for sandals and was soon across. I followed, finding the water strong and more than knee deep in the middle but by facing upstream, edging sideways, and using poles for support the crossing was safely made.

On the far bank we both felt much happier and were able to properly admire the luxurious growth of trees and bushes lining the river. We found a jeep trail that led back to the mouth of Walnut Canyon and entered a marvelous, fantastic, and awe-inspiring desert mountain world. After the vast spaces and huge vistas of the open desert we were suddenly in a confined world, the spreading sky reduced to a strip of blue high above the huge rock walls that hemmed us in. As we wandered up on an old trail the canyon narrowed even more. Contorted, eroded rocks towered above us, twisted into weird shapes and looking as though they might topple and fall at any minute. They'd probably been like that for centuries, maybe thousands of years. One day though . . . but not today, please.

A creek ran down the canyon's sandy bottom. Flowers, cacti, and birds were everywhere. High above a flock of vultures circled. I counted seventeen at one point. The canyon was alive with dippers, doves, flickers, red-tailed hawks, Gambel's quails, hummingbirds, swallows, curve-billed thrashers, the oddly named phainopeplas, and beautiful, rich red northern cardinals. There were squirrels and chipmunks, too. This profusion of life was due to the creek. And the creek itself? Well, the creek must be due to a natural spring or snowmelt high in the mountains. But it wasn't. Not this creek. This life-giving creek was due to humanity's desire to travel in planes and automobiles; this creek was due to our craving for oil. Prospectors had come here with a drilling rig to bore a hole deep into the desert floor. Happily for the wildlife and for the desert and of course for hikers the drill hit water not oil. The prospectors went away, taking their rig with them. They'd left the new well open and the cold, clean, spouting water was the source of the creek. We filled our bottles and gulped down the beautiful, delicious water, glad not to have to drink the silty stuff out of the Gila. I actually had a gallon left from the last cache but filled up with another, as we weren't sure where the next water was. We were a walking advertisement for the need for water in the desert with the battered, squashed, empty jugs from our caches dangling from our packs.

Heading in to White Canyon, we came to the boundary of the White Canyon Wilderness. On the marker post was an Arizona Trail sign, the first we'd seen in many, many days. A jeep trail reached this point, and there was a lot of garbage around the trailhead. Not wanting to camp among this disfiguring and dispiriting trash we climbed a short way up a trail and stopped on a flattish section of rocky mountainside. There was just enough room to squeeze our sleeping bags between the cacti and the bushes. At 2,200 feet it was the lowest camp of the walk, though it felt as if we were high up in the mountains after the flat desert camps.

The site was spectacular with magnificent sandstone cliffs, peaks, and amphitheaters all around. The rocks were banded with different colors—brown, red, and cream—and glowed wonderfully in the setting sun. I lay in my sleeping bag as the stars came out into a now-clear sky. Crickets chirped melodically. A few mosquitoes, the first I'd seen, threatened to spoil the perfection, but they soon disappeared.

I woke to myriad bird calls. A thick crescent moon hung over a red sandstone peak. A huge slanting vertical wall of colored rock sliced off abruptly at one end soared into the sky. Just one steep gully split the vast stretch of rock. Turning, I saw another double-tiered wall. Plants grew on the sloping ledge between the cliffs. I realized that the trees that were visible high on such ledges, and on the tops of ridges were actually saguaros. This glorious desert rock landscape reminded me of the canyon country far to the north on the Colorado Plateau, most notably in the Grand Canyon, rather than the other mountains of southern Arizona.

In the east the horizon glowed. The rising sun hit the cliffs to the north, making them look like giant slices of vanilla and chocolate ice cream. The heat and dust of the desert brings up such images, I was finding. The thought of ice cream distracted me from an unpleasant but necessary chore—draining and dressing a deep blister on my right heel. I adjusted the ankle strap on my sandal, which I suspected as being the cause.

Surprisingly a dew had fallen, moisture from the recent storm I supposed, and the foot of my sleeping bag was damp. The sun dried it in a few minutes.

Jake set off first, as usual. I wandered up White Canyon after him, marveling at the landscape. After a while I had to pay more attention to where I was going, because the trail became hard to follow as it plunged into thickets of spiky vegetation. Soon it disappeared altogether except for occasional cairns. A voice hailed me. Jake was sitting on a rock in the dry creek bed at a point where the canyon divided. He'd already explored a short way up both branches, finding a trace of a trail up the left fork but nothing up the right. Despite this he reckoned the route went up the right fork but agreed we should take the left because of the trail. As it turned out he was right. The only description we had of the route was brief, on a Passage Information Sheet from the Arizona Trail Association. From the map we could see that we needed to cross the mountains to a jeep trail in Alamo Canyon. The question was how.

The bits of trail in the left fork were old and intermittent, and we soon gave up looking for them. The canyon bottom became choked with brush and boulders, so we made our way up the mountainside above. Cross-country hiking was fairly easy on the open, stony slopes though we had to dodge around the usual spiny bushes and cacti and ended up zigzagging all over the place. Tremendous views of glorious desert mountains stretching into the distance opened up. We were trying to get around Ajax Peak, one of the few summits named on the map, and descend to a jeep trail that the map showed in the valley on the far side. From high on the ridge above the left fork we could see a saddle just south of Ajax. We contoured over to it. We now knew exactly where we were. We just did-n't know where the trail went—there was no sign of it on the saddle.

Descending from the saddle we reached a dry dirt tank and a jeep trail. Not far along this the Arizona Trail came down from a saddle to the north of Ajax Peak. We'd gone around the wrong side of the mountain. A closer look at the ATA sheet would have prevented this. Not that it made much difference. Our route was superb anyway.

The jeep trail led to the southern boundary of Tonto National Forest and soon afterward a forest service road. It might have been forest land but there were no trees, just dusty, cacti-scattered desert. Jake stopped to camp, but I continued, exhilarated by the landscape. From the winding road there were views of some huge sandstone towers that soared into the sky to the southwest and in the other direction the terraced ramparts of the massive block of Picketpost Mountain, which lay just above the trail-head at the end of this section.

A stretch of foot trail led down into Alamo Canyon and along a dry wash to a windmill. The tank it fed was full of dirty water. No fresh water came out of the spigot, as there was no wind to work the pump. Having enough water for an overnight camp I would decide in the morning if I needed to take any water from the tank. By then the wind might be blow-ing. The trailhead was now only about five miles away, so I shouldn't need much water anyway. Paul Leech was supposed to meet us there, as was Bill Watson, the man who had given me all the information on water sources. A stream of e-mails had passed between Bill and Denise, and although I hadn't managed to get through to him on the phone, a meet-ing had been arranged. I camped above the windmill among rolling saguaro-dotted hills.

The scenery had made the day magical, as had the wildlife and plants. The ocotillos had bright red flowers and green leaves, a great contrast to

Hot weather walking in the White Canyon Wilderness.

the dead-looking gray sticks of a few weeks earlier. The stubby hedgehog cacti were in flower, brilliant purple blooms poking out of the sharp spikes. For the first time I came across the strangely named desert Christmas cactus, which has long, thin, multijointed limbs. Vultures floated overhead all day. Lower down many quail darted among the bushes and small lizards basked on hot rocks. I saw an occasional squirrel and one small snake. There were fresh javelina tracks with an accompanying rank smell, but I didn't see any of the beasts themselves. Again I thought how familiar these plants and animals were now, how I knew where to find them and when I expected to see them. The desert was no longer unfamiliar and that felt very satisfying. The joy now was in recognition rather than surprise. I was beginning to feel at home, to understand how nature worked here.

A woodpecker was drumming down in the canyon at dawn. A crescent moon hung above my camp; a few wispy clouds drifted across. I found Jake down at the windmill. He reckoned that he could climb up and turn the blades with his hands to get water. I watched as he clambered up the thin metal tower. Clinging to it with one hand he reached out with the other and began pulling the blades. Slowly the windmill began to turn. I could hear water gurgling in the pipes but only a few drips came out. After a while Jake gave up and climbed back down. We treated water from the tank, me with chlorine dioxide drops, Jake with a filter.

One and a half hours of easy walking down the wash in Alamo Canyon led to the trailhead where we found Paul camped with a welcome supply of orange juice. On striking his camp he pointed out a couple of small pale scorpions under his groundcloth. "They're the most poisonous kind," he said. I hadn't really thought about scorpions, though I knew they lived in the desert. I'd be more careful when lifting up my foam pad and any other items in the future. A large, impressive metal Arizona Trail sign with a big map and plenty of information stood at the trailhead in a grand situation with Picketpost Mountain rising up behind it. You wouldn't have known from the sign that there were very few trail signs between here and Oracle and really not that much actual trail.

Paul drove us into the little town of Superior, five highway miles away. After collecting our mail from the post office we found the only motel and checked in. Superior was a somewhat sad town. A huge copper mine rose above it. No longer in operation, it was once one of the richest mines in Arizona. Most of the stores in the town center had shut down. There was more life on the strip that lay along US 60, where passing traffic might stop. That's where the motel was, along with a few restaurants in which I was very interested.

Just after we reached the motel a car drew up and a tall, lean, wiry man got out and strode toward us. "Hi, I'm Bill." I'd left a note for him at the trailhead. After seeing it he'd been to the post office and the bank and then finally found us here. He'd brought beer—including some excellent English Bass Ale especially for me—and snacks of fruit, cookies, crackers, and cheese. We sat in the sun for several hours talking about the trail and hiking. Bill described the next seventy-five miles of the trail. He had maps printed out from his computer, complete with the Global Positioning System coordinates of the trail, and was amazed to discover that neither Jake nor I was using GPS. "You'll never find the trail without it in some places." As he wanted to check part of the route ahead he loaned me his GPS receiver and asked me to switch it on between certain points.

Bill was also amazed that Jake and I weren't hiking in heavy boots. Discussing our different attitudes we decided that he was a traditionalist, I was a lightweight traditionalist, Jake an ultralight hiker, and Paul a minimalist. Paul carried even less than Jake and admitted that he was uncomfortable at times but liked to do very high daily mileages. The prolonged picnic over, we continued to eat at a Mexican restaurant, courtesy of Bill, after which he returned home. After our five-and-a-bit-day Sonoran Desert crossing I was hungry and quite happy to spend time in town eating. I wanted this stop to be a real rest, unlike the stop in Oracle.

The next day was for chores. In particular I needed to take my clothes to a laundry for the first time since Patagonia, eighteen days ago. There hadn't been time in Oracle. Despite being generally run down Superior had an excellent market with a good choice of lightweight food suitable for the trail. I was also delighted to find a secondhand shop with a selection of paperbacks at ten cents each. I bought several, including a copy of

Shakespeare's *The Tempest.* At the library I downloaded several e-mails but barely had time to read them before the library closed and so was unable to send any replies. Two were from Denise, who I'd spoken to on the phone the night before. All was well at home. However, work was catching up with me. A publisher wanted to know where I'd be on April 25 so she could send some proofs that needed checking by May 5. I didn't know. Somewhere near the end of the trail? I rang to say I'd ring again from the next town in about ten days time, as I might have a better idea by then. (Which I did but in the end they realized trying to get the proofs to me was too difficult and sent them to Scotland instead. It would give me something to do when I got home.)

Jake had a family gathering to attend and was getting picked up that evening and taken to Tucson. He hoped to be back later the next day, but I wanted to start out fairly early. I also wanted to go back to solo hiking. I'd enjoyed being with Jake, and we'd got on well. The hike wasn't the same, though. Having a companion created a barrier between myself and the desert and the mountains, the wildlife and the plants. It was only a thin barrier, a slight veil, but I still felt slightly detached from the landscape. This hadn't mattered so much on the dirt roads south of the Gila River, as the roads themselves had separated me from the desert. I'd noticed it in the White Canyon Wilderness, though, and it was one of the reasons I'd gone on that last day and camped alone by the windmill. Only when I was alone could I fully relate to nature and think and feel about where I was.

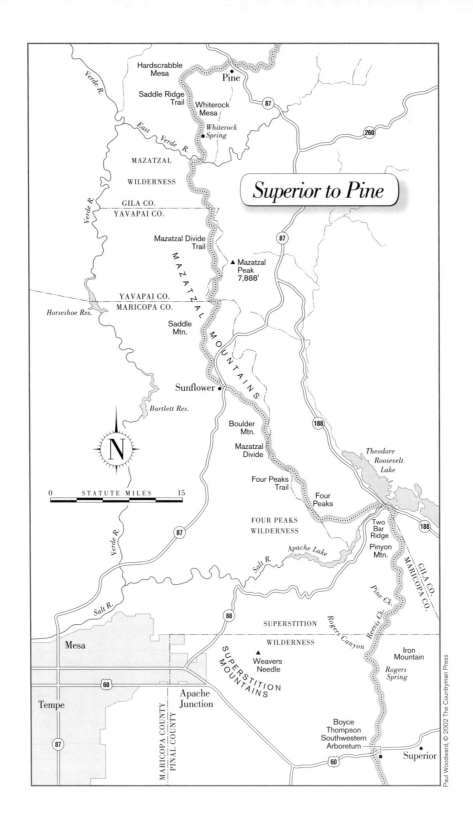

Hardscrabble Mesa

Pine

Saddle Ridge Trail

Whiterock Mesa

Whiterock Spring

87

260

MAZATZAL

WILDERNESS

GILA CO.
YAVAPAI CO.

Mazatzal Divide Trail

Superior to Pine

87

▲ Mazatzal Peak 7,888'

Verde R.

East Verde R.

Verde R.

YAVAPAI CO.
MARICOPA CO.

Horseshoe Res.

Saddle Mtn.

M A Z A T Z A L   M O U N T A I N S

Sunflower

Bartlett Res.

N

0   STATUTE MILES   15

Boulder Mtn.

Mazatzal Divide

Four Peaks Trail

Four Peaks

188

Theodore Roosevelt Lake

FOUR PEAKS WILDERNESS

Two Bar Ridge

Pinyon Mtn.

188

GILA CO.
MARICOPA CO.

87

Verde R.

Salt R.

Apache Lake

88

Salt R.

SUPERSTITION

Rogers Canyon

Reavis Ck.

Pine Ck.

Mesa

S U P E R S T I T I O N   M O U N T A I N S

WILDERNESS

▲ Weavers Needle

Iron Mountain

Rogers Spring

60

Tempe

MARICOPA COUNTY
PINAL COUNTY

Apache Junction

87

Boyce Thompson Southwestern Arboretum

60

Superior

Paul Woodward. © 2002 The Countryman Press

5

Superstitions and Mazatzals

SUPERIOR TO PINE

151 miles

North of the Picketpost Trailhead lie the evocatively and intriguingly named Superstition Mountains. These are steep, rough, rugged mountains, a complex mass of canyons, ridges, and peaks. The maps show a tangle of tightly packed, spaghetti-like contour lines. The maps are mostly brown, too, some completely so; there is little forest here. This is dusty, dry, harsh, hot, cactus country. Compared with other Arizonan mountains the Superstitions aren't that big. The highest summits are only a touch more than 6,000 feet; most are much lower. The lack of elevation adds rather than detracts from the arid nature of the Superstitions. There are no cool, forested mountaintops. This is Sonoran Desert country, similar to the White Canyon Wilderness but much larger in scale.

The Superstitions are famous in Arizona, partly because they rise just east of Phoenix, their serrated skyline visible to millions of people, but mainly because of a strange story involving gold, murder, madness, magic, headless corpses, kidnapped doctors, Apaches, mysterious stone maps, and a host of larger-than-life characters: the tale of the Lost Dutchman Gold Mine.

Any words on this tale should start "it is said that" or "once upon a time," as there is far more fiction than fact in the many versions of the story. This is frontier myth, one of the stories that make up the legend of the Wild West. The key character, the mysterious Dutchman, did actually exist, though he came from Germany not Holland, and he was a prospector. His name was Jacob Waltz, his nickname, Dutch, presumably a corruption of Deutsch. Sometimes the gold he is supposed to have discovered is said to have come from a mine owned by the wealthy Spanish Peralta family from Sonora in Mexico, gold that was lost when the miners were massacred by Apaches. In other versions he finds the gold himself. One story has him hearing about the gold from a Dr. Abraham Thorne, who was kidnapped by the Apaches who had killed the Peralta miners and taken to their secret lair deep in the Superstitions. After treating the Native Americans' ailments the doctor was led out of the mountains blindfolded. At one point the Apaches removed his blindfold. All around lay bags of gold and skeletons. The doctor was allowed to take as much gold as he could carry before continuing, blindfolded again. Although he was now rich the doctor returned to the Superstitions time and time again, convinced he could find the rest of the Peralta gold. Failing to do so, he eventually went mad.

Once Waltz found the mine he is said to have made regular trips there, each time returning to civilization with bags of gold. He told no one where it came from and reputedly killed anyone who followed him. When he died, in the best adventure-story fashion, he left behind a map showing the location of the mine or, according to others, hints as to how to find it.

Since Waltz died in 1891 many others have searched for the Lost Dutchman Mine. Some of them have died, sometimes in unexplained circumstances, adding to the legend. However, according to Tom Kollenborn and the Superstition Mountain Historical Society, there's no evidence of gold mining in the Superstitions by the Peralta family or anyone else. Also, the local Native Americans were the peaceful Pima, not the warlike Apache. Jacob Waltz did make regular ventures into the Superstitions, never telling anybody what he found. And when he died some gold was apparently found under his bed. Where it came from no one knows, but presumably it was the source of the legend. The first gold seeker was Julia Thomas, in whose house Waltz died. She failed to find anything, of course. It seems likely she did find a way to make money by selling the story of the lost gold mine to a writer with the wonderful name of Pierpont Constable Bicknell. He could tell the value of a good story and wrote several newspaper articles about the Dutchman and his gold. Many of the story's elements started with Bicknell. The tale was soon picked up by other writers and now had a life of its own, a life that is still strong and thriving. Thousands of articles and many books have been written about the Lost Dutchman Mine; there are even quite a few web sites. People still go in search of the gold, convinced that the mine is there.

The hardheaded and practical scientists called geologists say that gold is very unlikely to be found in the Superstitions because they are made of a volcanic rock that doesn't contain minerals. But to add a recent twist to the tale, the U.S. Geological Survey has reportedly found signs that there may be minerals deep below the surface of the mountains. Just possibly volcanic activity pushed some of these minerals to the surface; just possibly one of the minerals was gold; just possibly Jacob Waltz found it; just possibly it's still there waiting to be rediscovered, just possibly.

Lost mines and hidden gold were not on my mind as I stared at the distant, jagged horizon of the Superstitions from the busy highway between Superior and the trailhead. I could see there was much worth seeking there: a spectacular landscape, wildlife, wild plants, the privilege of hiking through pristine mountains, of sleeping under starry skies with no sign of humanity anywhere. I didn't want to find or see any mines. I wasn't likely to either, as most of the Superstition Mountains are now a protected Wilderness Area and mining is prohibited.

First I had to survive the highway, which as usual was far more dangerous than the mountains. Cars and trucks sped by just inches away as I plodded along. The four and half miles to the trailhead were very long miles. A couple of diversions broke the fraught monotony. The first, on the edge of Superior, was a small walk-through cabin entitled "World's Smallest Museum." Inside was a fairly random collection of local curios and historical relics while outside was a scattering of larger items, mostly to do with mining. It was worth a few minutes time. I thought the castellated wooden facade the most interesting feature of this curiosity. The name was emblazoned on it in gold on a green background and flanked by a large circular thermometer advertising Coca-Cola and a metal sign, bearing a picture of a stagecoach, that read THE OLD WEST HIGHWAY WHERE HISTORY STILL LIVES. Two rather tatty barrel cacti in large pots stood on either side of the entrance.

Much farther along the road I found a much more serious institution, the Boyce Thompson Arboretum, which is dedicated to the study and promotion of desert plant life. There are various indoor exhibits plus interpretive trails through areas laid out with the plants from different deserts worldwide. I wandered around some of the exhibits and took the Sonoran Desert Trail, which enabled me to put names to some of the plants I was unsure about. But I hadn't time to see much, and the Boyce Thompson Arboretum joined the long list of places I plan on returning to "one day."

I said a welcome farewell to US 60, which I had no desire to see ever again, at a culvert that took the Arizona Trail under the road. I walked through this silver tunnel to a new world. Ahead lay desert and mountains and nothing but desert and mountains. I felt liberated. There was nothing to do except hike and camp and observe what was around me while I did so. My pack was heavy with nine days' worth of food. I could have left the trail to resupply, but I preferred to carry the extra weight rather than break the walk again. I wanted to stay in the wilderness.

A section of newly built trail climbed to a low, cacti- and rock-strewn ridge that provided extensive views. Behind me to the south rose the rock tiers of Picketpost Mountain, to the east, above Superior, ran a line of cliffs called Apache Jump. My eyes were mostly fixed on the view ahead—the enticing, ragged Superstitions. Toward their western end I could see Weaver's Needle, a thin spire of rock that features in the Lost Dutchman Mine legend. This striking landmark is visible from afar and has entered the story as one of the markers said to indicate the gold's whereabouts. One searcher even believed the mine was inside the Needle.

My constant companion.

The trail ended abruptly partway down the ridge. Bits of pink flagging tied to bushes showed where it would continue. I followed them down into the fine red-rock ravine of Whitford Canyon. An intermittent creek trickled through the sand. Walking up the canyon I was suddenly startled by two simultaneous, unconnected, and unexpected occurrences. Five little balloon-tired off-road vehicles came bouncing noisily down the canyon at the same time as rain started to fall. The ORVs were gone in seconds. The rain lasted half an hour. The day was cool and there were some clouds, but the rain was still a surprise. In my desert world it didn't rain. I almost felt affronted by it.

The trail in Whitford Canyon became a dirt road. A huge cottonwood tree came into view. Two longhaired, long-bearded men stood under it beside a truck and a jeep. They pointed out a hole in a branch above them. A bees' nest, one said. Sure enough, a cluster of bees was buzzing around it.

Leaving the road I dropped down into Reevis Trail Canyon. The map showed a Reevis Creek, Reevis Valley, Reevis Gap, Reevis Saddle, Reevis Grave, and Reevis Ranch. Who was this Reevis, and why was his name all over the map? Elisha M. Reavis (as everyone seems to spell the name except the U.S. Geological Survey) settled deep in the mountains in the late 1800s, a time when hardly anyone else ever went there. Known as the Hermit of the Superstitions he grew vegetables and fruit, which he packed out of the mountains and sold. Pictures of him show a wild, longhaired, long-bearded man. Not unlike the two men I'd met under the bee tree.

The day's canyons had an odd mix of cottonwoods and saguaros, often growing within a few feet of each other. There was plenty of water in the creeks, which was a good sign for the days ahead, the Superstitions being notoriously dry. Fresh green grass grew in places by the creeks, the first I'd seen on the walk. I'd forgotten grass was so bright. Strikingly scarlet northern cardinals, one of the most beautiful birds I've ever seen, watched me from the bushes.

Late in the afternoon the Reevis Trail Canyon widened into a shallow bowl. The trail zigzagged for two thousand feet up Montana Mountain. That could wait for the next day. I made camp, pitching the tarp in case of more rain. On the edge of the mountains and back in the wilds I felt relaxed and at ease. The town stops were disruptive. Although Superior had been far less stressful than Oracle I'd still had to deal with people and things, especially things. Phones, money, locks, keys, chairs, beds, televisions, computers, postage stamps, vehicles. Civilization seemed full of things. They overwhelmed me, cut me off from what mattered. Out here there were few things. Instead there was life and nature. Rocks, saguaro, cholla, stars, creeks, cottonwoods, whitethorn, prickly pear, vultures, northern cardinals. I knew which list I'd rather have. At that moment anyway. At other times civilization, or some aspects of it at least, would be very appealing. But it could be difficult to handle.

Cacti in the Superstition Mountains.

I woke to the sound of waves of wind roaring down the mountain-side. Clouds raced across the sky. The trail led steadily upward out of the Sonoran Desert and into chaparral and piñon-oak-juniper woodland. The southeastern side of the Superstitions is one of the few places in these mountains where there is enough water for trees to grow. That's why Elisha Reavis came this way. The map shows a sweep of green running north from Montana Mountain and fading out in the upper reaches of Reevis Creek. After many days in cactus country the woods were a big change. There were no saguaros, instead real trees with leaves and needles, not spines. From the top of the climb a dirt road led to the Rogers Trough trailhead on the edge of the Superstition Wilderness. Half a dozen vehicles were parked there. It was a Sunday, and I was to meet most of the owners during the next few hours, all hiking out after a weekend in the wilds.

The trail down narrow Rogers Canyon, over Reevis Saddle, and into Reevis Valley was rough and steep, showing the true nature of the Superstitions, mostly hidden here by the softness of the beautiful forest. The view ahead to stony brown mountains showed what most of the range is like. Oaks and sycamores hung over the pools in Rogers Creek. On the descent into Reevis Valley big ponderosa pines appeared, the north-facing slope sheltering them from the sun. Steller's jays, beautiful blue birds with harsh, ugly voices, screeched raucously in the branches of the trees. The valley itself felt very lush with a flowing creek and meadows thick with tall grass. I could see why Elisha Reavis settled here. Old gnarled orchards and the remnants of the foundations of the ranch house are the only traces of his enterprise.

I'd been following Arizona Trail and other trail signs all the way from Rogers Trough. Every trail junction was marked and route-finding in the Superstitions seemed easy. Note that word: seemed. Trail signs have an insidious effect. Why bother checking the map when they're there? Just follow the trail and look for the signs, secure in the knowledge that they'll point you in the right direction. Which is fine until one isn't there. I ambled down Reevis Canyon looking at the trees and the grass and feeling relaxed and happy. On and on I went until I became gradually aware of a growing unease. Not wanting to lose my pleasant reverie I tried to ignore it. The entreaties emanating from somewhere in my head grew stronger. Think, something in my brain said. Think. Eventually, reluctantly, I thought. This is the wrong way. Damn.

What had alerted me to my error was my habit of studying the map before leaving camp. From somewhere near the ranch I should have climbed to Reevis Gap, I seemed to remember. But I was slowly descending. The map showed my memory was correct, unfortunately. But how had I missed the trail? Back up the valley I went, looking carefully for the trail junction. It appeared just where it should have. However, there was a log lying across the trail that obscured the junction when approaching from the other direction. If you weren't looking for it, and I hadn't been, you wouldn't have seen it. There was a trail sign though, an Arizona Trail sign on a tree. It pointed down Reevis Valley. The wrong way. That was worse than no sign at all. The sign was screwed in place. A few seconds with the little screwdriver on my Swiss Army knife and it was realigned.

A steep, stony climb led out of the valley, up the slopes of aptly named Boulder Mountain to a saddle, then descended equally steeply and stonily down to Pine Creek. The way was rough but the scenery superb with distant views across the wilderness and close ones of the cliffs of Boulder Mountain. As I reached Pine Creek a figure appeared carrying water containers, a bearded man with tied-back long hair and hiking boots, running shorts, and a blue shirt. A large dome tent sat in a clearing not far away. Ed Lawrence was from Ashland, Oregon, a town where I'd resupplied on my Pacific Crest Trail hike eighteen years ago, where he worked in performance theater. He said he hiked only in designated wilderness areas but was interested in the Arizona Trail. I asked him about Walnut Spring, where I was planning to camp. He'd never camped there, he said, as a friend hadn't liked the smell of the water and he, Ed, never filtered water. I could always treat it, I thought. The alternative was to haul water from here, a lot of water as Walnut Spring was the last water source for about ten miles.

On the short climb from Pine Creek an impressive mountain with four distinct summits appeared away to the north. This was Four Peaks

Mountain, a major landmark in central Arizona, where I'd be in a few days. Walnut Spring was hidden in a thicket on an open hillside. The water smelled fine to me, so I didn't treat it. I found a flat campsite next to a bush several hundred yards away, out of sight of the spring so as not to scare wildlife from visiting it. The views of Boulder Mountain and Four Peaks Mountain were tremendous.

Despite the fine campsite I was not content. The curse of a distant but approaching deadline was on me. I was supposed to meet Bill Watson at a road crossing in three days' time, at least fifty miles away across very rugged terrain. It had just taken me a touch under ten hours to hike sixteen miles, and I'd only had a few brief stops. The rough, steep trails were the main reason, though wasting an hour when I went wrong didn't help. To have any chance of making the rendezvous I was going to have to push hard over the next few days, not something I wanted to do.

A single mosquito whining around my head woke me in the early morning. Birdsong was a more welcome start to the new day. As the sky lightened I saw the clouds had cleared. There was no wind. Boulder Mountain was a black silhouette. As the first cool, gray light crept over the land the rock face slowly appeared, an uninteresting dull brown. Then the rim of the huge cliff caught fire as the first rays of the sun struck. Soon the whole mountain glowed gold. Heat, the landscape said, heat. And hot it was, one of the hottest days so far.

Most of the day's walk was in the full glare of the sun too. The cool woods were behind me. Here there were just stony slopes dotted with a scattering of cacti and bushes that gave little shade. The trail was very rocky, often faint, frequently steep, and sometimes in thick but low spiny brush. This made for slow progress and a growing number of scratches and weals on my lower legs that stung and itched.

There was no water. At least none that I could find. A spring called Klondike was marked on the maps, but I never saw it or even a sign pointing to it if there was one. This didn't surprise me, as each of my two maps had it in a completely different position, east of Pine Creek on the Forest Service one and west of it on the USGS quad. If the latter was correct I was probably nowhere near it. The trail guide described it as "impossible to find" too. Knowing I probably wouldn't find water until Cottonwood Spring, some ten miles farther on, I had drunk as much as I could before leaving camp and set off with two quarts. It was barely enough.

The long, flat-topped line of the cliffs of Boulder Mountain and the four triangular summits of Four Peaks Mountain dominated the views most of the day, the first slowly shrinking and fading into the distance, the second growing higher and more massive. There were no other really distinctive summits, just rolling brown hills dotted with shattered rock outcrops. The harsh beauty of the Superstitions was in the overall nature of the landscape rather than in individual hills.

This beauty was revealed in its fullness on Two Bar Ridge, a long broad spur running out from Two Bar Mountain, along which a trail runs, a wonderful rolling traverse, sometimes on the crest, sometimes just below, skirting little summits. The views were tremendous, and I had my first sight of the deep blue of huge Roosevelt Lake, looking startlingly bright and artificial, which it is, being a reservoir. Across the water the distant brown line of the Sierra Ancha Mountains rippled along the horizon.

Two Bar Ridge led out of the wilderness and changed immediately from foot to jeep trail. I was leaving the Superstitions. On the boundary fence I left a note for Jake, who was intending on dropping down east here to go to the little town of Roosevelt to resupply, asking him to call Bill Watson and say neither of us were likely to make the rendezvous. The rough terrain and heat were slowing me down. Jake, behind me as far as I knew, was unlikely to get there first.

The dirt road led down into the pleasant red-rock desert of Cottonwood Canyon. Ahead a smear of darker, richer green stood out against the faded paleness of the cacti and yuccas. Suddenly and delightfully the dusty arid valley became a deciduous wood in spring with fresh grass, clover, and even, almost unbelievably, dangling wild grapevines. Above was a cool canopy of green-leafed sycamore, ash, oak, and cottonwood. The damp ground even smelled like a forest in spring, releasing rich earthy scents with every step. Down this narrow strip of verdant luxury ran spring-fed Cottonwood Creek, dense waterweeds almost choking the slow-moving water.

Through the trees I could see saguaros and other cacti on the dry desert hillside that lay just yards away, a strange juxtaposition. In places saguaros and cottonwoods almost touched. The creek didn't flow far. As soon as it stopped the canyon became a dry desert wash. A short distance farther and the water appeared again and with it the strip of forest. Yet again the relationship between water and life was clearly visible.

Back in the desert again there were impressive red-rock cliffs above the slowly descending jeep trail. A final burst of green in the increasingly stark desert marked Thompson Spring. From above the spring there was a sudden view of Roosevelt Lake, now much closer, with a big sloping table of a mountain beyond known as Dutch Woman's Butte. The trail dropped steeply to the spring then went straight back up the other side. This was not a promising place for a camp, but I was tired and didn't want to haul water very far. On the far side of the creek two scrawny cattle, ribs showing through their skin, nervously watched, clacking their hooves on the stony ground. As I approached they ran off, tails high in the air. Not wanting to keep them, or any wildlife, away from water I left the trail and climbed the hillside above. After a few hundred feet I found a flattish patch of stony soil under a paloverde bush. It would do.

Less than a mile away lay a marina and a road along the side of the reservoir. I was almost back in civilization. But as I couldn't see them or hear any noise they might as well have not existed, at least for now. The night sky was spectacular again. Lying in my sleeping bag I stared at the stars and the silhouettes of saguaros and other desert plants feeling slightly sad. This would probably be my last night in the Sonoran Desert. The walk was about to change. Tomorrow I would climb up into the Mazatzal Mountains and stay high in them for many miles. These mountains are part of the Central Highlands or Transition Province that separates the Basin and Range region in the south from the Colorado Plateau in the north. The Transition Province runs southeast to northwest and features many large mountain ranges like the Mazatzals. There is desert, but overall this area gets more rainfall than other parts of Arizona.

The next day did not suggest that I was entering an area with more springs and creeks and pools. The night was warm, with a low of fifty-

Very hot weather on Two Bar Ridge.

two degrees. Oddly, it grew colder as it grew light, the temperature dropping to forty-six degrees in just twenty minutes. The mountains across
the lake turned from gray to a hazy pink as the sun began to appear.
Around me the cool gray-green of the desert plants brightened and
warmed into a golden green.

Not far from camp a trail led down to the highway. Knowing there
was a store at the marina I was tempted out of the wilds. Paul Leech had
told me not to expect much in the way of supplies, but a few extras
would be a nice supplement to my dwindling rations. The road was empty,
just a black strip stretching out along the edge of the dark blue water.
Boats bobbed in the marina, but there were none out on the lake. The
store was closed at this early hour. I walked out along a side road to a large
parking area and a low building that housed a visitors center. The lack of
people and traffic gave the whole place a slightly unreal air, as if it had
been abandoned in some mysterious disaster. Later, I knew, cars would
arrive, people would walk about, there would be engines, voices, laughter.
But for now it was like a ghost town. Inside the visitors center there was
life—a ranger sitting behind a long, leaflet-covered, curving counter. Various exhibits told the story of the reservoir and the Salt River Project of
which it is part. The ranger was more interested in talking about Scotland, once he learned where I was from. I guess he was bored with the
local history.

From the displays I learned that Roosevelt Lake was created in 1911
when the Roosevelt Dam was completed. The dam blocks the narrow
canyon down which the Salt River runs just after its confluence with Tonto
Creek. Building a dam in this remote desert basin surrounded by rugged
mountains was a huge enterprise that took six years. Before construction
could even begin roads had to be driven into the area. A temporary town
was built for the workers and the services they needed; it now lies under
the waters of the reservoir. The finished dam arcs one thousand feet
between the steep canyon walls and was initially 284 feet high. Additional
work in the 1990s increased its height to 357 feet.

As always when confronted with big dams I couldn't help but be
impressed with this feat of engineering. At the same time it left me cold.

My appreciation was logical, intellectual. The statistics said it all—how high, how wide, how long to build, how much money, how big. Roosevelt Lake was once the biggest man-made lake in the world. Most dams and reservoirs have some claim to having been the biggest somewhere, or the tallest, or widest, or first. Just making these claims shows that the figures are what matters. The dam builders, the engineers, want you to be impressed, want you to marvel at how they have tamed and controlled wild nature. And marvel I do. But I don't admire, I don't empathize, I don't feel ecstatic the way I do when I see a grove of saguaros curving around a hillside or a vulture floating high above or a mighty cliff soaring above a desert canyon. A dam is a very simple item compared to a tree.

Roosevelt Dam was built to control the Salt River, ending the droughts and floods that had made farming and habitation difficult, and to ensure water supplies for farming and the growing population of Phoenix and the Salt River Valley. As more and more water was needed more dams were built on the Salt and other rivers. Without dams and huge reservoirs central Arizona couldn't sustain a fraction of the people that live there now.

Back at the marina store I wandered around the few aisles, shopping list in hand. I was able to cross off bug repellent (just in case the mosquitoes became more of a nuisance), sugar, and trail mix, but that was it. Postcards, dried milk, wet wipes, and blister dressings would have to wait until the next store. Surprisingly, I could have bought stove fuel if I'd needed any. Unsurprisingly, there were various fishing and boating items; indeed, these made up most of the inventory.

The store did have a snack bar so, sticking to the long distance hiker's credo of never passing by an opportunity to eat, I ordered a second breakfast of scrambled eggs, hash browns, and toast with a couple of quarts of Coca-Cola to stop me from getting thirsty. Wandering outside I sat at a table under a sun canopy. A man sitting nearby was tying flies and taking an occasional bite out of a burger. If the flies hadn't told me he was a fisherman the thigh-high waders he was wearing would have. "Come far?" he asked, before telling me that he fished all over the state. The previous weekend he'd been down at Parker Canyon Lake. The name brought back memories. It seemed a long time ago. Much had happened in the twenty-four days and 320-plus miles since then. Then the walk had been new, young, and without any clear form. The landscape had been strange, a source of surprise and wonder. Now the walk was established and had a pattern. The wonder was still there, but it came from deeper within, a continued satisfaction at the complexity and beauty of the wilderness.

"I did a fifty-mile hike in the Mazatzals once," said the fisherman, breaking into my thoughts; they are much rougher than the Superstitions. There was some good news. Snow had fallen in the Four Peaks area two weeks ago. That should mean water in the creeks. Eventually, anyway. First there was a sixty-five-hundred-foot ascent straight up into the Four Peaks Wilderness. I could see much of that climb from down here. It looked very hot and very dry.

Glancing at a newspaper I saw that the forecast was for the weather to get hotter over the next five days. Oh well, I would be higher up most of the time and in woods where it should be shadier and cooler. Phoenix, I read, had had the third wettest March on record. Most of that was from the storm in which I'd arrived.

Before ending this brief contact with the edge of civilization I loaded up with a gallon and a half of water, enough, I thought, to get me to Pigeon Spring, the next likely water, seventeen miles away according to the trail guide but twenty-two according to the track record on Bill Watson's GPS.

A few miles of undulating trail traversed around saguaro-dotted, steep hillsides to a view down to the graceful curve of the suspension bridge that takes the road and the Arizona Trail over the narrow arm of the reservoir that reaches down to the dam. On the far side of the bridge steep open slopes climbed above the lake. Somewhere up there went the trail.

A very steep descent led down to the bridge. Once across a very steep ascent led back up. It was midmorning. The sun was high and hot and the trail ran straight toward it up a bare ridge with no shade anywhere. Even with my sun hat on and my umbrella up I was soon overheating. Sweat dripped off my nose, ran into my eyes, soaked my shirt. The water went down alarmingly fast. For one thousand feet the trail climbed relentlessly before finally easing off for an undulating few miles on a trail signed VINEYARD TRAIL, not that I could imagine vines growing on these desert hills, that eventually joined a dirt road. There were clusters of saguaros on south-facing slopes, but for the most part this was some of the most naked terrain I'd seen. To the south, across the deep Salt River Canyon, lay the Superstitions with Piñon, Two Bar, and Boulder Mountains all easily identifiable. However, at this distance the subtle and intricate beauty of the Superstitions couldn't be seen. They were just rolling brown hills all about the same height. Ahead, Four Peaks Mountain was much more distinctive.

The brief respite from the climb ended at a trailhead. A sign pointed up the Four Peaks Trail (Granite Springs Trail, according to the topo map). A short way on a lurid black-on-yellow sign leaped out at me. CAUTION, it said, FLASH FLOOD, TRAIL DAMAGE, ROLLING ROCK, FALLING TREES. The trail wound peacefully on through the chaparral. For a few yards. I quickly understood the meaning of the sign as the trail plunged into deep V-shaped ravines and crossed steep, loose slopes of eroded, stony soil. I skittered and slithered along, glad of the support of my hiking poles. Black skeletons appeared—the first small trees. The whole mountainside had burned. Without trees to absorb moisture and hold the earth in place there had been flash floods that washed out most of the trail. A tangled mass of spiky bushes, the first regrowth after the fire, added to the arduous nature of the climb. My legs were soon running with blood. I was horribly hot and sweating heavily, unable to use the umbrella because of the bushes and the need for careful balance. With little water left I was loath to drink much. Buckhorn Creek had traces of dampness but no actual water. A hope that there might be water in Granite Spring kept me wearily plodding uphill. It didn't. The shallow ravine in which the spring was situated had completely washed out. There hadn't been water here for a very long time. A sign lying upside down in the ravine bed told me the trail was unmaintained from here on. Dispirited and weary I camped on a slightly sloping, sandy shelf above the dry spring. I had just one and a half quarts of water left, and it was nine miles and about twenty-five hundred feet of ascent to Pigeon Spring. For the first time on the walk I had run seriously short of water. Ironically, mosquitoes buzzing around kept me awake. Where were they coming from? Some fetid puddle out of reach deep in the brush, I guessed.

When I set off early the next morning I had just a pint of water left. Above me rose 6,612-foot Buckhorn Mountain. In theory the trail went over the summit. In reality the trail had ceased to exist except for small, infuriating, overgrown traces that quickly disappeared. The climb was a desperately hot sweaty scrabble up steep, loose ground and through sharp spiny undergrowth that scratched my legs and tore at my clothes. It took one and a half hours and a great deal of water loss. I reached the sum-

Four Peaks Mountain. The steep bushwhack to the foot of this mountain was the hardest part of the walk.

mit sweat-soaked and very thirsty. Trickles of blood ran down my arms and legs. My mood was one of aggravation and worry. I cursed the bush and the mountain. Damn the thorns. Damn the rocks. Bloody awkward things. What the hell was I doing here anyway? And where was I going to find any water on this godforsaken mountain?

Suddenly the negative feelings were swept away in a rush of wings. A magnificent bald eagle, its white head shining in the sunlight, drifted over the ridge just fifty feet away and landed on a dead tree. I felt transformed. As I thrashed my way uphill I'd forgotten why I was here and what I was doing. I just wanted the climb to be over. The eagle took me out of myself, out of my self-pity and anger, and I once again saw the magic of the world around me. Why worry about being a bit thirsty? Why care about aching limbs, the sweat and blood running down my legs, the many miles to water? To be here high on a mountain ridge watching a glorious eagle soar past was what it was all about. The effort, the pain required to get here heightened the experience. I looked around. Tremendous views spread out on every side. I had that on-top-of-the-world feeling common to mountaineers, whether they hike up a trail or climb steep ice cliffs. A burst of adrenaline and elation stripped away my worries.

From the summit the remnants of the trail were easier to follow as it ran along Buckhorn Ridge toward the impressive, steep, rocky east face of Four Peaks Mountain. Although the ridge is mostly above six thousand feet the four great rock pyramids of the mountain still looked massive as they rose to 7,657 feet on Brown's Peak, the northernmost and highest summit. The mountain, protected in the Four Peaks Wilderness Area, lies at the southern end of the Mazatzal Mountains, which I would traverse over the next five days. This wilderness is supposed to have the densest population of black bears in Arizona, though I saw no signs of them.

Four Peaks Mountain dominated the view, drawing me on along the ridge toward its huge buttresses and deep gullies. To the south the Superstitions were smaller now, slowly fading away in distance and time, already part of my past. To the west, the organized, straight lines on the edge of Phoenix could be seen, far below and far away—rigid, regimented, another world.

At Alder Saddle (I liked the name, alders grow by water), right under the cliffs of Four Peaks Mountain, the back of a sign appeared. TRAIL NOT MAINTAINED AHEAD the front read. It looked as though the difficult section was over. And it was, an excellent trail traversed around the eastern slopes of Brown's Peak. There was better to come. As I descended into a little dip I heard a faint but familiar sound. I stopped. There it was again. Water trickling. Unexpectedly and wonderfully a tiny creek with a couple of small pools ran down the little ravine. The sight overwhelmed me with joy. Nothing in the world could have been more welcome. My mouth was dry and sticky; my tongue clove to the roof of my mouth in traditional lost-in-the-desert fashion. The pint of water was long gone. Gratefully I sat by the creek and drank. The water tasted amazing. I could feel it spreading through me, a delicious wave of cool wetness. The feeling of relief was enormous. Only as I relaxed did I become aware of just how tense and worried I'd been. I felt I had gone closer to the edge of real dehydration, of serious problems, than I liked or should have. Many more miles without water and I could have been in trouble.

High up on the north and east faces of Brown's Peak white speckles marked patches of snow, the remnants of the fall two weeks before that the fisherman had told me about. That storm must have been the same one that dropped snow on me in Molino Basin in the Santa Catalinas. I'd drunk the storm then. I was drinking it now. I felt fond of that storm.

Behind me Buckhorn Ridge rose gently to Buckhorn Mountain. The ghostly gray silhouettes of burned trees ran along the ridges, stretching their dead branches into the sky. Here and there a few strips of tall conifers—ponderosa pine, Douglas fir—had escaped the fire but most of the big trees were dead. The chaparral was quickly recovering though, with a dense spread of bushes, many fresh with the green of spring.

Refreshed, relaxed, and happy I continued on around the eastern shoulder of Brown's Peak. Far below Roosevelt Lake shone in the sunlight. There was water in almost every drainage, however small, so when I finally reached Pigeon Spring I didn't really need it. From a broken concrete tank, partly covered over, water dribbled into a cattle-churned morass. The water was green with algae; however, once dipped out from below the surface, it was quite clear. I left with one and three-quarter gallons, probably more than I needed, but I didn't want to run short again.

From Pigeon Spring a dirt road ran along or close to the crest of the mountains. A large signboard explained the huge burned area that still spread out all around. The Lone Fire burned roughly sixty thousand acres in just six days in the spring of 1996. The cause was a camper's fire at Pigeon Spring that got out of control. Strong winds and very dry brush ensured that the fire spread rapidly. Twelve hundred fire fighters tackled the blaze with everything from shovels to planes and helicopters.

The dry and stony road was hard on the feet, but I was able to stride out in a way I hadn't been able to for days. Around me chaparral-covered slopes ran out to brown hills. Two white-tailed deer trotted across the road. A large flock of ravens appeared. I counted at least a dozen. I smelled the reason before I saw it, a bloated, stinking, dead cow crawling with flies lying on the edge of the road. The ravens circled overhead and watched me from the branches of small trees. I was happy to let them return to their feast. High above, vultures were approaching. Between them they would strip the carcass in a very short time. Scavengers are often disliked and regarded with disgust, yet without them life would be impossible. They rarely kill, merely clean up what has already died or is dying. After seeing that cow I felt grateful to them.

After a few miles on the road I stopped. I'd been out eleven hours and that was enough. Sunflower, where I was due today, was still about ten miles away. I hoped my message had reached Bill Watson. Camp was on an open hillside dotted with scrub oak above large Bull Basin. When I stood up brightly lit Phoenix looked surprisingly close. But lying in my sleeping bag I was alone in the wilds except for a faint glow to the west. The constellations began to appear—Orion, Capella, Gemini, Ursa Major, Cassiopeia. As on many nights I fell asleep watching them.

The dirt road meandered uneventfully along, skirting below Bull Mountain and through Little Pine Flat to a trailhead. Here the Boulder Creek Trail plunged steeply down the mountainside to the northwest. The first part of the descent was rough, rocky, and very overgrown. In places the trail was a tunnel under the bushes. The vegetation clung and stuck and tore, as usual. Stinging, bleeding legs were now so normal I hardly noticed them. At least this was downhill.

Lower down the walking became easier, and I was able to look beyond the next step. Big sycamores grew near the creek bed in which there were pools of water. The first mule deer I'd seen, larger than the whitetails, with distinctive big ears clearly visible, bounded through the trees. My mind was on Sunflower. Would Bill be there? Would he have left a note? Was there a phone? I hurried on.

The trailhead came into view at half-past noon. A vehicle was just about to leave the parking lot but stopped when the driver spotted me. I was barely in time; it was Bill. He'd just left a note for Jake and me. Denise had e-mailed Bill to say I was about half a day behind schedule after I'd rung from the marina and left a message on the answering machine at home. I, of course, didn't know that the rendezvous had been rearranged for midday today. I was glad I hadn't decided on a long lunch stop somewhere.

Bill had soap, washcloth, and towel, as well as plenty of water so I could have my first proper wash in six days. He'd also brought a range of drinks—orange juice (of which I drank a quart), various soft drinks (I drank a Coke), and beer (I had none—I'd probably have gone to sleep)— and fresh fruit. After six days of dried food the latter was very welcome. I ate a banana and packed two apples and two oranges for later, despite the weight. As I also filled up with a gallon and a half of water, my pack was noticeably heavier when I set off again. Bill said he'd meet me in Pine, my next supply point, and loan me the GPS again so I could follow the line the Arizona Trail would take in places where it hadn't been built. "Without a GPS," he said, "you'll never find the route."

There was nothing at Sunflower except a couple of buildings and some road construction work. The trail bypassed all this, running through a culvert under the road then heading back into the wilds. The brush with civilization was much lighter than it had been at Roosevelt Lake and barely disturbed my mood. Ahead lay the Mazatzal Wilderness, the largest in Arizona at two hundred and fifty thousand acres. Beyond Sunflower it was like walking through a giant city park with huge grass meadows dotted with neat juniper trees and just the occasional patch of exposed rock. The urban effect was enhanced by the sound of traffic on the highway, which I could see not far away. Soon though, I reached the mouth of a canyon, a cleft in the hillside that was a gateway back into the mountains. A creek flowed out of the canyon, but it was dry once I passed Cat Spring, just a little way into the narrow rocky ravine. Cliffs rose high on the canyon walls while the floor was dense with bushes and trees, including piñon pine, sycamore, and a tree new to me, the Arizona cypress.

Finding nowhere to camp on the narrow, overgrown canyon floor, I climbed out of it at its head before settling on a small flat patch of bare earth just big enough to lie on. It was a good site, softer and more comfortable than many recent ones, but once I'd made camp I noticed masses of large reddish black ants crawling everywhere. I scattered a few grains of sugar on the ground to distract them from my food and hoped they'd slow down once it grew cooler. The ants were more fascinated by my water bottles than the sugar, crawling slowly all over them. Did they know there was water inside? Or did the cool surface attract them? Guessing what an ant made of a water bottle was impossible. Entering into the heads of some creatures can seem easy, though of course you never know whether you've really succeeded. With invertebrates I've never been able to establish any sort of rapport at all. They are just so different. Other insects were also abroad. The pleasant chirp of crickets was all around. Less pleasant was the occasional mosquito.

All the insects faded away as the temperature dropped. Thirty-seven degrees was just too cold. I found it chilly as well and stayed in the sleeping bag in the morning until the sun reached me. Dawn was strangely quiet. I was used to a lot of birdsong. Here there was just the occasional call. Otherwise all was silent.

The day was spent going deeper and higher into the Mazatzals. A system of trails—Saddle Mountain, Sheep Creek, Thicket Spring—took me past the rugged rock block of Saddle Mountain and deep, cliff-rimmed McFarland Canyon to the start of the amazing twenty-seven-mile Mazatzal Divide Trail. Twisting around drainages and skirting summits on steep and rocky ground this grand, high-elevation traverse stays mostly above six thousand feet. The lay of the land is so complex that to stay high the trail winds so much that hours of walking results in little straight-line distance. It was a joy though to be able to stride out on a good trail through fine forests with wonderful views. For the past few weeks the only easy walking had been on dirt roads, the trails being rocky and overgrown.

Although rough and rocky the Mazatzals are also lush and rich with forest. All day I was amazed at how green the hills were. Ponderosa grew everywhere, and there were stands of dark Douglas fir quite low down on shady north-facing slopes. At the same time cacti, especially prickly pear, grew high up on slopes exposed to the sun.

The name *Mazatzal* is Native American. Depending on who you consult it means either "land of the deer" or "empty space in between." Apparently it's pronounced "mata-zel." Locals, however, often pronounce it "mad-as-hell," which probably describes how you'd feel if you tried to go cross-country over this densely vegetated steep and stony landscape.

Out of the forest the views were extensive. Big, bulky Mazatzal Peak, built of layers of colored rock, lay ahead. Looking back, Four Peaks Mountain rose above lower hills. As was so often the case I was walking away from one mountain and toward another.

Unsurprisingly, the high-level trail didn't have many water sources, and there were none in the first nine miles. Needing water before I camped, I was pleased to see a sign for Bear Spring and even more pleased when four hundred yards down a side trail I found the spring had water in it, albeit rather stagnant-looking with barely any outflow. But it would do, and I filled up with one and a half gallons. A mile farther on I camped in a grove of tall ponderosas on a saddle just south of Mazatzal Peak. At 6,650 feet it was my first camp above six thousand feet and in the forest since the one on Dan Saddle sixteen days ago. The soft forest duff felt quite luxurious after the desert gravel I'd grown used to. The immediate surroundings were quiet, but high overhead I could hear aircraft flying in and out of Phoenix.

Camped on another saddle the next night I watched a procession of lights descending into Phoenix. Silver tubes packed with people speeding through the night sky, rushing from city to city, country to country, continent to continent. Big, clumsy lumps of metal, those planes could never come close to the delicacy, subtlety, and power of a bird such as the raven. Yet they were still wonderful. It was amazing that people could be transported so fast and so far through the air. In a month I would be one of those people, hurtling back home. But that was in the future, a future beyond the walk, beyond the mountains, the desert, the forest, a future not yet holding any meaning.

The day had been mostly in forest on another succession of named, signed trails—Mazatzal, Red Hills, Brush. Once I'd passed below the still-shadowed cliffs of Mazatzal Peak the hills were lower, rounded, and wooded, less defined, less rocky. Only a brief glimpse of the cliffs of North Peak broke the sameness. Instead of mountains and rocks the most interesting things were trees—the fine ponderosa pines and Douglas firs—plus very occasional wildlife sightings. The most memorable of these began with a harsh, piercing cry. I looked up as a common black-hawk, a bird I hadn't seen before, wheeled past just a hundred feet away, the distinctive white band across its tail clearly visible. Every so often white-tailed deer darted away in the trees with a gentle rustling sound as they scuffed up the leaves and brushed against bushes. Otherwise the forest was empty and silent.

The sky slowly clouded over during the day, and distant views were hazy. The clouds meant it was cooler though. I was surprised at how much less thirsty I felt than when walking under a blazing sun. Ironically, there was more water than there had been in many days. Brody Seep, North Fork, Hopi Spring, and Horse Camp all had water. At the latter a blue tarp weighed down with rocks covered a mound of something—camping gear I supposed. A little farther on I met the owner. A large hound bounded down the trail toward me followed by a fit, sun-tanned man carrying a tiny daysack and clad in boots, skimpy shorts, and a tank top. Just out for the weekend, he told me. It's good having these mountains so close to a big city. Weekend or not, big city or not, he was the only person I saw all day.

The last water of the day was Brush Spring, a large pool full of leaves and insects, both dead and alive. I took my now customary late-afternoon gallon and a half and walked on in search of a campsite. The place I chose, on that high saddle, seemed a good site with flat ground and a bit of a breeze. However, although a mile or more from any water there were more mosquitoes than at any other camp. Closing the sleeping bag's hood was too hot, so I ended up sleeping with my shirt over my face. It was not a good night. Under the cloudy sky the temperature fell only to fifty-two degrees, not enough to slow the mosquitoes down. Then the gentle breeze grew into a gusty wind that shook and rattled the tarp. Just before dawn I was awoken by one side flapping wildly. A stake had pulled out. I reset the tarp and decided I would have a hot drink and set off. Pine lay about twenty-five miles away and with little food left I wanted to be there that evening; an early start was a good idea. I also wanted to escape the mosquitoes. When I went to light the stove I found the valve slightly open and the fuel bottle empty. I couldn't imagine how this had happened. Had I not fully shut it down the night before? I hadn't been that tired. Or had I accidentally knocked it during what had been a restless night? Either way I was now short of fuel as well as food. This was my ninth day out from Superior, and I'd hiked nine to eleven hours every day. That this camp hadn't worked out well suggested that I might be getting careless and was probably in need of a rest.

For breakfast I shook the last of some granola out of a plastic bag, added a packet of instant oatmeal Bill had given me plus a few pieces of dried fruit, and poured water over the mix. The resulting sweet, gooey sludge would have to get me through several hours as I had little other food.

I was camped at the head of Bullfrog Canyon down which a steep trail dropped two thousand feet to the East Verde River, a wide but shallow stream easily crossed dryshod on rocks. The river was relaxing and restful with leafy sycamores and other trees lining the banks. There was a gentle, slow, languid feeling about the place, a great contrast to the stark, tense harshness of the mountains. I sat in the shade of a big tree and watched the river swirl by. I could have stayed for hours. But Pine beckoned, so I hauled myself to my feet, heaved the pack on my back, and started a long, slow climb back up into the hills. North of the East Verde

River the nature of the Mazatzals changes, the range ending in a series of huge, flat-topped mesas. The ascent across Polles Mesa was on gently sloping bare red rock and earth dotted with small junipers, a strange somehow unreal landscape with no edges. A few hundred yards in any direction was the farthest I could see. It felt as if that landscape could go on forever, an endless slope that never reached anywhere. In fact it led to the steep rim and small broken rocks of Whiterock Mesa at the base of which lay White Rock Spring, a pencil-thick stream of water running out of a pipe into a wooden tank. I wedged a water bottle under the flow and filled up a quart.

Whiterock Mesa became the narrower Saddle Ridge, which consisted of more gently sloping terrain, this time covered with strange, twisted, broken, volcanic rock. Even the cairns that marked the trail looked weird. The broad shoulder led to Hardscrabble Mesa and a farewell to the Mazatzal Wilderness. Once out of the protected area a jeep trail immediately appeared, leading to a dirt tank with some grubby water in it. Cows stood around it, watching me.

Pine lay to the east. The Arizona Trail curves south of the town to a trailhead. I took what seemed a direct route into town, linking a bewildering series of dirt roads and jeep trails, only some of which were on the map. I passed several dirt tanks, all of them full and rich in waterbirds, mainly ducks. One had a great blue heron that flew up, squawking loudly in a huge circle, flapping its great wings, long legs trailing and long neck extended as I approached, but was back perched on a post in the water before I was out of sight. Near another tank four elk, the first I had seen on the trip, ran through the trees. These magnificent, large deer are the same species as the red deer common in the Scottish Highlands. They grow bigger in the forests of the United States, however. In Scotland the red deer live mostly on open hillsides, as most of the forest is gone and overgrazing prevents any regeneration. With no natural predators and numbers kept high for stalking, as organized deer hunting is called in Scotland, red deer are, sadly, a problem. Reducing the deer numbers is key to the restoration of the forest, which would ultimately be better for the deer. The forest is, after all, their natural habitat. The name *elk* can be confusing for Europeans, as it's used in Scandinavia for the deer called moose in North America. In the Cascade Mountains on my first U.S. hike, the Pacific Crest Trail, I'd been asked by others I met if I'd seen or heard any elk. Thinking they meant moose I'd said no. "But they're all over the place," came the reply. It took me a while to realize that the red deer I was seeing all over the place were elk.

Eventually I hit a highway and stumbled wearily down the final slopes into the town, my thoughts fixed on two things—food and lodging. Without passing either I reached a junction on the highway. Which way to turn? There seemed to be more businesses to the left so I went that way. I passed a variety of stores but no motels or cafés that were open. A gas station marked the end of town. I went in. The heat and bright lights were disorienting, and I stood there feeling dazed for a few minutes. The woman behind the counter couldn't say if there was motel in town but thought there might be a campground out the other side. Wearily I plodded back down the highway. Almost out of town again and feeling tired and fed up I saw a row of cars outside a building. A café? Maybe. I tried to hurry on but my legs wouldn't go any faster. As I drew nearer I could read the sign outside: THE RIM CAFÉ AND MOTEL. I stumbled into the hot, bright interior, rich with the smell of cooking and tobacco smoke. Again I felt a little confused and stood there awhile adjusting to the atmosphere and wondering what to do. A waitress said she thought the motel was full, the owner, Clark, confirmed it was. The last room had just gone. Damn. If I'd turned right instead of left when I reached the highway I might have gotten it.

"There are motels in Strawberry, a couple of miles away," said Clark, "I'll fix you a lift in a while." I sank gratefully onto a seat and ordered a meal. A little later a guy came over and said he'd drive me to Strawberry. As we climbed into his pickup he suggested trying a place just a half mile up the road first. "It isn't really ready yet," he said, "but I know the new owner." Just outside Pine we reached the High Country Inn, a Swiss chalet–style wooden lodge set in tall pines. The owner, who had a European accent that went with the decor and the architectural style, had a trailer to rent for what seemed a rather steep $50 a night. I took it. I was too tired to argue, and it was within walking distance of town. That was its only good point. The trailer was in desperate need of renovation. The fittings were tatty, which didn't bother me, but the heat didn't work, which did. Even worse, the shower only stayed hot for a minute. The owner admitted he was so new here that he hadn't worked out how to adjust all the controls in the trailer, let alone repair anything. The bed had three thin blankets. I woke cold in the middle of the night and climbed into my sleeping bag. The temperature was forty-three degrees.

A dangerous walk along curving AZ 87 led into Pine. Trucks and cars raced by as I edged along the side of the shoulderless road, unable to see around the next bend. Walking that half mile, repeated several times over the next day and a bit, was undoubtedly one of the most dangerous things I did during the hike.

A standard town day followed. Pine had all the necessary facilities and for once they were within reasonable walking distance of each other. The town was friendly and pleasant, maybe not as upmarket as Patagonia but it certainly felt more prosperous than Superior. Snuggled in the forest, it had a sheltered air that open desert towns such as Superior and Oracle lacked.

Before starting my chores I rang Denise. It was wonderful to hear her voice. I had a letter from her too, which made me think of home. How far away it seemed. Not just in distance but emotionally and mentally as well. The walk was now what I did, what I was. I didn't think about it anymore. Walking through the mountains each day and sleeping in the wilds each night were the norm. It was the towns that were the aberrations.

Retrieving my box meant I could change into clean clothes. Washing my hiking garments was essential. Being dirty didn't matter in the wilds, but it can become uncomfortable. My sweat-soaked shirt was so stiff it practically stood up by itself. My shorts were filthy and rough with ingrained dirt. I was surprised at how clean they came. Were these pale, shining garments really my trail clothes?

Bill, whom I'd rung the night before, turned up at lunchtime and bought me a meal in the Rim Café, my second of the day there. He left me with his GPS plus a list of the points he'd programmed in when hiking the route the previous year. These waypoints, as they are called in GPS jargon, marked where the Arizona Trail would be built. By walking from one to the next I could follow the approximate line of the trail-to-be. The next time I would see Bill would be back in Phoenix after the walk was over. Jake, I learned, was about a day behind. By coincidence, a friend of Bill's had met him on the dirt road not far beyond Pigeon Spring on the day I'd met Bill in Sunflower. I half expected him to see him in Pine.

I devoted the afternoon to shopping. I needed six days' food plus a few other items. Most came from the just-adequate grocery store. I was glad to be able to buy some more insect repellent. Of course I had no idea that mosquitoes weren't to be a problem from here on. One delight was a fruit and honey stand where I bought masses of dried fruit. Another was a bookshop, A Book For All Seasons, where I found a secondhand copy of Edward Abbey's *The Monkey Wrench Gang*, appropriate reading as I approached the area in which this comic environmental thriller is set.

Chores over, I repaired to the Rim Café, which had become my base. It was too far to keep walking back to the trailer, which, in any case, was cold and unwelcoming. I liked the rough-and-ready, friendly atmosphere of the plain, unpretentious café. Most of the customers were regulars so I stuck out a little, especially when I opened my mouth. I don't think non-American accents were common here. Various people chatted with me, usually asking me what I was doing and then sometimes expressing disbelief that anyone should want to walk in the mountains. One guy, Dan, was more interested in talking about the political situation in both Europe and America. I met him several times, usually he had a gun magazine tucked under his arm. He'd been in the army, stationed in Europe in the 1970s and since then a policeman, involved in exposing corruption. Now he was a pro-militia, pro-gun Republican who quoted the Second Amendment and talked about returning to the values of the Founding Fathers. At the time of the walk the political parties were selecting their candidates for the next presidential election. Dan's choice was Alan Keyes, a Republican who he said had little chance. Although we didn't agree on many things we had friendly discussions and did find some common ground, such as a distrust of big government and big business. My limited knowledge of people with his political views, gained mainly from newspapers, suggested they were paranoid and dangerous extremists. It's always easy to stereotype those you haven't met. Meet them face-to-face and often it's apparent that you are both human beings and do have things in common. Dan was a case in point. He was honest, genuinely concerned, and wanted to bring about political change that would better the world. To a great degree we had opposite political views, but we managed to discuss them without rancor. I learned something about his political beliefs and understood a little better why people think like that, which is always valuable.

Early the next morning I was back in the Rim Café for my fifth and last meal there. The regulars were talking about how it was now allergy season and discussing what medications they were taking, all through a thick haze of tobacco smoke, which they seemed to ignore as irrelevant to their concerns. Another topic of conversation was the heat, specifically the high temperatures in Phoenix—it had hit ninety degrees—very hot for this early in the year. One woman said, "Eighty is enough; I don't do heat." At home, I thought, eighty is heat, eighty is strip and lie in the sun weather, eighty makes headlines.

Just before I left an object was brought into the cafe, a gift for Clark, that at the time I thought was just a curiosity. I never expected to see or hear about it again. I certainly couldn't have conceived of the worldwide attention it was to receive in the coming months. The artifact in question was an imitation stuffed fish called Big Mouth Billy Bass that plays songs such as "Take Me To The River" while its tail twitches and its mouth opens and closes. There was a general air of amusement and bemusement at this piece of unbelievable kitsch. "My husband's a game warden. I must get him one," said the woman who didn't do heat. That this slight and only temporarily amusing bit of plastic, reminiscent of a small child's toy,

gained notoriety as a favorite of world leaders such as former President
Bill Clinton and Prime Minister Tony Blair, seems incomprehensible.

My departure from Pine was a slow process. I had mail to post and
e-mails to send. Just one e-mail arrived, telling me that Ben Nevis, the
tallest mountain in Scotland and the U.K. as a whole, had been bought
by the John Muir Trust, a conservation body of which I was a member—
heartening news. Taking wild areas off the market and out of the control
of developers and government alike seems to me the best way to ensure
they are conserved for the future. If publicly owned, then wilderness
should be legally protected so that politicians can't decide to mine it, log
it, build ski resorts on it, sell it cheap to their buddies who've just given
them small fortunes, or any of the other things politicians are likely to
do with something they don't understand or value. In this respect I think
the U.S. Wilderness Act is one of the finest pieces of legislation enacted
anywhere.

Cheered by the Ben Nevis news I finally managed to leave Pine, some
forty hours after staggering in tired and hungry. I'd enjoyed my stay in
the friendly little town and I felt relaxed and refreshed. Now it was time
to continue the walk.

6

Forests and Lakes: Across the Mogollon Plateau

PINE TO FLAGSTAFF

97 miles

On leaving Pine I left the landscape of the walk so far. The rugged, stony mountain ranges I'd been crossing almost daily for almost five weeks were behind me. Above Pine, a long line of broken cliffs can be seen jutting out of the forest. This is the Mogollon Rim, a steep, two-hundred-mile escarpment, two thousand feet high in places, that marks the southern edge of the huge Colorado, Plateau, which covers one hundred and thirty thousand square miles of Arizona, Utah, Colorado, and New Mexico. The plateau is a mix of high desert and forest split by many deep and spectacular canyons, including the incomparable Grand. In height it's mostly from four to six thousand feet, though many of its mountains are much higher. Climbing onto the plateau would mark a big change in the walk. No more saguaros, no more javelinas, no more open Sonoran Desert. Instead, a new world of forest and canyon to learn about.

First came the Mogollon Rim. Before climbing through the cliffs the Arizona Trail heads east along the Highline Trail, now a designated recreation trail, but back in the late 1800s the means of travel between homesteads in the forest below the rim. After seventeen miles the Arizona

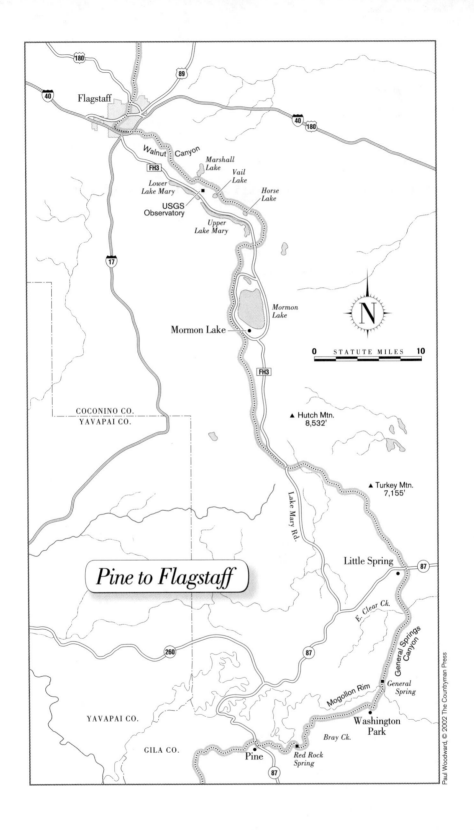

180

89

40

Flagstaff

40 180

Walnut Canyon

FH3

Marshall Lake

Vail Lake

Lower Lake Mary

Horse Lake

USGS Observatory

Upper Lake Mary

17

Mormon Lake

Mormon Lake

N

0   STATUTE MILES   10

COCONINO CO.
YAVAPAI CO.

▲ Hutch Mtn.
8,532'

▲ Turkey Mtn.
7,155'

Lake Mary Rd.

Pine to Flagstaff

Little Spring

87

E. Clear Ck.

260

87

General Springs Canyon

Mogollon Rim

General Spring

YAVAPAI CO.

Washington Park

Bray Ck.

GILA CO.

Pine

Red Rock Spring

87

Paul Woodward. © 2002 The Countryman Press

Trail leaves the Highline Trail and heads up through the cliffs to the plateau above.

The Highline is a well-made, well-used trail that undulates through the forest on the slopes below the cliffs. Others were about, and I met several day hikers, a backpacker, and passed someone's camp. The walking was easy, and there were good views of the shattered pinnacles, towers, ridges, and cliffs of the Rim rising out of the trees, the pale red-gold sedimentary rock contrasting with the dark foliage of the forest. In places the escarpment could be seen rippling along mile after mile after mile until it faded into the distance. Below to the south a green wave of forest rolled away to the ragged Mazatzal Mountains with the distinctive pyramids of Four Peaks Mountain tiny but clear in the far distance.

Much of the day though I was in the forest, often among huge and magnificent trees—towering ponderosas and massive Douglas firs. The forest walking was relaxing, soothing, almost hypnotic as the big trees cast their shade, the sunlight flickered through the branches, and nothing much seemed to happen. Lost in a pleasant reverie I was abruptly brought back to reality when a big, dark vulture suddenly appeared, flying low and fast through the trees in front of me. Startled awake and alert by the mean-looking bird with its wickedly curved beak, I wondered why it was there. A carcass of something nearby? A few steps farther and I came upon a dead skunk lying in the middle of the trail. Cue Loudon Wainwright III, whose catchy singalong song about roadkill, "Dead Skunk (in the Middle of the Road)," ran through my head for the rest of the day.

Water was abundant. Bear Spring, Pine Spring, Poison Creek, Bray Creek, East Bray Creek, North Sycamore Creek, West Chase Creek, and Chase Creek were all flowing. I drank from each except Poison Creek— the water looked fine, but the name put me off. It was good not to have to haul water. I did carry a gallon and a half the last few miles of the day— the habit was almost automatic—but I didn't need to as I ended up camping near an unnamed creek. Big cumulus clouds had slowly covered the sky during the day, and a gusty wind had sprung up so I pitched the tarp. A single mosquito appeared. I lit one of the mosquito coils I had bought in Pine and watched the thin thread of aromatic smoke drift across the campsite. There were no more mosquitoes. The moon rose, throwing strange patterns of juniper foliage and pine branches on the tarp that flickered and shook as the wind moved the trees.

The hard, rhythmic drumming of a woodpecker woke me at dawn. As I sat up the bird flew off with a raucous cackle as if to say, "Now I've woken you I can go." I yawned and stretched after a far better sleep on the forest floor than I'd had the last two nights in the trailer. Two squirrels ran across the soft ground, rustling the fallen pine needles, then one chased the other up a tree, their claws clicking on the bark. The sun's rays slanted through the trees and onto the tarp.

A quiet forest day followed. After the mountains and the desert, walking in the forest felt gentle and easy, a stroll rather than a hike. This was partly due to the softness of the trail, packed pine needles, earth, and the occasional tree root being much easier to walk on than hard stones and rocks. But it was also because the forest itself was cool and relaxing, undemanding on the eye, a kaleidoscope of leaves, needles, branches, and filtered sunlight. There was no searing brightness, no harshness, no rough and rugged landscape that said This is serious terrain, hiking here is tough. The forest, like all forests, had a sense of mystery that deserts and mountains lack. The trees closed in around me. Views were confined to one or two directions, when they occurred at all. In a forest you don't know what may lie just ahead, around the next twist in the trail. I walked in a dreamlike state again, alert yet somehow soporific.

My route soon left the Highline Trail and climbed steeply up the Rim beside a ravine, down which crashed the infant East Verde River. At the top stood a large sign marking the Battle of Big Dry Wash, fought in July 1882, the last battle between U.S. forces and Apaches in Arizona. Why the sign is here I'm not sure, as it says the battle was fought seven miles away. Just beyond the marker lay General Springs Cabin, a restored Forest Service building built in 1918. The general was George Crook, who led the U.S. Army in the Indian wars of the 1870s and 1880s. Passing through this area, Crook used a spring near the cabin, hence the name.

Beyond the Mogollon Rim the forest stretched away over gently undulating terrain. This was a new type of scenery, the high, flat Mogollon

Plateau. The trail ran down General Springs Canyon beside a creek full of melt from the many snowbanks lying in shaded areas of the forest. There were deep pools and a pretty little waterfall. The banks were edged with damp grassy meadows. The desert seemed another world. A few flocks of noisy Steller's jays broke the silence of the otherwise quiet forest. Leaving the creek I climbed up a steep trail to Battleground Ridge and joined a dirt road. A concrete aqueduct and a power line, first seen on the ascent to the rim, appeared. These intrusions into the wild feel of the forest came in and out of view as I continued along the broad grassy top of the ridge. The forest was soon not so wild anyway. Stumps appeared, showing that selective felling had taken place, which, while producing noticeable effects, is far preferable to the devastation of clear-cutting. I was now in the largest ponderosa pine forest in the world, one that stretches from the Mogollon Rim all the way to the Grand Canyon. Much of this forest has been heavily logged, but large sections are still intact. Elk droppings were everywhere, and I saw two herds of five or six animals watching me from the trees.

Battleground Ridge came to an abrupt end above East Clear Creek's steep-sided canyon. A short, precipitous descent led to the flat bottom of the canyon and to the creek, a sizeable stream with some deep pools and several banks of sparkling white gravel. A few cliffs jutted out of the trees, but for the most part the canyon's slopes were densely forested. A brief but strenuous climb led up the far side to a short walk across flat ground to an empty, snow-scattered campground, still closed for the winter.

Looking back I could see across the East Clear Creek canyon to forest that ran to the horizon. There were no hills in sight. For the first time I couldn't look back to places I'd been on previous days. The walk before Pine had vanished. It really did feel part of the past. I'd grown used to looking back and seeing the mountain ranges I'd crossed. That was over now. The walk had changed.

The next three miles were a corridor lined with rocks and logs on both sides, a lot of trailwork over such a distance. These miles crossed broad Blue Ridge. From the northern edge I looked across more rolling forest to distant, hazy, snow-splashed mountains, the San Francisco Peaks, highest in Arizona. These were the mountains I'd looked at from the North Rim of the Grand Canyon many years before and wondered what it would be like to hike to them. Soon I would find out. I might not be able to see mountains I'd already crossed, but the mountains to come would be in view for much of the next week, pulling me on through the forest.

I dropped down from Blue Ridge to another closed campground set in a steep-sided bowl in the ridge's walls. I'd thought there might be water in the ravines running down the sides of the bowl, but they were dry. I walked out of the mouth of the bowl, to Elk Tank and for the first time took water from a dirt tank. Just as I was packing away my full bottles three dogs appeared and started excitedly splashing around. A woman appeared soon afterward and then walked off, dogs following. Having seen no one all day and feeling as though I was in a remote area, seeing someone walking her dogs was a bit of a surprise. When I checked the map, however, I saw that a highway lay close by and that a ranger station and ranch were nearby as well. This is an illusion that forests often give. Go just a short distance from roads, houses, and even villages and you can believe you are in a remote wilderness.

I camped not far from the tank under some big ponderosas. At 6,900 feet this was my highest camp since that on Dan Saddle in the Santa Catalina Mountains, three weeks ago. Height meant cooler temperatures, and for the first time in weeks I wore my down vest. The water from Elk Tank was murky so I ran it through a coffee filter. It still came out brown, but the paper filter turned brown, too, so at least some dirt was being removed. The water tasted fine in spite of the color, though I treated it with purifying drops just in case. After all, I had seen those dogs playing in the water and there were tracks of many other animals on the muddy banks. The highway was about a quarter mile away, and I heard the occasional vehicle but wasn't disturbed by any lights.

As I did most evenings I checked the maps and my itinerary for the next few days. Fifty miles, said my notes, for the distance from Pine to Mormon Lake, the next supply point. How I arrived at that figure I now couldn't understand, as it was clearly wrong. I'd already walked thirty-five miles and I was barely halfway. However, I'd also reckoned on sixty-five miles, and four days from Mormon Lake to Flagstaff. Looking at the maps I now thought it more like half that. I shouldn't have been surprised at the mistakes. That's what happens if you plan a walk from small-scale maps in an atlas, which is what I'd relied on for areas such as this that weren't covered by the trail guide or the Arizona Trail Association passage sheets. The large-scale topographic maps I used when hiking I'd picked up in Tucson just before the walk. I hadn't had time to look at them closely before sending them off in my supply box. Overall, my pre-walk estimates hadn't been far off, but this time I seemed to have misjudged. However, on checking my supplies I decided I had enough food for two more days and so should still reach Mormon Lake without running out. In the flat forest high-mileage days should be possible, as long as I didn't lose my way. I'd just walked nineteen miles in nine and a half hours without hurrying and with many stops to look at trees and streams and wildlife and to take photographs.

The next day I walked for just forty minutes longer but covered eight more miles, twenty-seven in total. This was primarily because the walking was easy, being on dirt roads with little ascent, but it was also because I was mostly in featureless forest with few views, so I stopped less often and took fewer photographs. An early start helped, too. It was now light soon after 5:30, and I had woken at daybreak to jays screeching loudly near camp and a woodpecker drumming.

The foot trail ended abruptly in Jacks Canyon, as Bill had said it would. My route now depended on his GPS. I switched it on and got the bearing for the first waypoint and began walking cross-country. The arrow that pointed the way swung wildly at times and froze at others, especially in dense forest. I quickly learned that it was easier to transfer the bearing to my compass and follow that, switching on the GPS again when I neared the waypoint. When I picked up trail signs and a dirt road I felt unjustifiably pleased with myself. I'd never navigated like this with a GPS before. Now that it had worked for this short section I felt surer about using it for some of the longer section ahead where there was no trail.

There were occasional dirt tanks in the forest, and all the ones I looked in had water, which was good to know. At one point an old lava flow covered the forest floor, with trees growing out of the cracks in the flat surface. Beyond this strange, cracked pavement the strong smell of burning wood wafted through the forest, and I came to an area that had burned so recently that the ground was still smoking in places and felt very warm to the touch. Most of the big ponderosas seemed to have survived, though many had blackened trunks. But all the bushes and grasses had gone, suggesting the fire had swept through the area quickly, burning up anything small but leaving the big trees. I traveled through the area quite fast myself, just in case the fire should start up again. I had once almost walked into a big forest fire on the Continental Divide Trail in southern Montana. A Forest Service crew had taken me out in a pickup, racing through the burning forest with trees bursting into flame and spitting lumps of blazing pine tar while glowing burned branches crashed down all around. The heat was tremendous, the short truck ride spectacular and frightening.

My first experience with forest fire went back further, to when I was a child growing up on the Lancashire coast in northern England, not a place known for woodland. Where I lived, though, a belt of pines a few miles thick ran along the coast as a barrier to the sea. A trail with the alluring—to a ten-year-old—name of the Fisherman's Path ran through the woods, and I'd wanted to hike it for some time. Eventually my father offered to take me. But when we got to the start a big sign said the path was closed due to a fire, and we could see smoke rising from the trees. I remember feeling disappointed but also excited. A forest fire meant these were wild, dangerous woods. Not long afterward we hiked the path and I noticed the blackened trees and burned undergrowth.

TEMPORARY END OF TRAIL read the notice at Gonzales Tank, a large muddy pool with the tall gray skeleton of a dead tree poking dramatically into the sky from the middle of it. A phone number was given for further trail information, which wasn't much use to me out here. The trail signs did indeed end, but the dirt road the trail followed didn't, and it was obvious from the map which other dirt roads I should take. I walked on through the forest. The one view of the day came at a high point where the very snowy San Francisco Peaks appeared, looking quite a bit clearer and closer than they had the previous day. I was hoping to climb

Mount Humphreys, the highest peak in Arizona. Looking at the snow I doubted I'd be going up if it didn't melt soon.

That evening I lay under the tarp on the edge of the forest watching elk grazing in the large meadows that surrounded muddy Pine Spring. I'd seen many elk during the day and masses of sign, both tracks and droppings. I'd also seen a few Abert's squirrels in the trees. These pretty animals have tasseled ears and distinctive tails that are gray above and white below. The commonest birds were flickers and woodpeckers, their characteristic dipping and rising flight making them easily identifiable as they flitted between trees. A solitary raven flapped overhead, the one bird that I saw in every environment on the walk.

The cool breeze that had had me pitching the tarp the evening before was a strong wind by morning, and the day that followed was one of the coldest and windiest of the whole walk. I recorded gusts of twenty-seven miles per hour, enough to make walking a little difficult and to shake large branches. I was only just warm enough in windshirt, trail shirt, long pants, and boots. The sun shone occasionally, providing a little heat, but soon disappeared back into the clouds. In open places I could see dark, swirling rain squalls racing across the land. None caught me until I was about to make camp, when it rained heavily for fifteen minutes and the wind blew even harder.

Before reaching that camp I had more forest walking to the little settlement of Mormon Lake. A mix of dirt roads, bits of finished trail, and cross-country sections on Bill's GPS route led through the trees. The walking was easy and the forest pleasant with some stands of large aspens, one of my favorite trees. I love the smooth white bark and the tall graceful shapes, the delicate green of the leaves in spring and the brilliant burst of color in the fall, a last flourish of delight before winter. These aspens were in bud, waiting for warmth and light to trigger the new leaves. American robins, which look more like the blackbirds of home with the addition of a reddish breast than like British robins, foraged on the forest floor while pretty western bluebirds called from the bushes. Elk sign was everywhere and nervous animals trotted off through the trees from time to time. On the dirt tanks I passed were herons, mallard ducks, and lesser scaup, a small duck with a distinctive glossy black head, black chest and tail, and pale gray back and sides. The forest wasn't totally flat. There were what the map called mountains, though they looked like rounded, forested hills to me. It's aesthetics I guess. They were high enough for mountains, some reaching more than eighty-five hundred feet, and many were steep sided. But the fact they were tree covered and smooth with no cliffs, ravines, talus slopes, narrow ridges, or other montane features meant they didn't seem like mountains to me.

WELCOME. MORMON LAKE VILLAGE. POP. 50–5,000 read the sign, reflecting the village's seasonal popularity. On this cold and windy day it was closer to the fifty than the five thousand. I'd been told I wouldn't be able to buy supplies, and although it was included in the information on services in the trail guide, there was a blank for every facility so I wasn't expecting much. It's always better to enter an unknown place feeling like this. Then you won't be disappointed, just pleased if there is anything there. And pleased I was when a large, dark brown wooden building appeared housing a store, post office, saloon, and restaurant. The last wouldn't open for two more hours, which gave me a minor mental struggle. Was it worth waiting? I soon decided it wasn't. It was too cold to hang about that long, and I still had miles to go. Instead I bought a couple of sticky buns and a soft drink and gulped them down outside. The store also provided enough—mac'n'cheese for a couple of dinners, various candy bars for snacks—to ensure my dwindling supplies would get me comfortably to Flagstaff, now about thirty-five miles away. There were even some items I hadn't found in Pine—candles, wet wipes, sunscreen. Not that I needed the latter at the time.

The store owner asked if I was a hiker and was I expecting mail? I wondered, How did he know? I guess my battered boots and trail-worn clothing rather gave me away. I wasn't sure about the mail. I said No at first and then Maybe as I couldn't remember if I'd left this address at home. I knew I hadn't sent my box or anything else here. The man opened the post office, situated in a corner of the store, and produced a postcard. Jake had mailed it just yesterday in Pine. He wrote that he'd missed me by only an hour or so at the Roosevelt Lake marina and then by a day in

Pine. Although he'd gotten a ride to the town of Roosevelt he'd had to walk all the way from there to the marina and what he described as the "uninformation center." Clearly he'd met the same ranger. Jake had complained before about how useless ranger stations were for providing information on the trail and on water sources. That's the problem with expectations. I didn't expect any help from these places so when I did get some it was a bonus.

Jake was staying at the Rim Motel. "What a choice place. I hope I survive the night," he wrote. I wondered what he meant. A dangerous motel? I hadn't noticed any Norman Bates types in the café. And Jake was hardly a double for Janet Leigh. Perhaps my cold trailer had been the best place to stay after all. Jake reckoned on being in Flagstaff in five days' time. I hoped to be there in two. It looked as though we wouldn't meet again.

North of the village lies Mormon Lake, or what is sometimes Mormon Lake. The water level in this huge, shallow lake fluctuates enormously depending on rain- and snowfall. When full it's the biggest natural lake in Arizona. As I walked past all I could see was a distant dark line that was probably water across a huge flat area of damp meadow and marshland. Above the would-be lake the skies were dramatic with towering white cumulus clouds, racing waves of ragged gray rain, and patches of deep blue. I had one glimpse of the San Francisco Peaks before they disappeared into the clouds. Was it snowing up there?

I followed the road next to the sometime lake past scatterings of houses, then returned to the forest to camp below a wooded bump graced with the name Pine Grove Hill. There was no water nearby but that didn't matter as I'd bought a gallon at the store. I'd only drunk half a pint plus a soft drink all day, as opposed to the quart an hour I'd been drinking on hot days in the desert and mountains to the south.

The cooler weather affected how I slept as well as how much I drank. For many weeks I'd left the top of my sleeping bag open at the shoulders and used the hood as a pillow. This night I woke in the dark and felt something wasn't right. It took awhile to realize I was cold. The temperature was thirty-four degrees. I pulled the hood of my sleeping bag tight around

my face and drifted back to sleep to the sound of a coyote chorus echoing eerily through the trees, the yips and howls sounding very close. Awake
again at dawn I lay in my sleeping bag awhile, watching my breath con-
dense into spurts of gray in the cold air and waiting for the sunlight that
I could see brightening the treetops to filter down through the branches
and warm me. Ever so slowly the sunlight crept down, creating an ever-
changing, complex, three-dimensional texture of bright light and dark
interwoven branches that was fascinating to watch but didn't provide any
warmth. Bored with waiting I slipped my arms out of the sleeping bag,
shivered in the cold air, quickly pulled on my fleece pullover, and lit the
stove for a hot drink. A few minutes later the water boiled, and I turned
off the stove. The abrupt silence still startled me, even after all these weeks.
The stove's roar gone, there were just birds calling and the sound of the
wind high above, rushing through the treetops in big gusts. A faint whis-
per of wind passed by at ground level and disappeared into the distance.
The first rays of the sun finally reached me only to be almost immediately blocked by a big tree. Lately, I noted, this had happened a few times.
I needed to take more care in siting my camp. The desert had made me
lazy; I always had the sun early there.

Bill's GPS took me through the dense woods along the line of an old,
abandoned railroad. Rotting wood sleepers and stone embankments were
still visible in places, but the track was fast fading back into the forest.
Like the mining remnants I'd seen in the Santa Rita Mountains this intrusion into the wilds had softened and been absorbed by the forest to the
point where it felt part of the place. Leaving the railroad I went cross-country and along dirt roads to a closed campground and Lake Mary Road.
With no landmarks I simply followed the GPS directions, walking from
waypoint to waypoint. Each marked a point where the trail, when built,
would change direction. There was often nothing identifiable at these
places. Finding them with a map and compass would have been impossible. Of course I could have simply taken a compass bearing on the campground and walked through the woods to it, but I found it interesting to
follow the line the Arizona Trail would take and also to use the GPS. That
signals from small satellites orbiting Earth far above could guide me

through featureless forest seemed astonishing. Oh, I know the principles behind it and how it works, but that doesn't stop it from being extraordinary.

I knew too that GPS receivers were controversial and that some outdoors people didn't like them, feeling that it was somehow cheating or holding nature at a distance to use electronic devices in the wilds. I don't understand this view. GPS is a tool, just as a compass or a map is a tool. It's not essential, but in some places and circumstances it's useful. Using one doesn't impinge on the enjoyment of others or damage the environment, which are my criterion for whether something is unsuitable for the backcountry or not. GPS isn't noisy or visually intrusive. It doesn't involve altering the wilderness in any way. That makes it fine as far as I'm concerned. I'll save my energy for objecting to ski resorts, motorized vehicles, clear-cutting of old-growth forests, overgrazing, and other truly destructive activities.

Why object to GPS any more than to nylon shelters, polyester clothing, gas stoves, and other products of modern industry that make backpacking easier and more comfortable? Okay, there are reasons to object to these. The pollution involved in their production is one. That they separate you from nature is another. Let's consider this last one first. In Norway there's a guy, an outdoor instructor, who shuns all synthetics, only using wool and cotton clothing and canvas packs and tents. Does this really bring him closer to nature? Well, if he says so then yes. But that's him. Not me. I've used all of those natural materials and products at different times. Did I notice any difference in my relationship to nature? Nope. Not a thing. Whether my underwear is made of wool or high-wicking, bi-component, wonderweave polyester doesn't affect my appreciation of a bird or a bush one whit. (Well, it might if the wool itched like hell, which some does unless, um, given a high-tech treatment.) Tools are tools. Either they do the job or they don't. If they do, you can pay them little attention and get on with what you're really in the wilderness for. If they don't, you'll curse and swear at them and spend far too much time trying to get them to perform adequately. And that's the case whether they're natural or artificial. A leaking tent is a leaking tent whether it's made from silicone elastomer nylon or cotton. A cold sleeping bag is cold whether it's filled with down or high-loft hollow-core thermal polyester.

The pollution objection is different and more complex. Natural good, synthetic bad, is easy and slick. And wrong. Worldwide, more than 10 percent of the pesticides and nearly 25 percent of the insecticides are used on cotton, more than on any other single crop. Sheep, John Muir's hoofed locusts, are a major cause of overgrazing worldwide. Synthetics, of course, are made from oil, with all that that entails from spills to air pollution. Nothing we make has no effect; nothing is environmentally pure. The answer doesn't lie with choosing this product over that one. It lies with fewer products. It lies with making products last, with wearing products out and then recycling them, with handing products on when finished with them. Organic cotton and fleece made from recycled plastic bottles is worth buying, but in itself it's not nearly enough. Much more important is for people concerned about the wilderness and the environment to get involved in campaigning, whether with a local group or a national or international one, and whether for less consumption, less pollution, clean air, more wilderness, or something else you feel strongly about. It all helps. It's all necessary. And it's important to get out and enjoy the wilderness so you never forget what you're fighting for and why.

It's surprising where thinking about GPS can lead! But thoughts such as these did occur on and off throughout the walk. I've always found that spending time in the wilds, especially weeks or months at a time, makes the value of these places very clear and with it the necessity for protecting the whole environment—wild, semiwild, and developed. It seems a cliché to say that we are part of and depend on the environment, that everything is connected and intertwined, yet many people still seem to believe that this isn't so, that humanity can exist apart from the rest of nature, that the destruction of species and habitats, even the climate, doesn't matter and won't affect us. Repeating the same message may seem tedious, pointless even, but it needs to be done, and done in such a way that others listen and find it interesting and even entertaining. That's the challenge. It's all too easy to sound self-righteous, superior, and pompous, all too easy to put people off rather than attract them. At the same time it's also easy to compromise ideals and values so as not to offend, which is even worse.

From Lake Mary Road a rough cross-country climb led to Anderson Mesa, a vast, flat plateau of forest and grassland dotted with small lakes, on which I spent much of the rest of the day, mostly on dirt roads. The only views were of the San Francisco Peaks, much closer now and looking far too snowy. Although this was a high wooded land there were reminders of the desert, painful reminders in the form of prickly pear and hedge-hog cacti, often half-hidden in the undergrowth. I had to carefully remove needles from my legs several times before I learned that I had to look more

The San Francisco Peaks, the highest mountains in Arizona, seen from the flat grasslands of Anderson Mesa.

carefully here than in the desert where the cacti were usually very visible and easy to avoid. I'd already grown used to the pleasant idea that every bush and shrub wasn't just waiting to stab or scratch me and had stopped worrying about brushing against them.

The lakes on Anderson Mesa were like smaller versions of Mormon Lake, shallow and marshy, their size varying with evaporation and precipitation. Most are fenced to keep cattle out and so are a haven for wildlife. Three lay close to my route: Horse, Vail, and Prime. Ducks— mallard, goldeneye, lesser scaup—and coots drifted about on all three. Every so often a pair of mallards would splash into the air and fly low over the reed beds, a classic wetland image. There were herons, and delicate-looking, fork-tailed, sharp-winged swallows skimming over the water catching insects.

At Vail Lake I spotted three animals grazing at the edge of the water. Through the binoculars I could see they were pronghorn, those wonderfully graceful, deerlike animals, often wrongly called antelope, though they are in fact the only members of their eponymous family. Although I hadn't moved since I first saw them, and was standing on the edge of the trees and not very visible, the pronghorn soon sensed I was there and bounded across the grass and into the forest, wriggling under the cattle fence rather than jumping it. At least they could do this here. Pronghorn numbers have declined in Arizona, in part because of their inability to jump high fences or to go under them if the lower strands are too close to the ground. Other causes of their decline are overgrazing by cattle, which reduces the available food and makes it easier for coyotes to prey on the fawns, as the grass doesn't grow high enough to hide the young pronghorn. I had seen pronghorn once before, in the Great Divide Basin in Wyoming. But that had been fifteen years ago, and it was wonderful to see them again.

Just beyond Prime Lake I passed the domes and towers that house the telescopes of a USGS observatory. Operated by the Lowell Observatory in Flagstaff, the facility is here because the dark skies are unpolluted by urban lights. Beyond the observatory the lakes ended and the forest became more dense. After collecting water from a small, muddy dirt tank

I camped on the rim of deep, steep-sided Walnut Canyon, only three or four straight-line miles from Flagstaff, reckoning this was as close as I could get to the city and still camp where I liked. I could have continued on into Flagstaff, but that would have meant arriving late and feeling tired. Remembering how confused I'd felt in tiny little Pine this didn't seem a good way to arrive in a city that was bound to be overwhelming. Also, it was Saturday, and I wouldn't be able to collect my box and any other mail until Monday, so again there was no advantage in arriving tonight. Given what happened the next day I was to be very glad I'd made this decision.

A cool breeze was sweeping through the trees, but rather than pitch the tarp I slung my ground cloth between two trees as a windbreak and slept next to it. That way I could still see the sky and the trees and remain more in contact with the forest. A full moon rose into the sky, its pale light slipping through the silent, dark trees to form ghostly white patches on the forest floor. The only noise was the occasional burst of an engine somewhere in the valley below and the occasional blast of a train's horn. Even with this it was hard to believe I was only a few miles from an interstate and a city busy with Saturday-night revelry.

My night above the invisible city was quiet and cold. The temperature fell to twenty-eight degrees, below freezing for the first time in twenty-five days. In the morning my water bottles crackled with ice. A rumble of traffic came from "down below," as I thought of civilization, though it was only six hundred feet lower, but the noise was easily drowned out by a woodpecker drumming, which is how it should be. The drummer was joined by some squabbling jays and then other birds, and the traffic was forgotten. A dozen or so mule deer wandered through the trees and began to graze just a hundred feet away, oblivious, at first, to my presence. Then one started casting frequent glances in my direction as if aware something wasn't quite right. The jays squawked and rustled. The woodpecker drummed on. More deer appeared. One looked toward me and snorted a warning but didn't run. Slowly the deer moved away, grazing as they went. Something made a loud, very fast rattling noise I couldn't identify. Other birds called. The forest was coming alive with the sun's warmth. Flagstaff did not exist. The camp felt wonderfully relaxing with the birds and the deer and the sunshine and the trees, the background noise of traffic and trains somehow part of another unreal world. Parallel universes? Definitely.

Flagstaff did exist of course, and later that day I was in the thick of it, trying to adapt to a faster and noisier world without woodpeckers or mule deer. Trying to get there I had wondered if the city was real, as it was singularly hard to find, which seemed odd given its size.

By foot Flagstaff was maybe six miles away, yet the walk took five hours. If I want an excuse I can say it was because I spent some time on photography early on, but actually that only accounted for an hour at most. Mainly it was because I got lost and wandered around for some time, unsure of where I was and unable to find Flagstaff. This seemed

Camp on Anderson Mesa with my groundsheet used as a windbreak.

ridiculous and not a little surreal. In the past weeks I'd found small pools, tiny creeks, springs hidden in dense vegetation, remote trails, and concealed canyons. And now I couldn't find a city, a city that was vastly bigger than all the other places I'd had to locate put together and multiplied by a thousand. How could this happen? How could a city vanish?

The day had begun conventionally enough with a steep descent into narrow, flat-bottomed Walnut Canyon. A beautiful pink-and-gray Coconino sandstone cliff rose out of the canyon with the sun just rising through the trees above it. A short way along the canyon turned east and bigger, more dramatic cliffs appeared, the most distinctive of which was Fisher Point. Following Arizona Trail signs I climbed to the top of Fisher Point and then eastward along the canyon's rim. This is the Arizona Trail route for equestrians and anyone who wants to bypass Flagstaff. For once I didn't want to avoid a city. It had things I needed. The Arizona Trail route through the city hadn't been signed but I did have a sketch map showing where it ran, as part of the Flagstaff Urban Trail System. I expected to find a trail branching off the bypass route and heading for Flagstaff but none appeared. Eventually I decided I'd gone too far and retraced my steps back into the canyon. Casting around I found an Arizona Trail sign pointing up a clear trail in a side canyon. Further junctions, however, were unsigned. Unable to find these trails and dirt roads on my maps, all I could do was guess. A few times my choices petered out, and I had to backtrack. I kept hearing traffic thundering along not far away, but I couldn't reach it. Suddenly I saw big bright trucks apparently flying through the trees, a stream of color flashing along I-40. The trail I was on promptly headed in the opposite direction. Abandoning it I traveled cross-country for a while, paralleling the interstate, until I reached a dirt track heading toward the highway. Cyclists, joggers, and dog walkers came by, adding to the confusion, but there was still no sign of the city. Feeling foolish I asked a walker the way to Flagstaff. He indicated the way he had come. A creek appeared with a manicured trail next to it. I followed it under I-40. The sound of trains was now loud, but there was still no city. I knew I had to be on the Urban Trail System, but I still couldn't work out which way to go.

Finally and with great delight and relief I saw a paved road and some buildings. Flagstaff did exist after all. I headed downtown, only a short stroll away. Somehow, though, I'd ended up west of the center rather than east, which is where I should have been.

Downtown, I was glad to discover, was very compact. I found an old brick hotel, appropriately called the Monte Vista, that while slightly shabby had some character and wasn't just a soulless, cookie-cutter modern hotel designed to process businesspeople. The rooms were sixty dollars a night, which after the trailer in Pine seemed a bargain, especially as they were huge. With great pleasure I dumped my pack in a corner and sprawled on the big bed. Flagstaff had proved a very elusive city, but I'd managed to find it.

Flagstaff is the third-largest city in Arizona but still tiny compared to Phoenix and Tucson. The population is made up of fifty thousand residents and the fifteen thousand students at the University of Northern Arizona. I liked Flagstaff. It was about as big as a city should be allowed to get—large enough to have all facilities but not so large that it couldn't be quickly escaped. The name comes from the Fourth of July celebrations in 1876 when lumberjacks flew the Stars and Stripes from a tall ponderosa pine. The Santa Fe Railroad, which runs right through the town, arrived in 1882. The trains add a touch of difference to the town and are exciting to watch as they trundle through. They are noisy though, especially the horns, and can be heard everywhere. Route 66 runs through Flagstaff as well and is heavily signed as a tourist attraction. The downtown is well preserved, consisting mainly of attractive old buildings. Their typical, Spanish-influenced, Southwestern style hasn't been ruined by modern add-ons of ugly concrete and glaring neon. New buildings have been mostly constructed in the same style so they blend in rather than clash.

Wandering around in the evening I noted promising bookstores and outdoor shops plus many restaurants and cafés. I felt very detached, almost like a visitor from another planet, as I ambled about, staring into shop-windows and watching people striding purposefully about. It would be nice to do that, I thought, but how do you work out how fast the traffic is going to get across these awfully wide and busy roads? I put off shopping until the next day when I expected to be more awake and alert and used to the traffic and the large numbers of people. I was capable enough to find a decent restaurant, the Café Espresso, where I dined on good Mexican food and drank an excellent local microbrew, Mogollon Superstition Pale Ale. With that name I couldn't resist it. Back at the hotel I rang Denise from a pay phone in the lobby. While I was talking to her a burst of aggressive shouting came from a poolroom just off the lobby. The desk clerk quickly vanished into a back room. The shouting continued and then a big, muscular, bald-headed guy in a tight T-shirt and jeans and red eyes that suggested far too much alcohol rushed out of the poolroom and stomped past me looking furious. No one followed, and the shouting ceased. It was all over so fast I had no time to feel worried. Life in the city, I thought.

The next day I had to be more organized. The post office was a block from the hotel, which was great. Until I found that the one that held general delivery mail was two miles away. I took a taxi so I could bring back my awkward box. The cab took awhile to arrive and when it did it already had a passenger. I quickly realized that it was more like a bus than a normal taxi as we drove around the town picking up people and dropping them off. At the post office I found my box along with letters from Denise and Hazel. I read about snow on the mountains at home with more in the forecast. On the television the night before I'd heard a forecast for snow here. Above Flagstaff I could see the white-capped San Francisco Peaks. Snow on the mountains in Scotland; snow on the mountains in Arizona. They had something in common. I missed my family. I'd been away for more than six weeks now, by far the longest period since we'd been together. But as much as I wanted to see them I was aware that I didn't want the walk to end, a dilemma that would be solved when I reached Utah.

Flagstaff had a marvelous bookstore, one of those in which you can browse for hours, finding more and more books to read. Only the knowledge that I had to either carry or mail any books I bought prevented me from buying dozens. Exercising strict discipline I managed to keep my purchases to four—another Edward Abbey *(Black Sun)*, a Sierra Club guide to the southwestern deserts, a book of Arizona tales and, for light reading, a Tony Hillerman detective novel set in New Mexico (it was a desert landscape so there was some connection with the walk).

Books are essential to me. I am addicted to reading, one of those people who reads labels on food packages if there's nothing else available. I couldn't imagine not having something to read in camp. Sometimes I carried three or four books, adding a few extra pounds to my load, but I never resented the extra weight. Rather than buy books in advance and mail them in my supply box I'd decided to buy as I went along, which left me dependent on what I could find in the mostly small towns along the way, which led to an interesting, unusual, and eclectic reading list. Authors I read in Arizona included Edward Abbey, Colin Fletcher, John le Carre, Patricia Cornwell, C. S. Lewis, William Shakespeare, Poul Anderson, and Kinky Friedman. And I also had along, of course, various natural history guides.

Much more mundane than books but just as important was food. I found some rather expensive but easy-to-cook and tasty freeze-dried trail food at the outdoor stores. (In one an assistant who was interested in the walk asked me about supplies and showers. "You look very clean," she said. It was amazing what the first shower in a week and some clean clothes could do.) Groceries, however, were not to be found in downtown Flagstaff, since they were far too uninteresting for the tourists. I had to walk a fair way along wide streets lined with wooden houses and well-tended gardens before I found a supermarket, but when I did, it (Basho's) was excellent, with a far wider selection than I was used to, much of it organic. The problem was to avoid buying too much. Again I reminded myself I had to carry it and so was able to ignore most of the stuff in the store. Anything canned or bottled was out immediately, as was anything fresh. Dried foods were my staples, and even here I went for the lightest, highest-calorie items.

One of the greatest pleasures of town stops was not having to eat dried food. On the trail it tasted fine but once in a town I instantly had a great desire to eat fresh food; food with a texture that wasn't slimy slop. Most of the tiny towns along the trail had only one or two eating places. Flagstaff had a plethora of them, though most looked fairly mainstream and predictable. Searching for somewhere a bit more interesting to eat my dinner I found a place called the Alpine Pizza. Rock music was playing, and it was dark and gloomy with crude wooden tables and seats, most heavily carved with names and slogans. The walls were adorned with climbing photographs. Pizza and beer seemed the only food and drink for sale. The atmosphere was alive and exciting, unlike the restrained, polite nature of most restaurants. I ordered—no table service here—and sat down on a hard bench in the half-dark. The pizza was large and tasty. The beer—Oak Creek Nut Brown Ale—was pretty good, too. While I ate I watched a young woman carving her name and a date on the wall next to her in between bites of pizza and swallows of beer. A large party left, one of them going to the counter to pay, proffering a credit card. "We don't take plastic." Shaken and shocked the woman was at a loss for words. Clearly this was unbelievable. A hasty whip-round produced the required cash. Someone nearby remarked how astonishing it was that such a dive could be such a success when it clearly flouted all business rules. That's why, I thought. It's different, individual, not a corporate-designed, safe, bland, instantly forgettable, boring institution.

Supplies bought, laundry done, my box and other mail ready to send, by evening I was ready to head up into the San Francisco Peaks and impatient for the next day. A day and a half in even as pleasant a city as Flagstaff was enough. I watched the weather forecast on the TV in my room. Winds gusting to fifty miles per hour, snowstorms with, possibly, thunder and lightning. The trail didn't seem quite so attractive. I went to sleep without deciding what to do. Morning brought the answer. Snow was driving down out of a dark gray sky. People scurried about the streets with hoods up or struggling to control umbrellas. I would stay another day. Suddenly I was able to really relax. I spent much of the day sitting in cafés reading newspapers and books. In between I walked around Flagstaff looking at the old buildings and watching the trains. A nice town, I thought, a nice town.

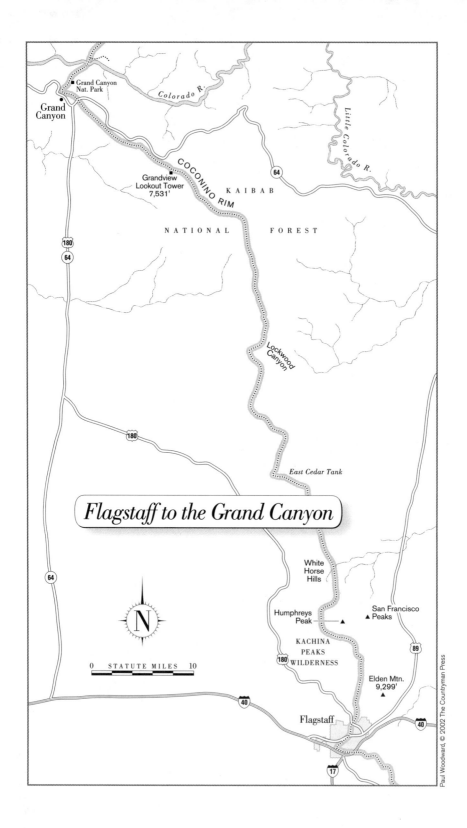

Grand Canyon

Grand Canyon Nat. Park

Colorado R.

Little Colorado R.

64

COCONINO RIM

KAIBAB

Grandview Lookout Tower 7,531'

NATIONAL   FOREST

180
64

Lockwood Canyon

180

East Cedar Tank

Flagstaff to the Grand Canyon

White Horse Hills

San Francisco ▲ Peaks

Humphreys Peak

64

KACHINA PEAKS WILDERNESS

180

Elden Mtn. 9,299' ▲

89

N

0 STATUTE MILES 10

40

Flagstaff

40

17

Paul Woodward, © 2002 The Countryman Press

7

In and Out of the Wilderness

FLAGSTAFF TO THE GRAND CANYON

107 miles

Leaving Flagstaff wasn't quite as hard as arriving had been, but the city did try to hold on to me. In trying to keep things simple and not get caught up in a network of minor streets I took a long but apparently straightforward way out of town. Busy, noisy Route 66 led to quieter Switzer Canyon Drive. Big brash car showrooms lined the mouth of this thoroughfare. Farther along the road, away from the traffic speeding down Route 66, I passed slightly smaller, though no less brash, secondhand car dealers. Then, as the road grew narrower and there was less traffic, small, subdued churches appeared. Car worship was clearly the dominant religion.

Continuing along Switzer Canyon Drive, I was surprised to come out on San Francisco Street, as this was the street on which the Monte Vista Hotel stood. I could have been here in a quarter of the time. And I was now in the maze of smaller streets I'd been trying to avoid. Somewhere I'd missed a junction. I turned resolutely northward and tramped on, passing a hospital with a red-and-white helicopter on the roof behind which the San Francisco Peaks rose into a deep blue sky. The previous day's storm had long gone; it was hot and sunny again. Soon there were more trees and fewer houses. A park appeared with a dirt trail running through it.

The trail led to larger Buffalo Park; the route I was seeking into the San Francisco Peaks lay just to its north. A notice announced TRAIL SYSTEM AND EXERCISE COURSE. Fit-looking cyclists and joggers sped around the dirt paths, some of the latter stopping at various marked points to undertake a designated exercise—calf stretches and the like. I looked beyond the park to the forest and mountains. I'd rather get my exercise up there, I thought as I plodded along, feeling slow and heavy compared to the lightly clad, unencumbered athletes.

Another sign marked the Beale Wagon Road and told me that Lieutenant Edward F. Beale with a hundred men had built the first federal highway in the Southwest between 1857 and 1860. The road ran from Fort Smith in Arkansas to Los Angeles, cost $200,000, and became one of the three main routes for settlers headed for California.

What the sign doesn't say was that Beale, clearly an imaginative man, imported twenty-five camels and used them as his beasts of burden, figuring that they would cope as well in Arizona as they did in North Africa. Handling the strange creatures was not easy, so Beale also brought in African camel drivers, one of whom, Hadji Ali (a name that became Americanized to Hi Jolly), became quite well known, eventually settling in Arizona. Beale felt using camels worked well, but his curious experiment remained unique, others sticking with traditional mules and horses.

Beale's route across northern Arizona had been used by Native Americans before him. The Atlantic and Pacific Railroad (now the Santa Fe) and Route 66 both followed in Beale's tracks. Although used until the 1940s the Beale Wagon Road ceased to be important when the railroad arrived in 1882.

On the far side of Buffalo Park lay the national forest boundary. A foot trail led invitingly into the cool, dark, mysterious woods. The city was behind me now; the wilderness lay ahead. The trail led past the huge, steep boulder fields on the western flanks of Elden Mountain, a massive, very steep-sided, wooded hill with a collection of communications masts on its summits. The chaotic heaps of boulders half-hidden in the trees reminded me of the mountains to the south, especially the Wilderness of Rocks in the Santa Catalinas.

Beyond the boulders I traversed the lower slopes of the gentler Dry Lake Hills and then began climbing beside Schultz Creek. A dirt road paralleled the trail on the far side of the creek. Every so often a mountain biker came bouncing down the rough trail. I guessed they climbed up on the road. A notice said that the Schultz Trail was built by motorcyclists in the 1970s along the line of an old road and was open to motorbikes but not ATVs. The mass of narrow tire tracks suggested that it was mostly used by mountain bikers now. I'd much rather deal with bicycles than the roar and stink of motorbikes, though it did occur to me that at least I would hear the latter coming.

As the trail eased off near Schultz Pass a young mountain biker, dressed in the usual bright-colored clothing, greeted me in an English accent. He was on holiday here for two weeks, staying in Flagstaff, and was ecstatic about the mountain biking but "gutted" that he had to go home soon.

Just beyond the pass lay muddy, murky Schultz Tank. As this might be the last water for a while I added five quarts to my load. With a now much heavier pack I continued slowly on up the hillside and into lower Weatherford Canyon where I found a flat area to camp in the midst of a magnificent grove of tall aspen. Above me lay a beautiful bowl, curving perfectly below the mountains. Patches of snow lay in shady areas and the ground was damp, but Aspen Spring, just below my camp, was dry. Cool breezes drifted down from above. This was probably a cold-air sink, but there was nowhere else flat enough for a camp. Others had thought it a good site too. An old fire ring lay nearby, filled with half-burned logs. I was right about the cold. By 8:00 P.M. it was just thirty-six degrees. It was also absolutely silent. No wind, no birds, no animals, no water. Just the loud, obtrusive scratch of my pen scrawling across my notebook's paper. I'd never before noticed how noisy it was. The drone of a plane far above cut through the quiet. I looked up. Stars shone in a black sky through the latticework of the leafless skeletal silhouettes of the aspens. I shivered with delight (or maybe cold). It was wonderful to be here, wonderful to be back in the woods and out of the city. Later the moon rose, and the aspens glowed a ghostly white.

I was now high on the southern slopes of the San Francisco Peaks at 8,850 feet. These are the highest mountains in Arizona, and their summits still rose almost four thousand feet above me. The Peaks are really one mountain (on the USGS map the name is San Francisco Mountain) that curves in a huge horseshoe around the deep Inner Basin. The four main summits are more than 11,000 feet, the highest, Humphreys Peak, reaching 12,633 feet. The mountain is the remnant of a huge volcano that may have reached 16,000 feet before its top blew off. The area around the San Francisco Peaks is rich in lava flows and cinder cones, at least one of which was active as recently as eight hundred years ago.

The Peaks were named by Spanish Franciscan missionaries, probably in the sixteenth century, in honor of St. Francis of Assisi. They have older names, those given by the Native Americans to whom the Peaks are sacred. Thirteen different tribes revere these mountains. To the Navajo they are Dook'o'osliid, the Sacred Mountain of the West, one of the four sacred mountains that mark the cardinal points around their country. The Hopi call the Peaks Navatekiaooi, the Place of Snow on the Very Top, and say that the kachina spirits, which are central to their beliefs, dwell there. Being sacred to Native Americans hasn't stopped the desecration of the mountains by a ski resort on the western slopes and an open-pit mine on the eastern. The mine produces white pumice stone used mainly to stone wash jeans so that consumers can buy them already faded. For this the mountains are defiled.

Thankfully they are now afforded some protection; most of the area now being in the Kachina Peaks Wilderness, established in 1984, with the boundary carefully drawn to exclude the ski resort. The pumice mine looks like it will probably be closed down, ironically because, in the 1990s, the owners applied to enlarge it. This request so affronted people that a coalition was formed between Native Americans and environmental groups such as the Sierra Club to fight the proposal. The campaign was successful, and an agreement was reached. The mine would shut in return for a payment of $1 million from the federal government. The mining company also has to restore the site, though they do have ten years in which to remove and sell the pumice that has already been mined. The next stage is to have the Peaks declared a Traditional Cultural Property so that mining can never take place there again.

Kachina was the ninth designated Wilderness Area that I'd hiked through on the walk, having already visited Miller Peak, Mount Wrightson, Rincon Mountain, Pusch Ridge, White Canyon, Superstition, Four Peaks, and Mazatzal. These are "official" wilderness, set aside by the federal government to remain forever wild with no development of any sort: no logging, no mining, no ski resorts, no "improvements." Some came into being after the Wilderness Act of 1964, some, such as the Mazatzal, created in 1940, were in place long before that farsighted legislation.

What though is wilderness? What does the word mean? It goes back a long way, being derived from the Old English (Anglo-Saxon) *wildeor,* meaning "wild animal," which became the Middle English *wildern,* meaning "wild." At some point the suffix "-ness" was added. Thus "wil(d)deorness"—the place of the wild animals. Appropriately enough one of the first known uses of *wildeor* is in the Anglo-Saxon epic poem *Beowulf* (which itself probably means "bee wolf," a creature that wolfs down honey, in other words, a bear) written between the seventh and tenth centuries. The hero, Beowulf, the archetype of all the "sword and sorcery" superheroes, searches for a savage and dangerous monster, the mother of another monster, Grendel, that he had killed. In Seamus Heaney's superb translation Beowulf and his followers hike

> up fells and screes, along narrow footpaths
> and ways where they were forced into single file,
> ledges on cliffs above lairs of water-monsters.

Eventually they come to a "dismal wood" with "mountain trees growing out at an angle above grey stones." In front of them lies the lake in which the monster lives, a lake full of weird and wonderful creatures including "wyrmas ond wildeor . . . serpents and wild things."

That the word *wilderness* comes from descriptions such as this is wonderful. It is so apt. Don't you want to tread those footpaths and venture into that dismal wood? I know I do. (Diving into the lake to fight the monster, as Beowulf does, is another matter. I'll wait until I find a magic sword.)

The wilderness link between Beowulf and Arizona may seem a trifle tenuous. But there are other connections. As I've said, *"Beowulf"* means bear, and the bear is a key animal for wilderness. Knowing that bears are out there says "here are wildeor" indeed. And there are bears in Arizona, particularly in the wilderness areas. We can go further. Theodore Roosevelt, the president who created Grand Canyon National Monument (as it then was called), after standing on the rim and looking down into the Canyon, gave his name to a stuffed animal forever after known as the teddy bear. And teddy bears, as everyone knows, really are "bee wolfs," with a great love of honey, none more so than the most famous teddy bear of all, Winnie-the-Pooh, who of course lived in a wood on a hill, a wilderness.

Yet more links can be made. We've seen that Beowulf journeys through the wilderness in search of Grendel's mother. At the end of the poem, as an old man, he goes into the wilds again for a final, fatal fight with a dragon that guards a treasure hoard buried in a "stone-roofed bar-row." The dragon had been roused to anger by an intruder who found a way into the barrow and took a "gem-studded goblet." Buried treasure? The Lost Dutchman's Mine comes in here, another hoard that is hazardous to seek though the dangers lie in the harsh landscape of the Superstition Mountains. Given the fantastic nature of some of the lost mine tales the appearance of a dragon would hardly be surprising. As the Beowulf story shows, tales of hidden gold go back much further than the Lost Mine. Maybe Jacob Waltz brought these stories with him from Germany— *Beowulf* is a Germanic tale after all.

Beowulf's journeys to fight monsters and the adventures of the prospectors in search of the Lost Dutchman's Mine both can be connected to long distance hiking. All three activities embody the concept of the quest, a challenging, purposeful journey into the wilds, into the unknown. The quest must be long and difficult, the outcome uncertain. "We have arrived here on a great errand," says Beowulf after traveling across the sea to seek out the monster Grendel. With all these activities, how they are carried out is important. The quest's fulfillment, whether the end of the trail, the killing of the monster, or the finding of the gold, sums up all that has gone before, all that has led up to that point. How the journey is undertaken matters more than its outcome. The meaning is in the process, not the conclusion. For the long distance hiker the journey is all. Reaching the end is just the point where you stop. How the end is reached affects the quality of the experience. Walking the whole way—no rides, no skipped sections—makes for a more satisfying journey. For Beowulf how he fights the monsters is crucial. He is in a heroic tradition that says battles must be fair. Because Grendel fights without weapons Beowulf announces he will do so too. This is not Odysseus tricking the Cyclops. Such tactics would be shameful to Beowulf. As to the gold seekers, it always seems to involve a single prospector or a small group armed with little more than picks and shovels. The words of Robert Service, written in the far-off Yukon, come to mind: "Yet it isn't the gold that I'm wanting / So much as just finding the gold." It's the search, the quest, that counts.

The word *wilderness* itself first occurs in the thirteenth century in *Brut,* a poem about the history of the world, by a writer named Layamon. In that time, wilderness would have referred to woodland, as that was where wild animals lived. However, the word became better known after its use in the first English translations of the Bible in the fourteenth century, when it was used to describe the desert areas of the Middle East. The basic meaning was clear: a wilderness was an area inhabited by wild animals and therefore uncultivated and uncivilized.

The 1964 Wilderness Act defines *wilderness* as "an area where the earth and its community of life are untrammeled by man, where man himself is a visitor who does not remain." *Webster's Dictionary* gives several definitions: "a tract or region uncultivated and uninhabited by human beings"; "an area essentially undisturbed by human activity together with its naturally developed life community"; and "an empty or pathless area or region."

These phrases describe wilderness, tell us what it is in an objective sense, but they don't tell us what the word means emotionally. They also reflect current attitudes about wilderness, which are often, though not always, positive. In the past the word more often had negative connotations. This dichotomy is due to different perspectives, different values. To some a wilderness is a place to be cultivated, civilized, inhabited, exploited even. If this can't be done it is useless, worthless. To others it is a place of beauty, a place where nature is revealed untouched and unharmed. Both views are valid. It just depends on your point of view. To me, *wilderness* is a magical word, redolent of all that is finest in the natural world. It means long hikes, beautiful campsites, and encounters with wildlife; it means arriving breathless on a high summit with the world spread out below, threading through a desert canyon with ancient rocks piled up overhead, walking through a dark and mysterious old-growth forest; it means mountain ridges, forest pools, tumbling creeks, a fragile butterfly on an equally fragile flower, a bear rooting through the undergrowth, a forest of tall pines, the wild cry of a mountain lion, the howl of a wolf, a vulture soaring high overhead. I can't define *wilderness*, the word encompasses too much, but I know what it is. And I know that it exists in many places, small and large, and that it can't be contained in a bureaucratic construct, however well meaning. Wilderness is where you can go and feel you have escaped civilization, where you can be in touch with the rhythms of the natural world and know that they underpin everything we do and everything we are, however cut off from them we may often appear to be.

The San Francisco Peaks have a special place in the history of ecology and natural history as it was here during the summer of 1889 that the biologist C. Hart Merriam worked out his concept of life zones. Merriam proposed seven zones, defined by the type of vegetation that grew at different elevations, from the Lower Sonoran (100 to 3,500 feet) to Arctic-Alpine (above 11,500 feet). Six of the zones are found in the San Francisco Peaks area. The concept has been refined and developed since Merriam's day, but the basics remain the same. At certain elevations at certain latitudes certain vegetation types grow. Other factors, such as aspect (the direction a slope faces), rainfall, and soil type play a part, but Merriam's life zone principle is still sound. I'd seen how it worked over and over again in every mountain range I'd crossed. Now I was seeing it in the range where the concept was developed.

In Arizona, Merriam's Arctic-Alpine zone is only found on the summits of the San Francisco Peaks. This small area of tundra is fragile and easily damaged. Because it is far from any similar area some of the plants have evolved into distinct, unique types. To protect these hiking is allowed only on trails above timberline.

My planned route up the Peaks was via the Weatherford Trail, a road built in the 1920s by rancher John Weatherford so that vehicles could drive up the mountain; it has long since been closed to traffic.

The day of my proposed ascent dawned cold and clear. The temperature was twenty-seven degrees. Frost coated the inside of the tarp and the ground was white and crisp. A fine white tracery of cirrus clouds covered the sky. I could hear trains in Flagstaff and the rumble of traffic, sounds that hadn't reached up here the previous evening. Birds started calling, and a woodpecker drummed loudly. The sun lit the treetops and began to filter down through the branches. Before it had reached my camp, hemmed in by steep slopes, I had packed up and was on my way.

The old dirt road ascended the side of the canyon in a series of long, sweeping switchbacks. Upward progress was slow but the views and the trees made up for it. Flagstaff appeared at times, far below, with the green of the forest rolling away beyond it. Ahead rose the big wedge of Fremont Peak. The forest was superb with masses of aspens of all sizes and huge ponderosas and Douglas firs. Higher up I found some old friends from hikes in other mountains: dark-needled, spire-shaped subalpine fir and gnarled, twisted limber pine.

Much of the trail was covered in snow, knee deep in places, which made walking difficult. For the first time since the early days of the walk on Miller Peak my boots were soaked and my feet cold. I postholed slowly on, back and forth across the slope. There were no other tracks. In places I edged carefully across runnels of hard snow, knowing that a slip could send me sliding down into the steep ravine below. After three and a half hours of hard work I reached Fremont Saddle at 10,800 feet. I'd walked just four miles. From the saddle I stared across the deep Inner Basin to

Humphreys Peak and the inside curve of the horseshoe of summits. Steep, snow-covered slopes dropped sharply down into the forest. I could see the line of the trail climbing up the east face of Agassiz Peak and then traversing across snowy slopes to a saddle below the south ridge of Humphreys. It looked too far, too steep, and, especially, far too snowy. I wasn't equipped for this. No gaiters, no ice ax, no crampons. The route crossed several obvious avalanche paths. I had no idea how stable the snow was. I turned back. My attempt on the San Francisco Peaks was over. Fremont Saddle would be the high point of the walk.

An hour and three-quarters later I was back at my campsite. On the descent I took a couple of shortcuts, the first one down a steep snowbank to avoid a long loop of trail. The snow was firm and slick, so I went down with my weight on my heels, slamming them into the snow to

The San Francisco Peaks from Fremont Saddle,
at 10,800 feet the high point of the walk.

make steps. This worked fine until I was almost at the bottom. I suddenly plunged knee deep into soft snow and then rolled forward onto my knees as my poles disappeared into the drift. Crouched with my head down the slope and my pack trying to push my face into the snow I had quite a struggle before I got the pack off and staggered to my feet. When I tried to retrieve my poles, made in three sections so they could be shortened for carrying on the pack, the bottom sections pulled out and remained buried. I had to dig for them, kicking the snow away with my boots. I probably could have walked down the trail in less time and with less effort. Still, it's traditional for shortcuts to take longer. The second shortcut, an eight-hundred-foot descent straight down steep slopes to Aspen Spring, taken to avoid another long switchback, went smoothly, however, and did save a little time. It was easier to go straight down the snow than zigzag across it.

My minor mountaineering venture over, I set off along the Kachina Trail, the route the Arizona Trail will probably follow, which curves around the southern slopes of Fremont and Agassiz Peaks. The trail undulated along through forest and big meadows at around nine thousand feet with good views all around. Buoyed by the easy walk and fine scenery I shrugged off the morning's climb. It hadn't been wasted. I'd seen the Inner Basin and stood high on the rim of the Peaks.

My positive mood became hard to maintain when I reached the Arizona Snow Bowl ski resort. Huge, empty parking lots full of piles of dirty snow heaped there by snowplows greeted me, the flat, hard, unbroken tarmac and concrete an intrusion in the flowing curves of forest and mountain. I crossed the blank wastes. A few buildings appeared. Above them rose the tangled, ugly metal junk of the ski lifts. Streaks of old grubby snow still covered parts of the slopes. The scene was desolate, bleak, and unattractive, as out-of-season ski resorts usually are. A solitary minibus was driving around the parking lots, trying to find a way out to the highway. Snowbanks blocked most of the exits, but eventually the driver found a short, steep, muddy bank and risked the descent, scraping the chassis on the rough ground. More interesting were prairie dogs, plump, ground-dwelling members of the squirrel family. Several of them sat on their haunches on the bare ground that surrounded the ski resort, watching me cautiously as I walked past.

Beyond the ski resort there was no trail, just the dark, dense forest hanging on the steep western slopes of the mountains. The easiest route would have been to drop down to the west and follow dirt roads through the trees. But that sounded dull, so as I had Bill's GPS and a list of waypoints I plunged into the dense woods. Snow, knee deep in places, lay under the trees. There was a lot of fallen timber too, half hidden in the snowdrifts. For the second time that day progress slowed to a crawl. You could hardly call it walking, this lurching stumble over fallen trees, this high-stepping, exhausting wade through soft snow, this flounder through broken branches. The GPS wouldn't work in the densest forest; the thick foliage blocked the satellite signals. In some places it reversed the bearing, pointing me back the way I had come. I used a compass between the waypoints but still needed the GPS to locate each one and get the bearing to the next point. I tried to remind myself that the road walk would have been boring. I wasn't convinced. Maybe boredom would be preferabe to this. After a couple of frustrating miles I reached a more open area with meadows and groves of smaller trees. Lew Tank lay nearby but was dry. With plenty of snow to melt this hardly mattered.

Camp that evening was on the edge of a meadow looking east to Humphreys Peak. A gusty cold wind blew through the trees, so I pitched the tarp in its battened down, storm-shedding configuration with just a low entrance to crawl through. Before settling in I hauled many stuff-sackful of snow to the camp and heaped them up at the front of the tarp. While I was doing this the slopes of Humphreys Peak began to glow in the evening light. Dropping the stuff sack I raced back to camp to grab my cameras and tripod. The mountain and the forest blazed a golden red in the setting sun. Slowly, the color deepened and darkened until the trees and mountain were silhouettes and the sky crimson and purple. The spectacular and beautiful sunset drew me out of myself. I forgot the day's frustrations and started to relax.

Back under the tarp I started the long process of melting snow. Enclosed in my nylon shelter I felt quite cut off. I was used to being able to see the sky and the forest. Coyotes calling nearby reminded me of the woods outside. After two hours I had a gallon of water, most of it needed for the next day. From this camp I would descend to lower terrain and leave the snow behind. I had been able to find out little about water sources. There were many tanks marked on the map but how many would have water was another matter. Dry Lew Tank wasn't reassuring. I also wanted to make up some distance. This camp was just eight miles from where I'd been the previous night. Grand Canyon Village, my next supply point, was seventy-five miles away. I had three days' food left and a reservation at a campground (made by phone in Flagstaff). In three evenings time I wanted to be there.

The night was warm but very windy, with the wind swirling around and buffeting the tarp from every direction. At 8,920 feet this was the highest camp of the walk, but the overnight low was only forty-six degrees. I wasn't surprised to see clouds covering the sky at dawn or that the

Evening sunshine on the San Francisco Peaks
from a camp near dry Lew Tank.

barometric pressure had dropped considerably. A weak, sickly yellow sun appeared over the shoulder of Humphreys Peak, showing that the clouds weren't very thick.

Leaving the peaks behind, the route continued through dense forest with deep snow. My feet were soon cold and wet again. I was meant to be mostly on dirt roads, but they were hard to find in the snow and even harder to follow when I did find them, even with the GPS. In places the going was just too difficult, with trees packed so tight I couldn't squeeze between them or masses of blowdowns that created a latticework of logs a few feet above the ground, and I had to go where the terrain allowed. Wanting to hurry I only checked the GPS at infrequent intervals and the altimeter not at all. The unsurprising though irritating result was that I missed my way and descended too far to the west, right into a small area of posted, fenced private property, the only posted area anywhere near my route. A gravel road took me back east, below the very steep slopes of the volcanic cinder cones called the White Horse Hills, to where a jeep trail headed up to a high, narrow pass. The forest on both sides of the trail had recently burned, and the blackened skeletons of the trees rising from black ground looked quite eerie.

The jeep trail climbed a narrow ravine to the pass and then descended an even narrower ravine on the other side only to peter out halfway down. The forest was thick with deadfall, so the easiest course was in the dry wash at the bottom of the ravine, which brought back memories of the many such washes I'd hiked through farther south.

The route wandered on northward, mostly on dirt roads though occasionally on new sections of the Arizona Trail. The land was much drier than around the San Francisco Peaks, and I was now in piñon pine–juniper forest. Every tank I passed was dry. Steep wooded hills rose all around, reminiscent of the Canelo Hills far away to the south. Behind me Humphreys Peak soared above the trees.

At a trail junction a bit of paper flapping on a signpost caught my eye. Idly curious I went over to it and was surprised to find my name. It was a note from Jake, or rather half a note—part had torn off and blown away in the wind. The remaining section read "Trail. I Kachina. See you at the Canyon. Jake. I have new shoes." I'd assumed he was still behind me, but he must have passed by while I was engaged in my futile attempt to climb the San Francisco Peaks. And he'd probably not spent two and a half days in Flagstaff. Checking the trail I did notice fresh prints in places and recalled seeing them before. I hadn't recognized the tread, however. Jake's note told me why. Since leaving Superior three weeks ago I had wondered if Jake would catch me. I'd doubted it after receiving his postcard in Mormon Lake, but now he was ahead and the question had reversed. Would I catch him?

As I tramped on the trees became more and more scattered. Past intriguingly named Missouri Bill Hill (who was Missouri Bill, and why does this hill bear his name, I wondered?) a view suddenly opened up of vast, parched-looking, pale yellow grasslands stretching away to the north with just a few small brown hills breaking the flatness. This was the CO Bar Ranch, the biggest section of private land crossed by the Arizona Trail. The owner, Babbitt Ranches, had given permission for the trail to cross the ranchlands on little-used primitive roads. And not just given permission. A very nice touch was a large wooden sign with the word "Welcome" on it. The Babbitts are a famous family in Arizona. I'd noticed their name on many of the stores in Flagstaff. In 1886 five brothers from Cincinnati, Ohio, bought a ranch near Flagstaff. Their cattle brand was CO, the initials of their hometown and state. A grandson of one of them, Bruce Babbitt, became governor of Arizona and then Secretary of the Interior in the Clinton Administration.

A long east-west running scarp divided woods from grasslands, emphasizing the change in the environment. A steepish descent led to a dirt road running along the base of the slope. I'd seen little wildlife all day, just a few elk early on, and I'd ceased to be very observant so it was with a shock that I suddenly noticed a big snake almost at my feet. The three-foot-long reptile moved slowly off the road. At first glance it looked like a rattlesnake, but the lack of rattles showed it wasn't. After checking my field guide I identified it as a gopher snake.

This late in the day I was more interested in water than animals. The Arizona Trail Association passage notes said that East Cedar Tank was "a reliable source of water." I hoped so. I hadn't found any all day and had little left. From the map I could see the tank lay about a quarter of a mile off the road up the scarp. Scanning the hillside I spotted something through the small trees that dotted the slopes. Guessing it was the tank I took a side track up toward it. A muddy dirt tank, the banks trampled by cattle, appeared. I could see a circular metal tank above. Into this water gushed, cold, clear springwater that tasted wonderful. I drank a quart and loaded up with a gallon and a half. The water in the tank looked healthy, too, full of water plants and small aquatic creatures—snails and beetles—crawling about.

A mile on from the tank I turned away from the scarp and headed out into open, sagebrush-dotted grasslands on a gravel road. A pickup rumbled up behind me and stopped. The driver, a man in a big cowboy hat, was not surprised to see me. He'd already met Jake earlier in the day.

East Cedar Tank on the edge of the CO Bar Ranch grasslands.

Jake hadn't been able to find East Cedar Tank, so the rancher had directed him to a tank near Tub Ranch, not far ahead. I'd noted that Jake's prints hadn't gone to the tank. Now I remembered that he didn't carry detailed topographic maps, just smaller-scale Forest Service ones. "What time did you meet Jake?" I asked. "Around midday," he replied. Half a day, I thought. Maybe I would see him soon.

A strong south wind swept across the grasslands in rippling gusts. The only shelter I could find for a camp was next to some junipers above a dry wash. The protection was more psychological than real. I felt quite exposed camping out here after all the nights in the forest, though I did enjoy being able to see a big night sky full of stars again. The weather had become unsettled, the wind blowing all day, clouds coming and going and with them big temperature variations. The rancher had told me it was forecast to be cooler for the next day or so and then to start warming up. Cool weather sounded good. Grand Canyon Village was now about forty-five miles away. It was easier to walk longer distances on days when it wasn't searingly hot.

Although my campsite appeared flat, masses of small lumps of baked-hard, dry earth lay under the grass. I woke many times as I shifted around to find a comfortable position but was tired enough to always drop back to sleep quickly. The tarp flapping noisily in the intermittent gusty wind didn't help me sleep either. A clear, flutelike, descending birdcall woke me at dawn. Scanning the nearby grasslands through my binoculars I spotted a small bird perched on a rather shaky bit of sagebrush. The bright yellow breast with a black V marking and the white eye stripe identified it as a western meadowlark. A kestrel flew by, hung briefly in the wind, then flew on. There was a wonderful sense of open space as the grasslands spread out all around. That meant there was nothing to stop the wind though, which gusted through camp at twenty-five miles an hour. It had shifted from south to northwest and was much colder than the previous day.

That wind became the dominant feature of the day, much of which was spent struggling against it in open country. I learned that my hat lifted off my head in gusts of twenty miles per hour or above, even with the neck cord cinched tight. The sky was cloudy and the temperature cool.

Despite the windshirt and long pants I wore I was frequently on the verge of being cold. Soon after I set off a pickup came by. "You'll be wanting to keep walking in this wind," said the driver. A young boy, age ten I guessed, stared at me in amazement. Hikers were probably unusual out here.

Beyond Tub Ranch, which the trail carefully avoided in a big curve of dirt roads, the walking was hard and unpleasant as I headed straight into the wind across three miles of open terrain. Swirls of dust blew up into my face. The strongest gust I measured was thirty miles per hour, but some felt stronger. Ahead I could see the mouth of a shallow canyon among some low hills. I plodded arduously toward it, hoping it would provide shelter. It did, and I entered the scattering of sparse piñons and junipers with relief. To the south a big cloud capped the San Francisco Peaks.

The mix of open forest and grassland continued as I went northward. A pronghorn darted across the plains not far away, surprisingly well camouflaged against the faded yellow and gray of the sparse vegetation. There were elk, too, looking much bigger among these small trees than they did in the ponderosa forest. I saw several more snakes, but again none were rattlers. At Lockwood Tank a flock of fifty-plus ravens, by far the biggest I'd ever seen, hung in the wind and swirled around each other. Occasionally one would land on a treetop, but for the most part they stayed in the air. For some reason many of them followed me for a while, a long rippling chain of black birds strung out raggedly behind. As I left the tank their numbers slowly dwindled, though the last few stayed with me for at least a mile. Perhaps they were just curious, or maybe they thought I wouldn't get far and would soon provide a meal.

A sign appeared in the sagebrush marking the southern boundary of Kaibab National Forest. The terrain didn't change but the dirt road did, becoming a foot trail and remaining so for five miles to the Moqui Stage Station, which lay a little off the trail. I made the side trip, but all I found were the foundations of a building, the remains of a stone water tank, and an information board that explained that this was one of three rest stops and horse change stations on the stagecoach journey between Flagstaff and the Grand Canyon in the period between 1892 and 1899. The journey took twelve hours and cost $20. Sometimes historical relics can conjure an impression of what the past was like. It didn't happen here. I tried, but I couldn't imagine stagecoaches trundling across the sagebrush and passengers alighting here to stretch their legs while new horses were harnessed to the coach. Maybe it was me, maybe battered by the wind and plagued by the insidious need to cover a lot of distance; I just wasn't in the right frame of mine to be inspired.

The route, an abandoned dirt road marked as the Arizona Trail with brands on wooden four-by-four posts, headed into Russell Wash, an attractive, shallow, grassy valley. The forest was changing, the juniper and piñon trees giving way to ponderosa pines. My main interest though was to find water for camp. I'd seen none since Lockwood Camp and only had three pints left. Maybe there'd be more in the ponderosas than in the dry juniper-piñon country. Disappointingly Anderson Tank, the first one in Russell Wash, was dry. A mile farther on I came to a metal stock tank. It was also dry. Nearby was a large, rusting, circular metal water tower with no outlet. I followed Jake's prints around it. Someone had put a rusted ladder against the side very recently, probably Jake. I could see the deep impression in the ground where the ladder had been lying. I banged the side of the tower and heard a hollow, empty-sounding deep boom. I didn't bother climbing the shaky-looking ladder.

Slowing down and feeling tired I decided to make do with the water I had, and camped in some ponderosa pines above the trail. I had just enough water for one hot drink and a meal that night, and cereal and a small drink the next morning. Large Russell Tank, said to always have water, was a couple miles away, but I'd had enough. Arriving there even more tired and in the dark didn't appeal. I'd been walking eleven hours with only a few short stops. According to the trail guide, the passage notes, and the forest service signs I'd walked about nineteen miles. I felt they were all wrong. I knew it was more than that. From the maps I reckoned it was more like twenty-seven.

The wind died down overnight and dawn came calm and clear. The sun rose, but a screen of young pines stopped it from reaching the camp. I'd slept well, the best for many days. No wind, flat soft ground, quiet—it was a great site for a peaceful night. The Grand Canyon was about twenty-three miles away, if the information I had was correct. That night I would be in a campground on the South Rim. And a week after that I should reach Utah. Eight days to go. I hadn't thought about finishing before. Suddenly it seemed close. I felt confused but only for a moment. I knew what I wanted. To see Denise and Hazel. Otherwise though I would be happy to go on walking.

A long, hard, tiring forest day followed. The "official" mileages were wrong again. When I talked to Bill Watson after the walk he agreed with me and said that his GPS route had given figures similar to mine for these sections. The day started pleasantly enough with a stroll up Russell Wash to Russell Tank, a depleted muddy pool. A father and son were fishing, with two rods apiece. They'd seen Jake late the previous afternoon. He couldn't be more than a couple of hours ahead. The anglers were from Flagstaff and said they'd never seen Russell Tank so low but "we haven't had a winter up here." I filled up with two quarts and continued on through the forest.

After a few miles I left Russell Wash and climbed gently to the top of the Coconino Rim, a five-hundred-foot line of steep, forested slopes and broken crags that runs southeastward from the Grand Canyon. The trail followed a very convoluted route along the Rim, twisting in and out of myriad little drainages. It was mostly in the trees, but occasionally there were views. And what views! The first sight of the promised land. Away to the north a long line of pinkish cliffs ended in a flat-topped butte and a sharp pinnacle, my first exciting, exhilarating sight of the top of the Grand Canyon, looking surprisingly and delightfully close. All around this searing line of color stretched the vast green blanket of the forest. It was hard to believe that the huge canyon was there, a great gash in the trees. I knew I wasn't far from the Grand Canyon but actually seeing the edge of the cliffs was wonderful. Inspired and energized I picked up speed, knowing I still had a long way to go before I was actually there.

Others wanted to see the Canyon as well, but from the air. A constant annoying buzz of small airplanes passed by just beyond the Rim, taking sightseers on a tour over the Canyon.

The forest was fairly uniform and uneventful. One short, steep switch-

backing descent into a drainage did have a sign at the top reading CAU-
TION: WALK BICYCLES. The climb up the far side was also steep and also
sported warning signs, the only ones like it on the whole walk. Farther on
I came out into an open, devastated area covered with stumps and many
small new trees; obviously an old clear-cut, I thought. I was wrong, as I
found when a neat sign labeled THE DYING FOREST appeared. An infesta-
tion of dwarf mistletoe had killed nearly all of the ponderosa pines in
this area, so the forest service had cleared the dead and dying trees and
replanted the area with seedling pines. Because the mistletoe can shoot its
sticky seeds up to sixty feet the new trees had to be more than that distance from any infected tree. In places sickly looking pines with bunches
of orange mistletoe hanging from their drooping limbs still stood forlornly.

I joined a neat white gravel trail, labeled the Mistletoe Interpretation
Trail and featuring many more signs, that led to a large, empty parking
lot at Grandview Lookout, a massive five-hundred-foot-tall metal fire
tower with a twisting metal staircase up the center and a small cabin at
the top. The tower is no longer in use, but visitors can climb up at their
own risk. I was tempted, but I still had a long way to go and contented
myself with some photographs. There were several fine Arizona Trail signs,
but they were all for the route south. From here to Grand Canyon Village
the trail was incomplete. Bill Watson had advised me to skip the built
section as it dead-ended in the forest. Instead he recommended following
a power line that led to the campground on the edge of the village. The
fisherman at Russell Tank had suggested the same route.

First I walked down the road from the lookout tower to the Grandview Entrance to Grand Canyon National Park. ENTRANCE FEES PAYABLE AT
SOUTH ENTRANCE OR EAST ENTRANCE read a sign. I wasn't going to either of
those. Oh, well. I found the power line and began what must be the most
boring, soulless, and monotonous walk in the park, a walk made even
worse by the knowledge that some of the most spectacular scenery in the
world lay not far away. The straight line of the service track below the
power line stretched into the distance. No route-finding was needed nor
was there any point wondering what lay ahead. Just the power line, that
was all. There was little wildlife, and it wasn't even peaceful. Through the

trees I could hear the rumble of traffic on East Rim Drive. The temptation to go and hitch was strong, but at the same time I knew I would resist. I wasn't going to break the walk now, and I knew this section would be over in a few hours.

I was trudging grimly onward, my mind miles away for once, when a figure in a dull, dark red top and off-white trousers suddenly appeared out of the trees a hundred yards ahead of me. "Chris!" The yell reverberated through the trees. Amazed, I realized it was Jake in a new set of his homemade clothes. He couldn't have appeared at a better time. If there was one point on the walk when I could have done with a companion, this was it.

Our first conversation, inevitably, was about how we'd gotten here. It turned out that Jake had taken the section of trail from Grandview Lookout that had been built, bushwhacking to the power line from where it ended. By a coincidence he'd emerged onto the track at a point just ahead of me.

It was twenty-three days since we'd seen each other. Walking on, we discussed our experiences since Superior. Jake had been only a few hours behind me a number of times and had arrived in Flagstaff during my second day there. He knew he'd passed me when my tracks veered off up the Weatherford Trail but didn't appear on the route farther ahead.

We reached Mather Campground on the edge of Grand Canyon Village just as it was growing dark. Jake had intended to camp out in the forest just short of this outpost of civilization, but as I'd booked a site he decided to join me in the campground. The place is huge, with a maze of roads and hundreds of sites. Stumbling abruptly out of the freedom of the woods into this very organized area was somewhat confusing. The open forest merged into the campground, and we suddenly found ourselves walking through people's campsites, apologizing as we blundered on. Eventually we found a road and set off down it hoping it led to the entrance.

"Have you done the Canyon?" The question was repeated as we wandered through the campground feeling dazed and a bit overwhelmed by the sudden mass of tents, campfires, vehicles, and people. Our trail-worn appearance was obvious, even to others who were camping. Of course, camping at a site with showers, laundry, and with a vehicle to carry all your stuff was not exactly the same as hauling everything on your back and camping in the wilds.

A guy hailed us and came across for a chat, inviting us to his site for a beer later. "I want to talk some more to you guys." Shortly afterward he drove past us, heading out to buy the beer. After what seemed miles the campground entrance appeared. The rangers had long gone home, but there was a list of allocated sites. Mine was number 273. We wandered the winding circuits of roads and then, with relief, found the right road, and then the site, and were able to stop. As I was staying two nights I pitched the tarp so I could store my gear. Jake was hoping to leave the next day and headed straight off for a shower and to do his laundry.

I'd been hiking for almost twelve hours and felt very tired. Maybe a meal would be a good idea. I hadn't eaten anything in hours. I heated some food but then found I couldn't finish it. Instead of feeling more awake I had an overwhelming desire to lie down. I was doing just that when Jake returned from his chores. I dragged myself upright, and we went off to see the guy who'd offered beer. Frank was delighted to see us. A big man, his hand enveloped mine when we shook. He and his buddy had just done their first ever backpack, a three-day trip in Bryce Canyon in Utah, and had found it very tough. When he heard we'd both hiked from the Mexican border he was incredulous. "Six hundred miles," he kept saying in astonishment. "Six hundred miles. I can't imagine hiking that." His home was in Florida where he worked in refrigeration, which I guessed was big in that state, and this vacation was to see some of the classic Southwest scenery. He and his buddy were considering a two-day trip into the Canyon but were clearly worried about how hard it would be. Suddenly finding myself with people was disorienting as usual, and I felt somewhat detached. The couple of beers I drank—something bland, tasteless, mass-market—probably didn't help.

Finally, at 10:30, very late for me on this walk, I slumped into my bag, only to sleep badly, waking many times during the night. Chattering, squabbling birds woke me at half past five in the morning, far too early after such a late night. Some ravens were especially raucous. "I'm sure they're noisier here than in the backcountry," said Jake.

Rising early made sense, however, as today we had to try to get permits for the Grand Canyon. Campsites below the rim are limited and sites along the popular cross-canyon trails, Bright Angel and North Kaibab, are often booked months in advance. These were the ones we wanted to hike as the bridge that connects them is the only way to cross the Colorado River without a boat, raft, or by swimming. Long distance hikers have a problem with permits, as booking ahead isn't possible when you don't know exactly when you'll arrive. Although a nuisance and hardly in keeping with a spirit of wilderness, the limited-permit system does make sense here. As most terrain is closer to vertical than horizontal and there is little water, good campsites are few and small in size. When far more people want to use these campsites than there is space for, some form of regulation is, unfortunately, essential. If, as I would guess is likely, the Arizona Trail becomes popular, some means of accommodating long distance hikers will become necessary.

The simple solution to the problem was to have a long hard day and cross the Canyon in one go. With six hundred and fifty miles of rough-country hiking behind me I was pretty fit and reckoned I could do this. But I really didn't want to. Rushing the Canyon in a day seemed almost sacrilegious. I felt I had to spend at least one night of the walk in the Canyon.

To do this I needed a site in the Canyon if I could get one. I had discovered that there are spare sites, usually due to cancellations, and that these are given out on a first-come, first-served basis every morning at the Backcountry Office, so that's where Jake and I needed to go.

Honed by weeks of backcountry route-finding and armed with a map of the village, Jake, and I set off for the Backcountry Office and promptly made a real mess of getting there. It began with a bus. Shuttle buses take visitors in and around the village, so in theory getting anywhere is easy. For most people it probably is but not for Jake and me. We caught the first bus that came along, which then went around the loop farthest away from our destination. Once we'd gone back past where we'd gotten on we kept a close eye out for the right stop and then got off at the wrong one. This was Jake's idea. I took control. "I've been here before," I said confidently. "It's this way." We marched off in the wrong direction. A building that shouldn't have been there appeared in front of us. Eventually we resorted to asking the way, an appalling loss of face for two experienced wilderness hikers, but we had to concede we weren't getting anywhere. Armed with definite directions we set off again. And went wrong again.

Finally we sorted out the seemingly incredibly complicated layout of the village and found the right way to the Backcountry Office, situated in an old railroad station. A small group of hikers was hanging around outside, waiting for their numbers to be called. We took tickets and wondered if this was all worthwhile. Most people, we quickly noticed, were not getting the sites they wanted. Many were not getting any sites at all. Some left smiling though while others were only making inquiries. Jake told me he'd met a guy in the laundry the night before who'd failed to get a site yesterday, which was not what I wanted to hear. The same guy had mentioned he knew of a hiker who'd set off to hike the Arizona Trail three weeks ago. That gave me something to think about. Three weeks ago. He should be somewhere around the White Canyon Wilderness by now. Setting out more than three weeks later than us would mean a hotter walk and much greater problems with water, we reckoned, wondering how he was getting on. Even though we knew nothing about him, not even his name, we felt an affinity. That he was doing a walk we were doing was enough. As with the participants in any activity, long distance hikers gravitate toward each other even though it is a solo or small group pursuit. There are long distance hikers' organizations with annual gatherings where off-trail and would-be hikers can get together and reminisce, swap knowledge, and plan for the next big one. At these meetings you can forget that most people think you are crazy.

While we debated the conditions facing the hiker behind us our numbers were called. We took places side by side at the two little booths, leaning our elbows on the wooden counter. The two rangers asked where we wanted to camp and pored over their paperwork, a mass of dates and names. I felt nervous. The only time I'd done this before, in Yellowstone National Park when hiking the Continental Divide Trail, I'd come close to having a row with the ranger and ended up with only part of the permit I wanted. This time I had the opposite experience, and I have only praise for the two rangers dealing with this early-morning set of would-be Canyon hikers. They were very patient and very helpful. And Jake and I ended up with sites in the Canyon, even if they weren't the ones we wanted. Jake's was a bit farther than he'd hoped to go in one day. He could stay there only one night, and so couldn't have a rest day in the Canyon. I'd wanted the same site Jake ended up with but for the following night. Fully booked, said the ranger. I explained what I was doing. The ranger thought for a while and then suggested I could camp on a side trail. It's a few miles off your route, he said, but once there you can camp where you like. Having no choice I accepted. On consideration I decided it was an excellent idea, as it meant I would visit part of the Canyon I hadn't been to before and camp in the wild, away from well-used campsites and other people.

Permits in hand Jake and I wandered off in search of breakfast. I couldn't believe that after camping where I liked for more than six weeks I'd just stood in line in order to be told where I could stay. Still, it was only one night.

Stomachs full, we risked taking the shuttle bus to the post office. This time we arrived successfully and began to feel we were coming to grips with this scattered holiday resort. In the post office I was surprised to discover that along with my usual box I had a much smaller one, postmarked Phoenix, that rattled. While I had an extra box Jake didn't have one at all, which was a blow as all his food for the next week was in it, food specially prepared so as not to need any cooking, just the addition of water. He didn't want to lose his campsite, so he decided to race around the store, grab whatever food seemed suitable, and head down into the Canyon. He was planning on a rest day on the North Rim in two days' time, when I should arrive there, and we expected to meet again fairly soon.

Jake was also desperate to leave the South Rim, which he was finding far more alien, overwhelming, and hard to cope with than I was, mainly because he hadn't been there before and hadn't expected to find a busy holiday resort here on the rim of the Grand Canyon. Having spent a few days here previously I'd been prepared for the abrupt change from the quiet of the backcountry. To me this was a town stop just like Flagstaff. I had no illusions that it had anything to do with wilderness or nature. I wandered around feeling detached. Somehow the noise and crowds and traffic didn't affect me too much. It was just there, in the background, a vague irritation. I still felt solitary, my head was still in the wilderness, though I guess this wouldn't have lasted if I'd stayed longer.

Back at the campground I sat down at a picnic table and opened the mysterious box. To my astonishment I discovered my first aid kit, the one I'd lost sometime during the first few days of the walk, along with a burst bag of trail mix, which explained the rattling. There was a letter too that told me how my first aid kit had been found, traced, and then sent here (some of this I had heard already from Denise). The tale was quite curious and showed the power of the Internet and how small, at least in terms of communication, our world has become.

The third day of my walk, when I hiked from Scotia Canyon to Canelo Pass, two hikers, Brad and Marc Buckhout from Phoenix, set off up Sunnyside Canyon toward Miller Peak. The start of our day's routes overlapped, but we didn't meet. Up in the snow on the Crest Trail the hikers found my tracks and were glad that I'd broken trail. In an open, snow-free area they found the little black pouch containing my first aid kit lying on the ground. I must have stopped there, gotten something out of my pack, and not noticed when the kit fell out of the lid pocket, where I carried it so it was easily accessible. Looking in the first aid kit the hikers found a prescription bottle of antibiotics I carry in case of infection. The label on the bottle gave my name and that of MacGregor's Pharmacy in Grantown-on-Spey. Brad, a general practitioner, probably looked more closely at the first aid kit than a nonmedical person would have done.

Back home Brad did a web search for Grantown, found the town's site, and left an inquiry in the guest book. As well as wanting to return my first aid kit, he was curious as to what I was doing in the remote and little-known Huachuca Mountains. And who was I anyway? An Arizonan who'd been on vacation in Scotland? (When starting his search for the owner he'd discovered a Chris Townsend living in Sierra Vista, the town closest to the start of the trailhead.) Or was I from Scotland? He had two replies to his inquiry, one from someone who didn't know me but was able to give my address and phone number and one from Molly Duckett at the Grantown Museum who knew Denise and phoned her to ask if I was in Arizona. Finding that I was, Molly e-mailed Denise with the information and queries from Brad. Denise then e-mailed Brad to thank him and tell him when I should reach the Grand Canyon so he could mail the kit back to me. As I hadn't yet spoken to Denise she hadn't told me to expect to see it here. So while I was hiking through Arizona at the rate of a few miles an hour messages about my lost first aid kit were flying in milliseconds through cyberspace between Arizona and Scotland, a distance of some eight thousand miles. And Denise knew what had happened to my first aid kit long before I did.

I phoned the Buckhouts to thank them only to discover that, appropriately, Brad and Marc were away hiking a section of the trail. However, I spoke to Karen Buckhout who very kindly invited me to visit and come over for dinner when I was back in Phoenix. I never made that visit—they were hiking again when I returned to Phoenix—but many e-mails have gone between us since, and I have friends in Arizona I have never met.

My air of detachment and generally bemused but benign feelings were upset, very upset, when I tried to phone home, a seemingly easy activity. Not here though. Here the phone companies seemed determined that making phone calls should be a challenging obstacle course. "We don't allow international calls," said one company. "Your credit card is not recognized," said another of the same card I'd used for all my phone calls and most of my purchases in Arizona. It was hard to imagine a phone company that had never heard of VISA. After trying five phone booths and walking a mile I changed tack and made a collect call, which involved convincing the operator that a recorded message would probably come on first but that when I spoke someone would answer. Finally I got through. And was cut off almost immediately. I tried again. "We don't allow international calls," said the operator. "I've just made one," I said politely though through gritted teeth. "You can't have. It's not possible." "I have." "No. We don't allow inter—" I hung up before I screamed at an undoubtedly innocent person who just happened to work for a confused, incompetent company. Maybe, I thought, as I couldn't have made the call, they wouldn't bill me for it. They did, of course.

I walked to a different phone booth and managed to get through again. But this time, although I could hear Denise she couldn't hear me. I gave up. At least she knew I was here. Later I bought a phone card, something I'd been reluctant to do, as I knew I wouldn't use all the time I paid for. It was from AT&T, the phone company who wouldn't accept my credit card. I had to call them to pay for the card. I did so with the credit card. I then tried making a phone call and paying with the card, just to see what would happen. "Your card is not recognized." "I've just paid for one of your phone cards with it." "Impossible. Your card is not recognized." The surreal world of phone companies was beyond me.

Buying supplies was thankfully far less frustrating than making phone calls. Babbitts General Store (yes, the same Babbitts whose land I'd hiked over) provided everything I needed. In the hiking department, where I went for stove fuel and freeze-dried meals, the sales assistant produced the GoLite catalog from under the counter and raved about their products, all of which he had except the umbrella, the one item I had. Babbitts, he said, didn't stock GoLite. I gathered he was carrying on a clandestine promotion of GoLite gear, though it turned out he had yet to go backpacking with it.

My prized purchase was a huge bunch of delicious grapes that I munched steadily while I sorted out my dried foods back in camp. Needing more than grapes to sustain me that evening I took the East Rim Trail back into the village. As the name suggests this trail runs along the edge of the Canyon. It's a wide, flat, smooth trail designed for people in street shoes. Winding through the trees right on the edge of the Canyon it gives superb views down into the depths and across to the North Rim. Since arriving I'd ignored the Canyon, wanting to get chores and necessities

done before I even glanced at it. I wanted to give the Canyon my full attention. I didn't believe it was possible to appreciate it without doing so. The
sun was low in the sky as I walked along the rim, throwing long black
shadows across the Canyon. To the west the buttes and cliffs dissolved
into a gray haze. I didn't look closely, content just to absorb the atmosphere. There would be time to think and feel more later.

Visitors thronged the village, packing the shops and restaurants.
Unable to get a table I watched them for a while. Many people gave the
Canyon only a glance before returning to the central attractions, the stores.
Some did look for longer and even strolled a short way along the rim
path before turning away. What had these people seen? What did they
think they'd seen? What did it mean to them? Why were they here? I
couldn't answer these questions, and I suspected most of them couldn't
either.

They'd come because of the Canyon's reputation, because it is a
"must-see" on the international tourist trail, frequently touted as one of
the wonders of the world. It's value as a tourist attraction is enormous.
Arizona is, after all, "The Grand Canyon State." It wasn't always so. Lieutenant Joseph Ives, who in 1858 became probably the first white man to
descend into the Canyon, wrote afterward that "after entering it there is
nothing to do but leave. Ours has been the first and will doubtless be the
last party of whites to visit this profitless locality." Forty-three years later
the Santa Fe Railroad reached Grand Canyon Village, and the tourist
boom began.

Grand Canyon Village is a classic honeypot, a famous place that
attracts masses of people, many of whom, probably most of whom, have
no real interest in wild places. It's just another stop on the tourist circuit.
Those who want to can learn a little from information displays and
exhibits about the spectacular landscape lying just yards away, those who
don't can enjoy the stores and cafés. The village may be in the national
park, may be on the rim of the Grand Canyon, but it's not part of it.
Rather, it's an urban tourist resort, a bubble of city life constructed so
that people can come, visit, and find the familiar, the known. Visiting
Grand Canyon Village means seeing Grand Canyon Village. The Canyon

itself is a just a pretty backdrop. It's hard to even see the Canyon from the other world of the village, really see it that is, really grasp some understanding of what it is like. For that you have to venture away from the bright lights and the crowds and contemplate the Canyon itself. Just a few hundred yards along the rim trails and the atmosphere and the scene changes, the village fades into the forest and the Canyon begins to dominate. Even better is to descend a little way below the rim, to be inside the Canyon even if only at the edge. Go farther, down to the Colorado, and spend a night there, preferably away from an organized campground, and the true nature of the place may start to reveal itself.

That evening my concerns were like everybody else's. I wanted to eat. Eventually I found space in a restaurant and had a meal, a meal that was a long time coming, so long in fact that I was given dessert free in return for my patience. When I left it was dark. The walk back along the rim trail was a revelation. In the dark the Canyon had a huge presence, even greater than when fully visible. Below the rim it was a gigantic black chasm that told of vast depths, a black crack in the earth that seemed to have sucked the blackness out of the sky, which was paler than the land below and bright with stars. As I moved away from the lights of buildings and cars I began to see a little more detail. The pale outlines of the highest cliffs sank into the darkness. Far below a few spots of light marked Indian Gardens Campground. Farther out and farther down another speck of light must be right at the bottom near the Colorado River. Higher than me was a single flicker of brightness on the North Rim. Otherwise all was a solid, seemingly impenetrable. In contrast the sky blazed with light. I'd always felt overwhelmed and awed when looking at the night sky and thinking of the unimaginable universe. Now, for the first time, I viewed the land in the same way. I felt a sense of real power, of the massive slow forces that had created this gash in the ground.

Mostly, I hiked the dark path alone. Occasionally people came into view and then faded away. A woman passed me, flashlight picking out the path ahead, hiking fast. Three people stood on the trail staring into nothing. "This is a night to remember," I heard one say quietly. It was indeed. The walk along the rim was quite cathartic. All the tensions and aggravations of the day fell away. Back at camp I felt completely relaxed and slipped quickly into a dreamless sleep.

The rim walk stirred in me a desire to hike into the Canyon that I'd so far suppressed, knowing I had other things to do first. The desire had to be kept in check a little while longer the next morning. I was up early and in a café the moment it opened. I had to wait for the post office, though. There I mailed my box for the last time. I wouldn't see it again until the walk was over. That done I set off back along the rim trail. The village was seething, far busier than the previous evening, with long lines for everything from stores to toilets. I was pleased to find a phone that was free. I called Denise, using the phone card, for a more organized talk than the attempts of the previous day. I also called Chris Brasher, whose company had supplied me with boots for the walk. He had hoped to join me for a few days, either here or closer to the end of the walk, but said he was unfortunately unable to do so. Generous as always, he asked if there was anything he could help with. Not really, I replied, the only problem I had was how to get back to Phoenix from the Utah border. This was a problem I'd decided to leave until the end as everyone I'd asked, from the Arizona Trail Association to various rangers, had known nothing about what happened beyond the Grand Canyon. Jake had found the same and called the final section "the black hole." Chris Brasher didn't know any more than anyone else, but his solution was simple. "Call a taxi," he said, "we'll pay." Finding one to call now looked like the real difficulty.

A young guy stopped me. "Are you hiking the Canyon?" "Wow." "Where, when?" He was hoping to day hike down to the river and back and was obviously feeling both excited and nervous. I chatted for a while, not wanting to seem rude, but feeling restless and very keen to leave the crowds and the noise and return to the wilds.

Finally he moved on. I had nothing left to do—no phone calls to make, no supplies to buy, no permits to get. I could return to the walk.

8

The Canyon

BRIGHT ANGEL TRAIL TO THE NORTH RIM

32 miles

Standing at the start of the Bright Angel Trail looking down into the vastness below, I thought of my first visit here, five years earlier. That two-week hike had been significant. It was then that the tentative idea for this walk had first occurred, then that I'd felt a desire to see what else Arizona had to offer. In one sense the whole walk so far had been to reach this point. I had looked ahead to it, relished it, dreamed about it. And now I was here. In just two days I'd have crossed the Canyon.

That first visit had caught me by surprise. I'd thought I was ready for the Canyon. I'd seen the photographs, read the books. Having visited other spectacular landscapes—Yosemite Valley, the Canadian Rockies, the Himalayas and the Alps—I knew how I would react to the Grand Canyon. Or at least I thought I knew. I didn't. It wasn't like that at all.

I can still remember the shock. Having arrived by bus at the South Rim I wandered over to the edge for a quick glance before heading off to the campground. I was completely unprepared for what I saw. As I approached a low parapet I was aware that an empty space lay beyond it, but not what an empty space it was. I reached the rim and there, suddenly, too suddenly really, was the Canyon, overwhelming and bewildering.

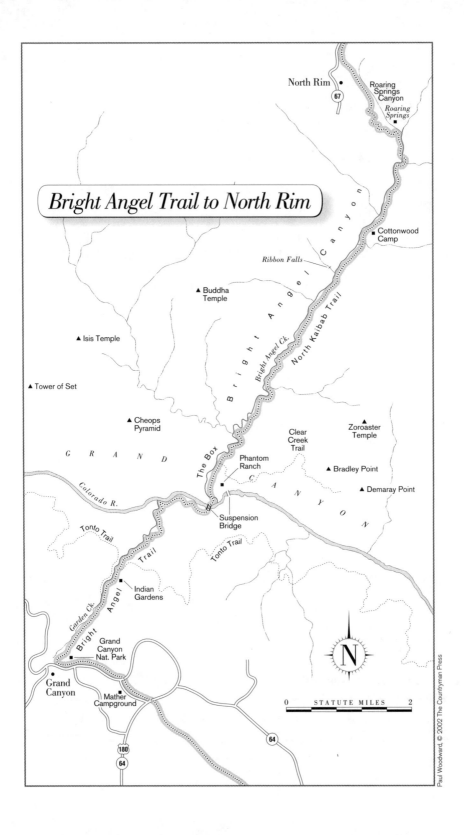

Bright Angel Trail to North Rim

North Rim

67

Roaring Springs Canyon

Roaring Springs

Cottonwood Camp

Ribbon Falls

▲ Buddha Temple

Bright Angel Canyon

▲ Isis Temple

Bright Angel Ck.

North Kaibab Trail

▲ Tower of Set

▲ Cheops Pyramid

Zoroaster Temple ▲

G R A N D

Clear Creek Trail

The Box

Phantom Ranch

▲ Bradley Point

▲ Demaray Point

Colorado R.

C A N Y O N

Suspension Bridge

Tonto Trail

Tonto Trail

Garden Ck.

Bright Angel Trail

Indian Gardens

Grand Canyon Nat. Park

Grand Canyon

Mather Campground

N

0   STATUTE MILES   2

180

64

64

Paul Woodward, © 2002 The Countryman Press

Beyond the little wall chaos reigned. The ground fell abruptly away into a confusion of glowing, multicolored rock towers, buttresses, cliffs, and terraces dropping into dark hidden depths then rising again in even more complex forms to the dark, tree-fringed far rim. To either side the contorted chasm disappeared into the distant horizon, a twisting slash in the flat, forested plateau. Unable to comprehend what I was seeing I stood there staring down, trying to grasp the scale, the pattern, of the world before me. I felt overawed, nervous. I had never encountered anything like this before.

Looking down again I could well understand those feelings. I was still awestruck, overwhelmed, excited. But this time it was different. Instead of an apparently disordered tangle of random features I saw buttes and side canyons and terraces, many of which I could name. The swirling shapes formed themselves into peaks and cliffs. Those faint pale lines were trails on which I'd walked. It was no longer an alien world.

From the South Rim you actually see only a small part of the immensity of the Canyon. In total it's around 280 miles long, a dark slash that runs almost halfway across Arizona. The width varies from four to sixteen miles. But it's the depth that impresses. From where I stood it was forty-four hundred feet down to the Colorado River. And the North Rim was fifteen hundred feet higher.

Walking in the Canyon is like mountain climbing in reverse, a description given so often it's almost a cliché. It's correct though. The Canyon is like an inverted mountain. On my first visit I'd found hiking from the high forested rims to the open rocky desert at the bottom strange. I was used to that now. I'd been doing it since the Mexican border. The difference here was that the forests grew on a plateau, not on mountaintops, and the desert was a narrow strip, not a wide valley between small mountain ranges. This was the opposite of a sky island.

It was half past one, right in the middle of the hottest part of the day, when I started down the Bright Angel Trail, a popular, maintained trail that begins on the edge of the village. The upper cliffs of the Canyon are very steep and for the first twenty-five hundred feet of descent long switchbacks cut back and forth. The immediate rock scenery is dramatic, the distant views spectacular. My attention, however, was drawn by the people, masses of them, most in casual clothes and carrying shoulder bags, carrier bags, sometimes no more than plastic water bottles. Most were ascending, just a few were still headed down. Exhausted looking, they labored upward, sweat soaked with glazed eyes and heads down, every step a huge effort, all joy gone, nothing left but a desire for this to be over. Some did look happy and cheerful, but they were few and far between. That's the problem with hiking to the bottom of the Canyon and back in a day. It's very easy, in the cool of the morning, to descend, to keep going

The Bright Angel Trail below the South Rim of the Grand Canyon.

down the steep trail, unaware of just how many thousands of feet lie above. Until you have to climb back up, a climb that occurs in the baking hot heat of the day. Unfit mountaineers tend not to get too far, turning back when they get tired. Unfit, unprepared canyoneers can easily descend farther than they can comfortably ascend, turning the long, steep, hot climb into a nightmare.

Two young men without daypacks, just water bottles in their hands, plodded slowly past. One glanced wearily at me, took in my large pack, and muttered one word: "Idiot." Like many people he and his companion were not wearing hats. I had on my battered, wide-brimmed cotton hat, veteran of two previous long distance walks. What would it be like to hike without a hat in this heat? I tried the experiment. Briefly it was refreshingly cool as the sweat in my hair evaporated, but in only a few minutes I could feel the sun pounding on my head and neck. And I was heading down. Those two men were heading up. I put my hat back on and felt cooler instantly. My umbrella would have been even more effective, but I felt that the trail was too crowded to use it without causing hassles for both others and myself.

As I descended the proportion of people who appeared to be enjoying the walk increased. These, I assumed, were those who had gone farther, knowing they had the ability to climb back up in comfort. Watching the endless procession of walkers ascending the long switchbacks I noticed that age and sex had little to do with how well people coped. Little children bounded upward gleefully, elderly people marched past, giving cheery greetings. If anything it was young adults who seemed to be suffering the most. There was a mix of languages—European, Asian, different versions of English, and more. A large party of French hikers strode determinedly past, rucksacks on their backs, hiking boots on their feet, muscular legs protruding from shorts. Others took the easy way up, riding on mules in long trains led by cowboy-hatted outfitters.

Because the Bright Angel Trail is so popular with casual and inexperienced hikers water sources are provided. Outhouses are available too, essential with this many people. Lurid warning signs show a hiker sans hat wilting in the sun, an attempt to get novices to understand what hiking in the Canyon entails. In several languages the signs warn "do not attempt to hike from the canyon rim to the river and back in one day. Each year hikers suffer serious illness or death from exhaustion." Some experienced hikers do make the round trip, but to do so you need to be fit and allow plenty of time. Superfit trail runners trot up and down in a few hours—that's exceptional.

The Bright Angel Trail follows a fault in the uppermost cliffs, though two tunnels have still had to be blasted through the rocks, down to Indian Gardens, where big trees and thick undergrowth line a flowing creek. This dark strip of green can be seen growing slowly larger and closer during the descent, the cool foliage drawing the eye and helping to keep the legs moving. The first people to come this way were Indians who grew crops beside Garden Creek. Then in the 1800s prospectors used the trail in their search for valuable minerals. Failing to find anything worth mining they turned their attention to tourists and began charging people to use the trail, which proved very lucrative. The gold they sought wasn't hidden in the Canyon, it was the Canyon.

Today Indian Gardens has a campground, ranger station, corral, and toilets, all partly hidden in the huge cottonwood trees that line the creek. The shade was welcome as was the water, and I rested here, watching the last few people head back up the trail. One hiker hailed me—the guy who'd spoken to me on the South Rim and who was now enjoying his hike to the river and back. I hoped he'd still enjoy it higher up. This was a test trip he said; next he wanted to backpack in the Canyon for a few days.

Beyond Indian Gardens the crowds vanished and between there and the Colorado River I met only three pairs of backpackers, all sensibly choosing to ascend in the cool and shade of late afternoon. Now that I had the freedom and space to look around and see where I was, my attention went from people to nature. I started noticing wildlife—fat lizards with black strips on their backs and dark heads that bobbed up and down when they sunned themselves on rocks, a long thin snake with yellow stripes down its sides slithering across the trail, ground squirrels darting through the bushes, a canyon wren calling from a rock. There were plants too, big clumps of bright yellow flowered brittlebush, the tall green flower spikes of the century plant—a type of agave—prickly pear and barrel cacti with bright pink flowers. I was back in the desert.

Indian Gardens lies on the edge of the Tonto Platform. This gently sloping terrace, lying about two-thirds of the way down the Canyon, is wide enough to give a feeling of space rather like that found on a plateau high in the mountains. Here all sense of being in a canyon vanishes. There are cliffs all around but, rather than confining walls, they make up separate mountains and ridges divided by deep side canyons. The flat, forested plateaus beyond the rims are invisible. I knew, rationally, that they

The view across the Inner Gorge to Zoroaster Temple.

were there but they didn't really exist down here; they weren't part of this reality, this complex, exciting, colorful mountain world.

Many of the mountains inside the Canyon soar four to five thousand feet above the Colorado River yet still aren't as high as the rims. These peaks have strange names for Arizona—the Tower of Set, Isis Temple, Cheops Pyramid, Buddha Temple, and, most impressive of all, Zoroaster Temple—names that would seem out of place elsewhere yet which, somehow, seem totally appropriate in the Grand Canyon. The formations were named in the nineteenth century by Clarence Dutton, a geologist who, inspired by the Canyon's overwhelming, incredible presence, decided to name them after Eastern deities.

The Tonto Platform is important to routes inside the canyon, because it provides relatively easy walking for many miles. Colin Fletcher hiked along it on his pioneering walk the length of the national park, described in his *The Man Who Walked through Time,* one of the best hiking books written, which I reread during the last week of the walk. It was also the scene for some of John Annerino's amazing runs through the Canyon, described in his book, *Running Wild.* I'd followed the Platform for four days on my first visit and had planned ever since to return and undertake a longer walk. This, however, was not the time; my route lay across, not along, the Canyon.

The trail wound down Garden Creek Canyon between dark rock walls then left the creek where it gushes down a steep ravine. Beyond the Tonto Platform steep switchbacks led down the ancient rocks of the Inner Gorge to the seething green waters of the Colorado River, a great sight. And this is so even though the Colorado is a controlled, tamed stream, its flow regulated by a huge dam just upstream of the Canyon behind which the waters fester in an ugly, stagnant reservoir with a dirty, scummy, bathtub ring. This is "Lake" Powell and below it lies the once beautiful and spectacular Glen Canyon. I was to see this reservoir just days after finishing the walk. It's a sad place. The bright blue waters have the superficial appeal of cheap, tacky jewelry, an appeal that vanishes once you look closely and see the artificiality of the place and the unnaturalness of the shoreline. Look at the photographs of Glen Canyon before its inundation and compare them with the pathetic reservoir that now lies there. Instead of a wild, incredibly beautiful, complex world lie the flat, featureless waters of a man-made lake. "Lake Powell," wrote Edward Abbey, "is a graveyard." For Colin Fletcher, who crossed it on his trip the length of the Colorado River, it is "superficially beautiful. Profoundly sad."

The appalling, shameful desecration of Glen Canyon has a lesson for those of us who want to keep such places wild and pristine: Don't keep them secret. Glen Canyon was dammed because it was "the place no one knew," in the words of that great conservationist David Brower. If more people had known about Glen Canyon it could have been saved. In *Wilderness and the American Mind* Roderick Nash writes, "Glen Canyon was lost through apathy." Not enough people cared because not enough people knew enough to care. There is talk of "loving the wilderness to death," but the effects of eroded trails, beaten down campsites, and crowds of people are slight when compared to the industrial vandalism of dams, mines, clear-cuts, ski resorts, and the like. Restoring the marks left by backpackers isn't hard. Careful management can prevent a great deal of the damage in the first place anyway. And without people, many people, to defend wild places they could be lost forever.

Incredibly, after Glen Canyon had been dammed there were plans to dam the Grand Canyon itself by, in Fletcher's words, "competent little men" with "no grasp at all of what they were proposing to do to the earth." The Grand Canyon, however, was well known, and David Brower and the Sierra Club waged a brilliant campaign that succeeded in stopping the dam from being built. Among the advertisements was the wonderful cry "Should we also flood the Sistine Chapel so tourists can get nearer the ceiling?" Theodore Roosevelt said on seeing the Grand Canyon, "Leave it as it is. You cannot improve on it. The ages have been at work on it, and man can only mar it." That's still true and always will be. Plans for damming the Canyon still crop up at intervals, though the threat seems slight now. There are also campaigns to remove the Glen Canyon Dam, campaigns that deserve support; if interested check in with the Glen Canyon Action Network (www.drainit.org) and the Glen Canyon Institute (www.glencanyon.org). Restoration of wild places is, I believe, a necessity.

There are too few left. Too many have been needlessly damaged or destroyed. What does it say about our civilization if we allow the most beautiful works of nature to be defaced and defiled?

Apart from restoring Glen Canyon itself the dam needs to be removed for the sake of the Grand Canyon. All the silt that once washed down the river and replenished the beaches in the Canyon now collects behind the dam. Without that material the beaches are disappearing. The dam has caused the extinction of some of the life in the Colorado, as well as in the Canyon. Water released from near the base of the dam is quite cold, while the river's temperature before it was dammed was warm. That's why today the river runs cool and green instead of warm, full of silt, and red, the red that gives the river its name—Rio Colorado, the Red River. Changing the pattern of releases from the dam has mitigated some of the harm, and experiments are underway to see if other changes could lead to restoration of the beaches. It would be better though to simply remove the dam.

Walking above the river, watching the complex swirling in eddies and backwaters, it is possible to forget what happens upstream. The river still looks wild. And this is the most dramatic setting for a river imaginable. It feels like the bottom of time. The dark, twisted rock that forms the walls of the Inner Gorge, Vishnu schist, looks ancient, looks weighed down and compressed by the vast layers of time lying above it. Time is physical here, visible in the cliffs that the river has sliced through and revealed over millions of years. The unimaginably slow process of erosion continues. The river is still cutting deeper into the Canyon. Every time a stone falls or a rock crumbles the Canyon changes. Ever so slowly it is being eroded away. Eventually it will probably flatten out and become a wide valley. But that is millions and millions of years in the future, a time when Earth in general will be unrecognizable from the one we know now.

Geologic time is incomprehensible, at least to me. The Vishnu schist cliffs are 1.7 billion years old. The Kaibab limestone that forms the top-most cliffs is "only" 250 million years old. Between these two formations, depending on where you are in the Canyon, lie fourteen more layers of sedimentary rock—limestones, sandstones, shales—all of them formed from the detritus left by a succession of ancient seas. The differences in color between these rocks and the rate and the way in which they erode are what give the Canyon its beauty and grandeur. The most sheer and colorful cliffs form the four- to five-hundred-foot-high Redwall, the major barrier into the Canyon. The rock is actually a pale limestone, but its surface is a rich, dark red, stained by iron leached from the rocks above.

Standing by the river, it would be easy to feel oppressed by the enormity of time, by the ages rising above you. What place does human life, all human life, never mind that of one individual, have in this inhuman time scale? Humanity has only existed for a flicker of the time these rocks have lain here. The Canyon itself is very young compared with even the newest rocks, formed no more than 10 million and maybe as recently as 2.5 million years ago. For a few seconds I felt the force of the rocks, felt their inconceivable age pressing down on my spirit. It was surprisingly easy to shake off, precisely because it was inconceivable. The time of the rocks was not my time, was not human time. I could no more relate to it than to an insect, with a lifespan of a few hours. Human time was my time and a year of it, unnoticeable in geologic time, was a long period. For me the two months of this walk made up a significant amount, and the two days I'd be in the Canyon were very important. And that mattered too. The rocks did nothing, could do nothing, with their time, they simply changed according to external events. I could choose what to do with my time. That's why I was here. Because I had chosen to be. Over the short period we have existed we human beings have chosen to do an amazing number of things with our time. One of them is to study rocks to find out how old they are, how they were formed, how they came to be where they are. So we can understand what the Canyon is and why it is. We give the rocks names, we work out how old they are, we study the fossils to see what lived when these layers of stone were beaches on the shores of shallow seas or silt at the bottom of the ocean. It is like the night sky in the desert. One reason the universe and the Grand Canyon can be overwhelming, can make the whole of humanity, never mind one individual, seem insignificant, is because we *can* explain them, because we have an idea of how big and how old they are. Somehow, I found that satisfying and reassuring. What you did with time was what mattered.

At the river I turned upstream, following a trail that ran along a terrace of rock. The sun was low, sending slanting rays of light across the Canyon that clearly showed the rough texture and detailed sculpting of the cliffs. The north side of the river was in shadow low down, the rocks dark and gloomy, but I was walking in sunlight, the bright rocks above me glowing gold. High up the pale cream cone of Zoroaster Temple rose above an amphitheater of tiered red rock. Two suspension bridges arced gently over the river ahead, one silver, one black. Standing on the first one, the Bright Angel Suspension Bridge, I watched the Colorado rushing not far below my feet, the swirls of the water mesmeric and fascinating.

A few rubber rafts were moored by the shore upstream. Those who have rafted the river say it is the only way to see the Canyon. One-armed Major John Wesley Powell first made the trip in 1869, in wooden boats not rubber rafts, when he led a party down the Colorado. (This is the same Powell whose name was used for the reservoir that now fills the canyon he described as full of "wonderful features," and through which, he wrote, "we glide hour after hour, stopping now and then, as our attention is arrested by some new wonder.") "The Great Unknown," he called the Grand Canyon. Since that first trip the river has become well known and there are many commercial rafting trips for which bookings have to be made far in advance. Edward Abbey came this way many times, anticipating one trip as "this suicidal journey down the river of no return," referring to the many rapids and the fact that once begun you cannot turn back (though of course there are places where you can climb out to the rim). Colin Fletcher rafted solo through the Canyon on his trip down the Colorado. He was mostly in the company of other rafts, but it was still an astonishing feat for a man in his late sixties who'd never rafted before. Perhaps the strangest trip was one described by John McPhee in *Encounters with the Archdruid* in which David Brower, the leading opponent of the dams, and Floyd Dominy, the man behind Lake Powell and the plans to dam the Grand Canyon, rafted the river together.

Rafting sounds thrilling, adventurous, committing, and, to me, totally terrifying. I can safely predict that I will never make a raft trip through

On the Clear Creek Trail.

the Canyon. I am so bad on the water that a gentle swell has my stomach turning over and my mind convinced that whatever vessel I'm on is about to capsize and that death by drowning is only seconds away. The thought of spending days running rapids on the Colorado is nightmarish. I'm convinced the best way to see the Canyon is on foot. I have to believe that; it's the only way I'll ever see it.

Across the river a small speck of civilization lies at the foot of Bright Angel Creek—an organized campground, a ranger station, some rustic lodgings known as Phantom Ranch, and sundry other buildings. This is the only tourist resort and the most popular place in the inner canyon, with both campground and ranch booked months in advance. Phantom Ranch was established in 1903, though back then it was a tent camp.

Those staying indoors in the ranch often arrive by mule in organized parties. Campers walk down and then usually walk back up the next day. I knew both places were full, but when I'd called Phantom Ranch I'd been told they did sometimes have a late cancellation or a no-show. It was now early evening. The closest place I could officially camp was several miles away and some fifteen hundred feet higher. I doubted I'd reach it before dark. The ranch buildings were brightly lit and rich cooking smells wafted from the windows. The temptation was too great to resist. Without really thinking about it, I found myself knocking on the door. A young woman appeared, didn't know if there was space, and went away to check. I hung around outside, unsure if I really wanted to be here or not. Through the windows of the bar I could see people drinking beer, eating, laughing, talking. Did I want to join this world, to leave the canyon for a night indoors? In the end I had no choice. "I'm sorry, the last bed has just gone." At the time this wasn't welcome news. The possibility of being able to stop, of not walking on into the dark, had seemed quite appealing. Later I was to be profoundly thankful to the unknown person who'd taken that bed.

As I walked away from the seductive brightness of Phantom Ranch into the growing darkness, the Canyon began to take control again. The rock walls were black now, the air drifting down Bright Angel Canyon a little cooler. Not far beyond the ranch I reached a trail junction. A wooden sign marked the start of the Clear Creek Trail. NO CAMPING NEXT 2 MI, it read. I began switchbacking up the steep talus slopes below Sumner Butte. Racing the dark, I climbed as fast as I could, though there was no way I could win. At the base of the steep cliffs of the butte the trail eased off and began to head east on the Tonto Platform. The narrow path curved around two huge bays below overhanging cliffs. Below me lay black space. I walked on in the increasing darkness, tapping ahead with my poles, and wondering just what I was doing here, with massive cliffs on one side and what seemed long steep drops on the other. There was nothing to do though but continue on into the blackness along the thin strip of flat ground separating these vertical worlds. Eventually the terrain to either side leveled out and I crossed wide, shallow, dry Sumner Wash, beyond which wild camping was allowed. But where to camp in this sloping, stony desert? I'd carried five quarts of water from Phantom Ranch, so I didn't need to go all the way to Clear Creek. I just needed somewhere relatively flat and cacti-free. I walked on in the gloom. High walls rose in the distance. The silhouettes of century plants appeared, then faded. The trail started to descend, gently at first and then more steeply. I stopped. How long would this go on? I had no idea. Just behind lay reasonably flat ground. I went back a few steps and left the trail in search of a site. Treading carefully to avoid cacti and spiky bushes I scanned around with my headlamp until I found a level patch of stony ground just big enough for camp.

Setting up camp was now automatic and quick, even in the dark, which was good as my heart was pounding and I was soaked with sweat. The camp-making ritual was soothing, creating a home a fitting end to the day. As always I started by unrolling my foam pad and lying on it to check that the ground was flat and there weren't too many lumps. That done I unloaded bits of gear and placed them either side of the pad. I then put my pack at the end of the pad and propped it up with my hiking poles so I could use it as a backrest. Sitting down I removed my boots and stood them beside the pad. Then I set up my kitchen where I could easily reach it. Feeling hungry I pumped the stove, opened the valve, let out a dribble of fuel, and lit it so that flames, bright yellow in the darkness, flickered and flared around the burner, heating the fuel tube. The stove hissed and sputtered. I opened the valve again and it roared into life, shattering the silence of the Canyon. I set a pot of water on the burner and returned to organizing my camp. My notebook, paperbacks, and maps I put next to the stove, on top of the nylon bag they lived in. My altimeter watch went next to them so I could check the time and, of more interest, the temperature. On the other side of the pad I placed my sandals and food bag. I pulled the sleeping bag out of its sack and shook it to fluff it up a little, then laid it on the foam pad and slid my bare legs inside. The thermometer still read sixty-six degrees, but my skin felt a little cool and would, I knew, soon feel distinctly chilly. Noticing that my arms weren't too warm either I rolled down my shirtsleeves then pulled on my fleece sweater. Sixty-six might be warm, but it was much colder than it had been all day and I could feel the difference.

Steam was now pouring from under the pan's lid. I lifted the lid and tipped in a quick-cook, freeze-dried pasta primavera. After stirring I turned the stove off. The food would rehydrate in the hot water. The silence brought me back to the Canyon. Darkness lay all around, a solid blackness that rose to a star-bright, blazing sky. I was now down in that black space I had looked into the night before. It still felt solid. It was solid. This was the Canyon without light, the rocks without color. But the cliffs were still there, hard and black, rising into the stars.

I leaned back against the pack and watched the sky as I ate my meal. There was no sound, no lights, nothing. I knew Phantom Ranch lay only a few miles away and that Grand Canyon Village was somewhere up there on the distant rim, but I couldn't see either. I was alone in the Canyon and felt as though for tonight it was mine. Dinner over I lay back and snuggled down into the sleeping bag to fall asleep watching the stars.

Gray light was creeping over the desert when I awoke. The harsh croak of a raven came from nearby. Then the big black bird itself flew low over me twice before landing on a bush about fifty feet away, from where it watched me, presumably to see if I were dead and a potential meal or maybe, if it was used to campers, to see if I would discard something edible. Looking around I worked out that I was camped in the mouth of an amphitheater somewhere between Bradley and Demaray Points. Across the Canyon the top of the South Rim cliffs shone in the first sunlight. Below them the rocks were dull, subdued, waiting for the day. One of the glories of the Canyon is the ever-changing light, the ever-changing shades of the rocks. There was color close to camp too, small, yellow, daisylike flowers and big pink cactus blooms. The dusty narrow trail lay about ten feet away. I had thought I'd gone much farther from it than that. A cactus wren sang from a nearby yucca. The sun crept down Bradley Point toward me. A few hundred yards up from camp, while digging a toilet scrape, I unearthed a decaying wood pencil. The lead was intact but the wood rotten. How long had it lain here?

Camp on the Tonto Platform.

Watching the Canyon come to life, the cliffs slowly brightening and glowing in the strengthening sun, I felt incredibly grateful to be here and very thankful there had been no beds at Phantom Ranch. How could a night under a roof compare with this? It was the most glorious campsite of the whole walk. I also thanked the ranger in the Backcountry Office who'd suggested I camp along this trail. My own choice would have been Bright Angel Campground near Phantom Ranch, where I'd have camped on a little rectangle of ground, complete with a picnic table, surrounded by identical sites. That would have been tame, semicivilized, safe. Out on the Tonto Platform was exciting and spectacular.

I couldn't linger though. I had to return to Bright Angel Canyon and then climb for fourteen miles and fifty-eight hundred feet to the North Rim. I set off back along the trail. Two backpackers were sitting on a ledge in the wash I'd crossed in the dark, gear spread out all around. Was this Sumner Wash? they asked. They'd obviously camped nearby and weren't sure whether they'd come far enough for camping to be officially sanctioned. While we talked two more hikers appeared, then another three, then two more, all heading for Clear Creek. The threesome stopped to talk. They were from Colorado and commented on the heat. The two on the ledge scoffed. This, they said, was cool and fresh—they were from southern Arizona.

In daylight the Clear Creek Trail had tremendous views down to the river and over to the South Rim. A few tiny, brightly colored rafts bobbed on the water, which was a constantly changing, swirling mosaic of different shades of green. On the far side I could see the zigzags of the South Kaibab Trail running steeply down to the Colorado. On this side the trail I'd followed the night before, around the back of the amphitheaters, was narrow, the black space I'd felt was a big drop, so I wasn't surprised I'd felt uneasy here in the dark. Just before the descent back to the North Kaibab Trail the cluster of buildings that was Phantom Ranch, half-hidden in leafy trees, appeared almost directly below my feet.

The Clear Creek diversion was over, an unplanned diversion that had turned out to be one of the high points of the walk. I took delight in that. It reinforced my belief that too much planning can detract from an adventure, that keeping to a strict schedule can mean possibly missing the most significant experiences. There has to be space for the unpredictable, the unforeseen. In this case bureaucratic requirements intended to control the whereabouts of backpackers had sent me off route to a spectacular wild camp. I relished the irony.

Back on the route again I started up the North Kaibab Trail next to Bright Angel Creek. The wonderful, evocative name came from Major Powell, who explored upstream in search of timber for oars. "We have named one stream, way above, in honor of the great chief of the 'Bad Angels,' and as this is in beautiful contrast to that, we conclude to name it 'Bright Angel.'" The reference is to the Dirty Devil River in Utah, so-called because it was "exceedingly muddy and has an unpleasant odor."

Above Phantom Ranch the creek runs through a narrow, twelve-hundred-foot-deep ravine, The Box, that slices through the steep rocks of the Inner Gorge. In places there is barely space for both creek and trail, a trail that in places was built by blasting away the rocks to avoid many creek crossings. Unsurprisingly, in times of flood there isn't room for both—the trail is submerged, and sometimes sections are swept away. On rare occasions, the waters bursting out of The Box have been known to inundate the campground and the flat delta of the creek.

On this day swathes of sunlight lit up The Box, making it seem quite cheerful despite the enclosing, oppressive walls. The tall, narrow, yellow-flowered stalk of a century plant shone bright against black shadows, picked out by a shaft of light. In a cool gray niche below a dark cliff grew a sacred datura, one large white flower open, the others closed up for the day. This slightly sinister-looking plant, also known as jimsonweed and thornapple, blooms only at night. The appearance is a warning: "Entire plant is toxic," said my field guide. Hazardous in a different way were the many prickly pear cacti with their bright pink flowers. Lizards darted and flickered everywhere. How many millions of generations of them have lived here amongst these warm rocks? I wondered.

I'd walked through The Box twice before and so was surprised at how long it took this time. I'd thought it was shorter. The imagined length probably had nothing to do with distance or time. My left ankle was

Bright Angel Trail in The Box.

hurting, sharp pains shooting through it. Being acutely aware of every step made time pass slowly. The pain had begun the previous day, but I'd ignored it, apart from taking some ibuprofen. It had been minimal earlier when I set out, but in The Box the pain increased and began to intrude. The immediate discomfort was unpleasant, but my real concern was that it would worsen and perhaps threaten the continuation of the walk. Although the journey was about what happened along the way I did want to complete what I'd set out to do. And I was so close, only some hundred miles to go. Surely my body wouldn't let me down now. That I could think this was interesting. For weeks now I'd taken my body for granted, or, more positively, I'd felt no split between mind and body, no feeling that my body was "other," was not "me." Fit and healthy, attuned to the trail, I'd relished how right I felt both mentally and physically. Now, suddenly, my ankle was external, something mechanical that might fail.

I plodded grimly on, trying to ignore the pain and concentrate on the nature around me. I came out of The Box into wide Bright Angel Canyon where a strip of green marked the line of the creek, and I could again see the great walls of the Canyon rising up all around. The sudden emergence into what felt like open space was a release, and I immediately felt more cheerful. I needed a rest. Not only was my ankle sore but my feet were so hot they felt like they were going to blow my boots apart. I settled in the shade of an ash tree by the rushing water of the creek and removed my boots and socks. The relief was immediate. I could practically feel them expanding. I examined my ankle. There was no swelling or discoloration. I decided I would continue in sandals. I couldn't imagine putting the boots back on. Ravens watched as I stuffed the boots into my pack, waiting for me to leave so they could come and scavenge any scraps I'd left, not that there were any.

Hiking in sandals was better for my ankle, though it aggravated the scar of a blister on the same foot, a blister caused by the sandals many weeks earlier. Despite the relief I slowed to half my normal pace. Every limb felt heavy, and sweat poured off me. I could feel the heat hammering at me. The air seemed solid, a barrier I had to struggle to pass through.

Yesterday the shade temperature had reached ninety-one degrees at Phantom Ranch. The forecast was for today to be even hotter. In the lid of my pack my thermometer read 116.

Bright Angel Canyon is beautiful. Rich green bushes line the creek with desert plants growing just yards beyond. A complex tangle of cliffs, side canyons, and buttes soar up on either side. Beavers live in the creek, and at one point the trail was muddy and wet as it passed the dense web of branches making up a dam, an unusual sight here in a predominantly desert land. I passed the sign for the side trail to Ribbon Falls, where the lime-rich waters of Ribbon Creek have built up a bright green, moss-covered cone of soft travertine rock below the cascade. A delicate swathe of mosses and ferns grows in the humid area around the falls. It's a lovely spot, but I had seen it before and today any extra effort seemed worth avoiding. I stayed on the main trail. At Wall Creek, a small trickle across the trail, a sign warned of flash floods. HIKERS CROSS AT THEIR OWN RISK! If the creek was in flood hikers should return the way they had come and report to a park ranger, continued the sign, finishing with the admonishment CAMPING OUTSIDE DESIGNATED CAMPGROUND SITES IS NOT PERMITTED. So, if the creek was impassable, hikers heading upward should return to Phantom Ranch, some seven miles back down the trail. Somehow I didn't think many would.

Just beyond Wall Creek huge green cottonwood trees appeared, signaling their eponymous camp where there is a ranger station, water, restrooms, and a campground. I stumbled into the shade of the trees, barely able to put one foot in front of the other. The temperature was ninety-four. I'd grown used to temperatures that, for me, were very hot, but I clearly wasn't acclimated to this. A few people were in the campground, all, I noticed, either stationary or moving unnaturally slowly. I'd seen a few hikers earlier, but beyond Cottonwood I wouldn't meet anyone. The North Rim was still closed, the facilities locked up. That seemed to discourage people from going much farther than here.

A few miles ahead the steep climb to the North Rim began. In this heat the ascent would be torture. Walking on the gentle trail down here was becoming an ordeal. A siesta was called for. I found a bench, lay down, and pulled my hat over my face. I dozed for maybe an hour then roused myself, hefted the pack, which seemed much heavier than it had for days, and hiked on, still slowly, still feeling as though I was wading through heavy syrup rather than walking in unresisting air.

The trail narrowed as I approached the start of the climbing, the rock walls beginning to crowd in on each side. Bright Angel Creek still rushed down the canyon. I had become used to its cheerful sound. However, the ascent to the rim abandons the creek for a side canyon. It didn't always do so. The original trail followed the creek up to the North Rim. This trail still exists in part. I'd descended it once and knew that it was hard to find in places and that some scrambling on steep rocks was required, not something I wanted to attempt with a heavy pack. There is little water on the old trail as most of the flow in Bright Angel Creek comes from Roaring Springs, which gush out of the base of the cliffs just above the confluence of Roaring Springs and Bright Angel Canyons. There is, however, virtually no water on the new trail, built by the National Park Service in 1926, as it mostly stays high on the cliffs, well above the canyon floor.

Roaring Springs is the water source for facilities on both the North and South Rims. For the latter the water is piped down Bright Angel Creek, across the underside of a suspension bridge, and up to Indian Gardens. Head pressure takes it that far, then pumping is required to bring it to the South Rim. The North Kaibab Trail runs past the springs and up Roaring Springs Canyon. The park staff who run the pumphouse live in a house that sits next to the trail near the mouth of the canyon. I knew there was a faucet outside the house for hikers. What I'd been unable to find out on the South Rim or at Phantom Ranch was whether there was any water at the North Rim. I'd been told that the campground and other amenities were still closed, but no one seemed to know about water or even if there was any snow left. This faucet was the last water before the rim, so I had to decide how much to haul to the top. As I didn't know how far beyond the rim the next water lay I was going to have to carry a fair amount.

As I approached the house I saw a table set up outside with a pink flower–patterned plastic tablecloth. On the table stood a red plastic barrel, a tray of mugs, and an empty coffee tin with a sign. HELP YOURSELF!

ICE COLD LEMONADE. DONATIONS ACCEPTED. I helped myself. Several times. The cool, sweet but sharp drink tasted amazing. I could feel it soaking through me. As I sat and drank I wondered what to do about water. Maybe the house's occupant would know the situation on the rim. I was reluctant to disturb anyone but even more reluctant to carry unnecessary weight. I knocked on the door. After a short delay a figure in a towel appeared at a window and indicated the door. I waited. The man, dressed now, opened the door. "I was in the shower when you knocked." I apologized. No need, he said. He was very friendly, and knew nothing about water on the rim though he doubted there was any. I filled up with a gallon and a half.

Slow progress along with the stops at Cottonwood Camp and here for lemonade had one benefit: The trail winding up Roaring Springs Canyon was in shade. The combined effects of lower temperatures and no direct sun was astonishing. Although the ascent is steep, climbing thirty-six hundred feet in 4.7 miles, my pace doubled. Suddenly, putting one foot in front of the other was no longer a huge effort. The roar of the springs accompanied me on the first part of the climb, which wound below the massive ramparts of the Roaring Springs cliffs, a huge prow jutting out between Roaring Springs and Bright Angel Canyons. I could see the water crashing down the canyon side in a series of cascades, green bushes nourished by the spray growing to either side then fading out into dusty desert.

Rather than following the canyon bed, as I'd done since Phantom Ranch, I was now high on the canyon wall with steep cliffs above and below. This is a spectacular trail and an amazing construction, especially where it had been blasted across vertical cliffs. On the far side of the canyon the buttes and walls still shone red and yellow in the sunlight, but dark shadows were slowly creeping up from the depths, snuffing out the color and turning the rocks dull and gray.

The most impressive section of trail runs along the base of the Redwall and then switchbacks up the huge cliffs on narrow ledges. Here you feel suspended in space, halfway up vertical cliffs. As I climbed the big drops to my right started to make me feel nervous, which was puzzling.

The trail was flat and fairly wide. Also, I'd been up it twice before and down it once, making it the most familiar bit of the entire route from Mexico to Utah. Thinking about it, I decided I was concerned that my still sore ankle might suddenly give way, or that a spasm of pain might cause me to stumble and fall off the trail. I told myself that this was very unlikely. My tall, unstable pack, with one and a half gallons of water sloshing about in bottles in the top, made me feel a little unbalanced too, but I wasn't nervous enough to want to stop and repack. The light was going, and I already doubted I would make the top before dark. I also felt tired, which I put down to the heat earlier, though the next day I came down with a cold. To overcome the weariness and nervousness and to help

Bright Angel Canyon.

maintain a steady rhythm I chanted a mantra under my breath. Not feeling very inspired, it was a very simple one—Concentrate, short steps, concentrate—but was so effective I kept it up long after I needed it and my tiredness had passed.

The first big trees started to appear where the trail switched from one side of the canyon to the other, crossing on a small bridge. Above, I could see the forest growing slowly thicker. Below, Roaring Springs Canyon stretched downward, a narrow, steep split in the cliffs. I ascended into piñon pine–juniper woods, passed through the Supai Tunnel, blasted through the rock, and went on in growing darkness to the final switchbacks through ponderosa pine and Douglas fir forest to the North Rim.

It was pitch black when I reached the trailhead. I could just see the outline of a large bulletin board in front of me. I took off my pack, found my headlamp, and switched it on. To my astonishment the first thing I saw was my name on a piece of paper. I peeled it off. It was, of course, a note from Jake. He'd stashed a gallon of water for me nearby, which he'd gotten from the ranger station, and was camped in the North Rim campground. A gallon of water. And I'd just hauled a gallon and a half all the way up Roaring Springs Canyon. I looked around. In the trees lay piles of snow. More water.

I shivered and realized I was quite cold. I was at 8,250 feet, back in subalpine forest, not hot desert, and it was night. A cool wind had been blowing for some time, but the effort of the climb had kept me warm. Now, stationary, I was quickly cooling down. I donned thick socks, fleece sweater, and fleece hat, shouldered the pack, and set off along the road to the campground. I had crossed the Grand Canyon, the section of the walk I had most looked forward to was over, and all I could think about was making camp and eating hot food.

Bright lights, swirls of smoke, and cooking smells marked the campground. Although still officially closed, with no running water, there were quite a few people. I passed several RVs—one with a TV flickering inside, the sound blaring out of the open windows—and many large tents. There seemed to be a large campfire at every site. At times the beam of my headlamp rebounded off the thick clouds of smoke drifting through the trees. The whole effect—glaring lights, loud clashing noises, flickering orange flames, hazy smoke—was phantasmagoric, as if some strange and mysterious rite was being carried out in the forest. The Canyon had been sharp, clean, hard-edged, pure. This dark forest was soft and blurred; dirty snow lay on the ground; noises, lights, smoke flowed around me, strengthening and fading. Nothing was substantial, nothing quite real. I wandered on, watching what seemed almost a show, something I was not part of, not connected to. Nobody spoke to me, nobody looked at me. I could have been invisible.

Wanting to camp somewhere quiet and away from the eerie atmosphere I walked on through the huge campground until I reached a section where the roads were still closed and there were no people. I would look for Jake in the morning. I made camp at the base of a big ponderosa and cooked a meal. I was so tired I could only manage a few mouthfuls. The day had been the hottest of the walk and also the longest, with twelve and a half hours between camps, and with the most ascent, a strenuous fifty-eight hundred vertical feet. Abandoning the food I lay down and was quickly asleep.

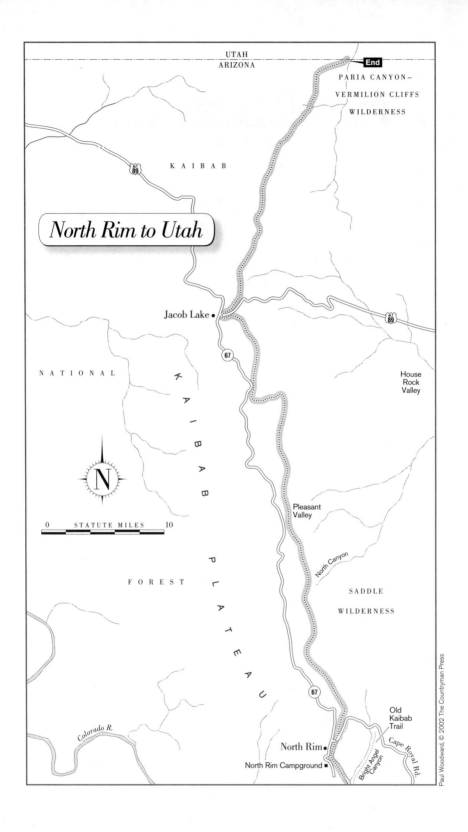

UTAH
ARIZONA

PARIA CANYON–
VERMILION CLIFFS
WILDERNESS

End

North Rim to Utah

KAIBAB

US 89

Jacob Lake •

67

US 89

House
Rock
Valley

N A T I O N A L

K
A
I
B
A
B

P
L
A
T
E
A
U

N

0   STATUTE MILES   10

Pleasant
Valley

North Canyon

F O R E S T

SADDLE

WILDERNESS

67

Old
Kaibab
Trail

North Rim •

Cape Royal Rd.

North Rim Campground ■

Bright Angel Canyon

Colorado R.

9

Winding Down

THE NORTH RIM TO UTAH

116 miles

Early the next morning I walked over to the edge of the trees to say farewell to the Grand Canyon. The dark depths of a long narrow side canyon called The Transept lay below, running down into Bright Angel Canyon. Oza Butte, on the far side of The Transept, caught the first rays of the sun. Much farther away, the long line of the South Rim was brightly sunlit. Beyond the Canyon, over the dark green of the forest and faint in the distance, I could see the hazy gray outline of the San Francisco Peaks. I'd walked between the mountains and the Canyon now. I knew what lay there and all the way south to Mexico too. I sat in the dawn and watched the Canyon slowly emerge into the day, then turned away and walked back into the trees. I was finished with the Canyon. Until next time.

In case Jake was still there I wandered around the campground, which seemed dull and mundane in the soft daylight, the sinister magic of the previous night long gone. There was no sign of him, which didn't surprise me. Knowing his liking for early starts, I guessed he was already hiking. I soon followed, beginning the last part of my journey, some hundred miles across the high, forested Kaibab Plateau. This is part of the Arizona Strip, that remote part of the state split off from the rest of

Arizona by the Grand Canyon and difficult to reach from anywhere other than Utah.

Kaibab means "mountain lying down" in the local Paiute Indian language, an interesting name for a vast, flat plateau, mostly more than eight thousand feet high. The highest of the five plateaus on the North Rim of the Grand Canyon, it's surrounded by lower desert lands, a great wedge of trees that supports much wildlife, including many mule deer noted for their size and their magnificent antlers.

The walking on dirt roads and trails was easy after the steepness and rock of the Canyon. The four days I spent crossing the Kaibab Plateau were a gentle coming down from the magnificence of the Canyon into a softer world of tall trees, grassy meadows, and sunlight filtered through green foliage. Until the very end of the walk the desert would now be a

Morning light in the Grand Canyon from the North Rim.

mysterious presence just beyond the forest, a presence occasionally glimpsed but always felt, even when hidden. The Kaibab Plateau is like a giant sky island. Once the elevation drops even a little the trees fade away and the desert returns, the desert that is really the dominant feature here. I was walking along a spine of forest just above the arid lands, a subalpine ecosystem dependent for its existence on the snow that its altitude brought.

Dirt roads led out of Grand Canyon National Park and back into Kaibab National Forest. A crowded truck stopped, the driver quizzing me as to where I was going. The truck carried a fire crew off to set a controlled burn, and they didn't want anyone nearby. Luckily, my route lay elsewhere. A few minutes later another truck stopped and asked me again. I saw no other people in the woods, just magnificent trees—ponderosa, Douglas fir, Engelmann's spruce, subalpine fir, and aspen, and much wildlife, including the first wild turkeys, strutting through the forest, and several beautiful Kaibab squirrels. They are a variant of the Abert's squirrels I was used to seeing and unique to the Kaibab Plateau, having been isolated for long enough to evolve distinctive characteristics in the form of bushy white tails and dark gray bodies.

I walked through rolling, low, wooded hills, very soothing on the eye after the harsh, bright, almost violent scenery of the Grand Canyon. Gentle walking was welcome because I'd come down with a heavy cold and felt lethargic and had no appetite. This landscape was placid, unchallenging, and restful. Concentration was required only at trail junctions. Otherwise I could daydream and dawdle along.

Scattered patches of old snow lay in shady areas under the trees. Sometimes they crossed the trail, impeding walking slightly but not enough to be more than a minor irritation. The snow did have one big advantage. It fed a succession of ponds, springs, and streams. I had no need to carry much water. The Kaibab Plateau is made of limestone, the same limestone that forms the top layer of the Grand Canyon. Limestone is porous, so permanent water is rare on the plateau. Eventually, it soaks through the rocks, emerging at places like Roaring Springs, where the layer of rock below is impervious to water.

At the boundary between national park and national forest I joined North Kaibab Trail 101, which runs almost all the way to Utah, and which is also the route of the Arizona Trail. For the first time since Grandview Lookout, Arizona Trail markers appeared. They were different than the ones south of the Grand Canyon, with a Kaibab squirrel on a green outline of Arizona surrounded by the words KAIBAB PLATEAU and ARIZONA TRAIL in green on a white background. These signs were mounted on brown carsonite posts. Since they were mostly white they were easy to spot from a distance.

The route ran down broad, grassy Upper North Canyon for many miles to a large pool formed by Crystal Spring, the last water for a while. I filled up with one and a half gallons and then left the valley to climb steep slopes to the edge of the Kaibab Plateau at East Rim View. The closed-in forest world suddenly opened up. Across the plunging depths of cliff-rimmed North Canyon lay a vast area of flat, pale desert cracked by the giant chasm of Marble Canyon, through which the Colorado River runs before reaching the Grand Canyon. Farther to the northeast the distant, bright pink Vermilion Cliffs rose beyond the deserts of House Rock Valley.

I found Jake sitting under a tree, staring out over the desert. We camped together under the trees near the rim. There was a trailhead nearby, and other campers arrived and pitched two tents a few hundred yards away. We watched them bringing armfuls of stuff from their vehicles.

That evening Jake and I swapped tales of our hikes through the Grand Canyon. On his rest day Jake had phoned the Forest Service and the BLM to inquire about water on the Kaibab Plateau. What he had heard was not encouraging. It had been a very dry winter, and he'd been told there was little water farther north. But he doubted that the office staff he'd talked to had any real information, suspecting they were mainly spouting the standard line. Some had even told him the Arizona Trail hadn't been built yet, even though the first section of the trail to be completed was here.

Quiet forest walking continued the next day. Again the trail, which was sometimes a foot trail and sometimes an abandoned logging road, cut across many dirt roads and other trails, making me glad of the regular trail markers. There were few distinctive places on the day's route. One was Dog Lake, a pretty little pool surrounded by tall aspens and conifers. A bank of snow lay under the trees, and the water was deliciously cold. Not that it was hot anymore. A cool west wind had sprung up at the East Rim View camp and continued all day, bringing in clouds during the afternoon. For several miles the route ran through the wide grasslands of Tater Canyon, so called for a failed attempt at potato farming during the late nineteenth century. There were more pools, including fenced Crane Lake, really just a large pond, so again water was not a problem. Maybe Jake had been misinformed.

A sign indicated a historic Forest Service lookout tree. Nearby lay a huge fallen conifer with a narrow wooden ladder running along the massive trunk. I looked at the small rungs, barely big enough for more than the toe of a boot, and imagined climbing high into the sky up such a ladder. Well, no, I didn't imagine it as I knew I wouldn't have gotten very far before turning back. Not without a safety rope anyway.

Seeing the fallen lookout tree reminded me, as so much on this walk had, of Edward Abbey. He worked as a fire lookout on the North Rim for four seasons, an experience described in his novel *Black Sun* and, briefly and salaciously, in an essay called *Fire Lookout* that appears in the collection *Abbey's Road*. *Black Sun* is a complex tale, a sad, elegiac story about love found and lost. It contains the most wonderful descriptions of the Kaibab Plateau and the Grand Canyon, descriptions that are integral to the story as it is in the forest that the protagonist, Will Gatlin, finds solace. There are detailed descriptions of life in the forest, of the slowness and quiet and simplicity. Abbey is clearly describing his own experiences, his joy in a basic, uncomplicated, but free way of life. I could relate to that. That's what the walk was giving me.

I ambled on through the undulating mix of forest, hill, and meadow. There was only one brief steep section, marked in advance with a sign that read CAUTION—CYCLISTS AND SKIERS—SHORT, STEEP GRADES. A brief climb in and out of a wooded canyon followed. Mule deer appeared more and more frequently, watching me from the trees or crashing off through the undergrowth at my approach.

Late in the afternoon a wildlife tank set in a square of concrete appeared. I filled up with the usual one and a half gallons for the last two hours of hiking. Shortly beyond Murray Trailhead I stopped to search for a site in the forest. I found a good spot fairly quickly and began to set up the tarp, as the cloudy sky might mean rain. However, I wasn't comfortable, something felt wrong. Was I too near the trailhead? I didn't think so. I looked around. The forest stretched away on all sides, a tangle of bushes and fallen branches covering the ground. I wandered around to see if I could work out what the problem was. I soon found it. The skeleton of a deer lay nearby, with enough skin and flesh left on the legs to attract scavengers including, possibly, bears. Maybe I had picked up a faint whiff of decay, enough to disturb me but not enough for me to recognize what it was. Now I knew it was there I would not sleep soundly here so I dismantled the tarp and set off again. A few hundred yards farther on I spotted Jake, camped just off the trail. I joined him and pitched the tarp again, partly over some infant ponderosas. I didn't need shelter though, as the clouds dissipated and the wind dropped during the evening, leaving a calm night and a starry sky.

"Did you see the turkey hunter?" asked Jake. "No." "He was aiming right across the trail." "Oh." I wondered if he'd been there when I walked past. Jake said he'd first heard a strange, unnatural noise. Looking around he'd seen a hunter dressed in camouflage sitting not far from the trail. The noise had come from a plastic turkey decoy that was almost on the trail. Anyone hiking by would be in the line of fire. Jake said he was glad to be wearing a red shirt and white cap. I reckoned my pale clothing, intended to reflect the desert sun rather than blend in with the forest, would stand out too, but knowing someone had been aiming a gun across the trail was a little disturbing.

I settled into camp feeling much more relaxed than I had for a couple of days. My cold was rapidly clearing, my ankle was much less sore, and the blister scar I'd aggravated in the Grand Canyon was almost painless, though it had blistered again and I'd had to drain and dress it. Overall it looked as though my body wasn't going to let me down. Utah was barely more than forty miles away.

Much closer and of much more immediate importance was the little settlement of Jacob Lake, where there was a store and café, the last near the trail. Jake had sent supplies there, which he needed as the food he'd bought in Grand Canyon Village had not proved as nourishing as his own carefully prepared rations. I could do with a little food too, though it wasn't essential. However, I did hope to find out something about the end of the trail and whether I could arrange a shuttle or taxi to pick us up. We also hoped to find out if there was any water on this last section.

Jake set off before me, and we arranged to meet at the café. I followed the trail for a few miles then took forest roads to Jacob Lake, guided by the detailed sketch map of the area printed on the back of the large Kaibab National Forest map. Arriving in the scattered, forest-hidden village I headed for the Jacob Lake Inn, which held both café and store, expecting to find Jake inside with a hot meal. He wasn't there. This was a surprise. He had the same map and had set off at least an hour earlier. I walked down to the visitors center. No Jake. I did, however, get the phone numbers of taxi and shuttle companies in the towns of Page and Kanab, the nearest settlements to the end of the walk. I needed to go to Kanab, as that's where I'd sent my supply box, while Jake wanted to go there en route to California. I wandered back to the inn, sat down at the bar, the restaurant being closed, and ordered a meal. It was a long time coming. The place was quite busy even though not fully open, the season not having really begun. The atmosphere was friendly, though, and I didn't mind the wait. I wasn't leaving until Jake turned up anyway.

The inn was old and had character. It was slightly dark inside and a bit disorganized, which created a feeling of welcome and coziness. I had the impression that the owners, the fourth generation of the family who'd founded the place back in 1923, were more concerned that visitors feel comfortable and at home, rather than in whether every candy bar was aligned exactly with every other candy bar and the furniture arranged so that visitors couldn't disturb it. There was no sterile, lifeless, don't-touch, instantly forgettable atmosphere here. I liked places like this. I remembered places like this. It is the corporate chains that are instantly forgotten. Individuality counts, diversity matters. Uniformity threatens nature, threatens

No water! Jake Schas in a dry Joe's Reservoir on the Kaibab Plateau.

freedom. Who wants everything, everybody to be the same? I don't. Who wants the world to be controlled, safe, boring, and bland? Outside lay an untamed wild wood, full, undoubtedly, of potential dangers but also excitement, beauty, adventure, and liberty. Compare that with the regimented ranks of factory trees, planted in ruler-straight lines in deep plowed furrows that mock the name of forest but which are replacing the true woods in all too many places around the world.

I'd been musing along these lines for an hour when Jake finally arrived, quite angry with himself. He'd taken a wrong turn, not having noticed the sketch map on the back of his map, and gone three miles out of the way before turning back. He was cheered by the discovery that his supply box had arrived safely and by eating a hot meal. We made various phone calls to taxi companies in the towns of Kanab and Page and ended up arranging a pickup at the trailhead in two mornings time. The end was suddenly near. This was the first time I'd made any arrangements for life beyond the walk.

Since leaving the North Rim I'd been slowly entering a strange but familiar state of mind, a sort of limbo between the walk and after the walk. Part of me wanted to remain inside the walk, not acknowledging that it would soon be over. Another part of me couldn't help but think ahead and move forward out of the wilds and away from the walk, mulling over the problems of getting home, of what I would do with any time left in Arizona, and, especially, the pleasure of seeing Denise and Hazel again. This dichotomy had occurred on previous long hikes so it wasn't a surprise, just an irritation, a distraction that distanced me from where I was. Overall I preferred the first me, the one who wanted to live the walk to its full right to the end, but I couldn't silence the other me, the one who was planning for life when the walk was over. I guess the second was needed. Thinking like this was preparing myself for the change to come, making it easier for me to accept a suddenly different life.

A man who overheard Jake and me talking outside the inn came over from a nearby vehicle. My accent had attracted him; he'd been born in London but had been living in the United States since he was six years old. He told me he still thought of himself as partly British. He now lived in Page, and he gave me his card, saying he might be able to arrange a lift south from Kanab.

Jake and I filled our water bottles and sorted out our packs. A group of turkey hunters, dressed in camouflage from head to foot, hung around nearby, eventually piling into a truck and driving off. To the north huge black clouds were building up over the forest. A big storm seemed likely. Ahead lay the area Jake had dubbed "the black hole," due to the lack of information about it. Now the name seemed literally correct.

Despite the apparently imminent storm Jake and I managed to drag ourselves away from the enticing fleshpots of Jacob Lake and head back into the forest. The plateau was now declining slowly, and our route followed the gentle descent. Sagebrush appeared in the meadows, piñon pine and juniper among the ponderosas. A few yuccas hinted of the desert.

Late in the day we camped in a long, narrow, wooded canyon. Utah was just twenty or so miles away. The clouds passed by with no rain and stars appeared. We slept under them, no need for tarps.

The walk, easy for the last three days, was not going to fade quietly away to the finish, however. The last twenty-four hours were to be quite interesting. It started when I woke suddenly at two in the morning to find Jake alert and buzzing with adrenaline and tension. "Did you hear it?" he asked excitedly. "What?" I replied, drowsily. "The screeching, the animal walking about. It passed just twenty feet away." I must have been deeply asleep because I had heard nothing, though it was probably the animal's cries that woke me. I didn't doubt Jake, though, his voice vibrated with stress and apprehension. He'd clearly heard something. We waited awhile, peering into the black night. Nothing. Whatever it was had gone. In the morning we decided it must have been either a mountain lion or a bobcat, both of which scream at times, according to the field guides. The canyon was narrow, and we were camped right in the middle of it, blocking the path of any creature that came this way. Our visitor had probably been out on its usual nighttime patrol and been startled to find two bundled humans lying in its way. Jake reckoned he'd heard it skirt past a little way up the canyon's side. We looked for tracks and other sign, but the soft pine needles that covered the ground showed nothing.

The other shock of the night was the cold. I woke before dawn to a temperature of twenty-one degrees, the lowest of the walk. There was thick ice in my water bottles. I'd stood them upside down, so water still ran out, to the sound of the tinkling and cracking of splinters of ice. A hot drink was really welcome. And for the first time I heated water to pour over my granola. While the stove purred I lay on my back and stared through the branches at the slowly fading stars. Birds sang nearby, and a woodpecker drummed rhythmically and noisily, the usual woodland dawn welcome. It was beautiful and wonderfully peaceful. I shall miss this, I thought. It has become normal. Wearing gloves wasn't but I needed them this morning. I'd hardly worn them to this point but now was glad I'd carried them all the way from Mexico.

We left our last camp with a quart or so of water apiece. So far we'd

Jake Schas fishing for water in Summit Trick Tank.

found water every day on the Kaibab Plateau. At the end of the canyon was a large tank called Government Reservoir. It was dry. This wasn't a surprise—the trail guide said it rarely had water. Across a vast meadow of sagebrush and grass and a dark line of piñon and juniper, distant pink and white cliffs ran along the horizon, cliffs that lay in Utah. The trail followed an abandoned dirt road along the edge of the meadow, just under the trees where it was still quite cool, to another tank, Joe's Reservoir. We had hopes for Joe. "May have water in the spring," said the trail guide. My notes from Bill Watson were stark and abrupt, however: "no water." Unfortunately Bill was right, and Joe was dry. We looked at the shallow, dusty depression dotted with clumps of grass that suggested it had been dry for a long time. On the chance that there was a muddy puddle at its heart Jake wandered out into the middle of the reservoir. He turned and held his arms out wide in a gesture that said "nothing." Arizona's reputation for dryness was lasting to the very end.

This was serious. We had to find water or return to Jacob Lake. Utah was just sixteen miles away. We consulted the maps. The Forest Service map showed a Summit Trick Tank about a mile away on the far side of the meadow. On the topo map it was marked as a cistern. There must be something there. A dirt road led across the meadow and then along the far side. Two large, rusted metal cylindrical tanks came into view in a beaten down area of hard, sparsely vegetated earth surrounded by a barbed wire fence. In front of the tanks was a dry open trough, behind them a large area of rippled metal on which the water gathered and then ran into the tanks. It was dry, as was the smaller of the tanks. We couldn't get into the big one at first. When hit it sounded hollow, but there could still be water in the bottom. Unable to find a side opening we climbed on top where we found a small circular inspection cap, bolted shut. A couple of rocks dislodged the rusted bolt so the nut could be turned. We dropped a pebble in. Splash. There was water in the bottom. Jake cut a large hole in an empty gallon water jug, filled the bottom with stones, tied the jug to a length of cord, and dropped it into the tank. It floated. A rank smell emanated from the disturbed water. Despite Jake dragging it about and jerking it up and down the jug came up empty. We tried my rigid quart size bottle. Splash. Jake jiggled it around on the end of the line then hauled it out. A few inches of very grubby, rusty, unpalatable-looking water covered the stones. It would take a long time to produce enough water for two of us.

Leaving the fishing to Jake I wandered about to see if I could find anything else. How did the water get from the gathering area to the tanks? I traced the line back. At the outflow of the metal sheet a recessed chute ran into a small, open area, maybe three feet long, covered with a metal grill, and then went underground. This must have been a settling tank for debris. When it was full the water would run down into the tanks. There was about ten inches of water in the bottom, clear water that looked easy to extract. We pried off the grill and filled our bottles. The whole diversion had taken an hour, but we had water. Relieved and cheerful we replaced the grill and the tank cap and returned across the valley to the trail.

The big trees were behind us now, and we walked through piñon and juniper woods to the forest boundary. This was the start of Jake's black hole, BLM land nobody had been able to give us much information about. We didn't have an adequate map. I'd been unable to get the topo map that covered this last section. It was labeled as a Utah map and unavailable everywhere I'd tried in Arizona. The Forest Service map showed little detail, and the only other map we had was a black-and-white printout from a CD, courtesy of Bill Watson. This showed the end of the Arizona Trail but not how to get from here to there. Bill didn't have any waypoints for this section. Indeed, he'd asked me to switch the GPS on at Joe's Reservoir to record the track from there to Utah.

Beyond the boundary fence we were delighted to find a good trail, well-marked with rock cairns and carsonite posts, that ran through an increasingly rugged and rocky landscape with many little canyons rimmed with little cliffs and occasional views of the much larger, dark red cliffs called Coyote Butte. The trail wound around the heads of these canyons and over small hills before arriving at a barbed wire fence. There was no gate. On the far side the trail was less clear, and there were no markers, just strips of ribbon attached to bushes and trees. Out to the north and

On the descent into Coyote Canyon near the end of the trail.

east lay the red rock desert lands of Utah, enticing and beguiling. Blue-gray piñon jays darted noisily through the bushes. Pretty meadowlarks perched here and there. A kestrel hovered overhead. The uncompleted trail gradually faded. In places there were cut trees and bushes that showed where it would run. Indeed, we felt that the trail makers had been unnecessarily enthusiastic with their axes, chopping back far more vegetation than seemed necessary.

Eventually we arrived at the western rim of Coyote Canyon. Somewhere down there in that broad desert valley was the end of the trail. We lost the last ribbons and traces of the trail at the start of the descent. But we were back in open desert now, and the walking was fairly easy. We descended through cacti—prickly pear, hedgehog, some with beautiful dark red flowers, and, for the first time in many weeks, cholla. Jake pointed out a well-camouflaged, squat, so-ugly-it-was-beautiful lizard with an armored head and short spikes all over its back and tail. "Horned toad," he said. It felt good to be back in the desert and good to be seeing new species in the last hours of the walk. Old friends were with us too. Ravens soared over the red rock landscape.

On the wide canyon floor we found a large, unfinished trailhead with blank notice boards, toilets, and a picnic area. There was no mention of the Arizona Trail anywhere. We walked out to the dirt road that ran through the valley. A sign read ENTERING UTAH, LEAVING ARIZONA. The walk was over, but there would be one last camp in the desert among the now familiar sagebrush, juniper, yucca, and cacti.

I lay in my sleeping bag staring at the stars, as I had so many nights before. Above us rose the impressive red rocks of Coyote Butte. It was a fine, wild place to finish. I felt quietly satisfied. The walk had been a success. Not just because I had reached the end, though that obviously mattered, especially at the moment, but because of the journey itself, because of the two months in wild country, because of an experience that was immeasurably valuable and that would deepen in the months and years to come.

The finish. With Jake Schas at the Utah border in Coyote Canyon.

Afterword

The immediate aftermath of the walk was a confusing mix of hectic activity and stultifying boredom.

Leaving the wilds proved surprisingly difficult. The expected taxi did not arrive so we walked toward the nearest highway, watching for the small dust cloud that would mark an approaching vehicle. Nothing. The valley wound on. We wound with it. Still nothing. On our right lay the red sandstone of the Paria Canyon–Vermillion Cliffs Wilderness. I gazed at it longingly. I wanted to both go home and go on hiking.

After a long eight or nine miles the highway appeared. Having no other choice we hitchhiked, waiting an hour in the hot sun for a ride that, when it came, was fast and terrifying. We reached the little town of Kanab where I said farewell to Jake, off to California and the Pacific Crest Trail. From Kanab a taxi took me to the little town of Page and then, the next day, to Flagstaff where I could catch a bus to Phoenix.

The landscape we drove through from Kanab to Page was spectacular. I wanted to stop, head into it, see what lay there. I was already missing the wilderness. We passed Lake Powell, the first time I had seen it. My eyes were immediately drawn to the ugly, pale bathtub ring around the shoreline that said that this was unnatural and man-made. The wide blue waters looked wrong, too. The desert scenery around the reservoir was impressive but shouldn't rise out of a lake. A sticker in the taxi read FRIENDS OF LAKE POWELL. I said nothing. I didn't know enough to argue. I had emotions but no facts. I guessed that if I spoke I would be told the reservoir was needed, that it provided water, power, jobs, and more. This would be true, too. I knew there could be alternatives, ones that didn't involve despoiling a beautiful place. There always are. It was just that I didn't know what they were.

I felt detached and somewhat passive during these few days. The world of towns and cars seemed too fast to deal with. Talking to strangers was hard too, though I don't think they noticed my discomfort. They probably thought I was always like this. In my head I was still on the trail.

The next day, back in the taxi, we headed south to Flagstaff on US 89, which stretched out long and straight through the deserts of the Navajo Indian Reservation. Every so often a small cluster of stalls selling jewelry and other artifacts appeared by the side of the road. There was little traffic. We made one coffee stop. The journey was long, too long. The scenery was interesting and often impressive, but that's all it was: scenery, a backdrop that could be glanced at or ignored. I felt no contact with it. I was outside it, cut off inside this hurtling metal box that raced down the black unnatural strip of road. I needed the ride. I wanted to go home. But I was already feeling separate from the wilderness.

As we approached Flagstaff the San Francisco Peaks came into view, far less snow on their summits now. In the city there was time to wander around for a short while before my bus left for Phoenix. Flagstaff felt familiar yet different. Again it was a stopover on a journey, but there were few similarities between the trip out and the trip back. In just one day I was traveling past country it had taken almost two months to walk. The bus rolled south. Out there the rumpled distant hills must be the Mazatzals and the Superstitions.

Two days later Arizona receded below me as the airplane powered into the sky. I watched the land fade away. I would miss the deserts and canyons and forests and mountains, the small towns, the friendly people, the hiking, life on the trail.

Back home it felt cool and damp, amazingly damp. I could see the moisture in the air. The Highlands were very green, rich with the colors of spring. Being with Denise and Hazel was marvelous, but I felt restless after only a few days. I knew I would. I was accustomed, physically and mentally, to hiking every day and sleeping somewhere different each night.

In the following months I often thought of Arizona and the walk, sometimes deliberately but mostly unintentionally. Something would trigger a memory, and suddenly I was back under desert skies or deep in ponderosa forest. The walk was part of me now, something I would never lose. The beauty of the country sent shivers down my spine for months afterward. Hiking through the wilderness I had felt whole, in tune with myself and nature, in a way I find impossible most of the time. It was, I felt, how I was meant to be, how, I supposed, humans were meant to be. After all, that is what we have been for much of our existence: nomads traveling the wilderness. My feeling that we should be part of nature and not separate from it was reinforced. Some contact with nature is, I think, essential for sanity, essential for well-being. It is also clearly necessary for our survival. Nature, I am sure, will continue. Whether humanity is part of it is another matter.

Some ten months after I started the walk I began to write this book, began to give concrete form to what had happened and what I felt and thought. Through the writing I relived the walk, relived the nights under the stars, the steep hard climbs, the snow in the mountains, the calmness of the desert, the beauty of the canyons, the magnificence of the forest. The pleasure of recollection was intense; it surprised me. As I neared the end of the book I found myself slowing down, prevaricating, avoiding finishing the walk again. For the second time I didn't want to stop, didn't want to leave the wilderness. I still don't. The answer is to go back. The next long walk beckons.

TRAIL NOTES

Facts and Figures

I reckon I hiked 800 miles, at least that's the nearest convenient round number. It's probably accurate within 10 percent either way (but I think more likely to be an underestimate than an overestimate). I can be more precise with how long the walk took—53 days. That's just more than fifteen miles a day. However, I didn't walk at all on seven days, which means I averaged a bit more than seventeen miles a day on the forty-six days I did walk. How far I actually walked on individual days varied from five (once) to twenty-seven miles (on three occasions).

A walk in mountains is always about ascent as well as distance, and I estimate that I climbed some 92,350 feet (as computed by my wrist altimeter—which, when checked against the contours on a map, seemed pretty accurate). On a few days the ascent was too small to measure, on a few others it was more than 4,000 feet. Just once it reached 5,800. The average, excluding rest days, was about 2,000 feet.

One of my aims was to spend as many nights under the stars as possible. I managed twenty-three. On another eighteen I slept under the tarp. Of these forty-one nights only three were in campgrounds, the others were in the backcountry. The remaining twelve nights were in motels and hotels at town stops.

Equipment

Long distance hiking is always tough on equipment and clothing. The hot, harsh, dusty terrain of Arizona is particularly severe. Spines and thorns tear at clothes and pack, abrasive dust and grit sneak in everywhere, and the sun makes some items almost too hot to touch. Durability was important, but so was weight. My final choice was for gear I thought would last the hike but which was also as light as possible. Nothing failed, so I was right about durability. I could have had lighter weight items in a few cases.

Footwear Footwear is the single most important piece of equipment for long distance hikers. Get this wrong and big problems can ensue. The rocky ground and spiny vegetation of Arizona meant that footwear would receive a real bashing, so it needed to be tough. It also had to protect my feet against the heat of the ground and allow sweat out so my feet would stay dry and cool. Leather is still one of the best materials for doing all

My boots at the finish.

this so I decided on leather footwear. The next question was whether to go for boots or shoes. I chose the former for the extra protection they provide against cacti and rocks. However, I wanted my footwear to be as light as possible too as the lighter it is the farther I can walk without feeling tired. This requirement eliminated 99 percent of the hiking boots made. Very few leather boots even came close to what I wanted. I was delighted, then, when, shortly before the walk, Brasher Boots, a British brand I'd worn on other long hikes, launched what is probably the lightest leather hiking boot available, the Supalite. A pair in my size weighed just two pounds and proved comfortable and durable. I ended up wearing them for forty days and six hundred miles.

Where the terrain seemed suitable (open ground, no dense vegetation, especially cacti and thorn bushes) and the weather was really hot I hiked in Teva Terradactyl sandals (twenty-three ounces). These were cool and had soles solid enough to keep out cactus spines. I hiked two hundred miles in them.

With the boots I wore Coolmax socks, figuring that this fast-wicking polyester would help keep my feet cool and dry. I carried two pairs of thin socks and one pair of medium weight (one and a half and three and a half ounces, respectively) and quickly found that the thicker ones were more comfortable, even in the heat, because they provided cushioning. They matted down quickly, however, and needed frequent washing, or at least rinsing. They were reasonably cool, but I think wool socks would have been better.

Shelter A tent seemed unnecessary for Arizona so I took a tarp (British-made Kathmandu Trekking Basha-Tent) made from silicone elastomer nylon. It weighed twenty-eight ounces and was very roomy. I could have managed with a smaller, lighter one. A ground cloth, stakes, and guylines added another fifteen ounces. My hiking poles doubled as tent poles. I used the tarp primarily to keep off the wind.

On many nights I slept under the stars. As the ground was usually dry I didn't often bother with the ground cloth, just using a three-quarter-length RidgeRest foam pad (nine ounces). This proved perfectly adequate, though it did look rather torn and battered by the end of the hike from being carried outside the pack where it was clawed by cacti and spiny bushes.

Sleeping Bag   A British-made Rab Micron 400 containing fourteen ounces of 750+ fill power goose down and weighing a total of thirty-one and a half ounces kept me comfortable in temperatures ranging from twenty-one to sixty-six degrees. The shell was quick-drying, moisture-shedding Pertex nylon. It was also black, which helped speed drying on the few occasions dew or frost made it damp.

Pack   I still haven't found a lightweight pack that will handle fifty-plus pounds comfortably (and I knew I'd carry this much when I had lots of water) so I ended up taking a heavy, 6.8-pound Gregory Shasta that I knew carried well and which had a large, five-thousand-cubic-inch capacity.

Kitchen   I like hot food in the evening and a hot drink in the morning so I carried a stove, the Optimus Nova multifuel model (17.8 ounces with windscreen). I ran it mostly on white gas, though for one week I used unleaded gasoline. With either fuel performance was excellent. The stove lit quickly, simmered well, and packed small.

For cookware I used an Evernew quart-size titanium pan (5.3 ounces), a stainless-steel, one-pint Cascade cup (4 ounces), and two Lexan spoons (1 ounce).

Water Containers   These were crucial. A failure far from a water source would have been serious. Because of this I started out with eight containers, rather than a couple of large ones, so that in the event of a leak I would still have plenty of water. To keep the weight and bulk down I took collapsible containers—four one-quart Platypus bottles (4 ounces), two two-and-a-half-quart Platypus bottles (2.7 ounces), a four-quart Ortlieb Water Bag (3 ounces), and a rigid one-quart Nalgene Bottle (5 ounces). I took the last because the wide mouth made it easy to fill from small seeps and trickles. It proved worth the weight. I found I didn't need all the other bottles and ended up sending three of the quart-size Platypus and the Ortlieb bag on ahead in my running supply box.

Water potabilty is a major concern on any hike, and some means of treating water is usually necessary. Not wanting to bother with a complex, fragile, and heavy filter I used Aqua Mira water purification drops (2.8 ounces), which don't leave a taste or any chemicals in the purified water and which are very easy to use. I didn't purify water when drinking from creeks high above cattle or human habitation or from any springs. I did treat water from cattle tanks, lowland creeks, and murky pools. I also carried an Ortlieb coffee filter and some filter papers (2.8 ounces) to filter out visible sediments.

Clothing   I hiked mostly in Berghaus Pertex nylon shorts that had zip-on long legs (total weight 8.8 ounces) for cold weather, spiky vegetation, and cool evenings in camp, and a Craghoppers Barkhan nylon shirt (12 ounces). I liked the shirt because it had large breast pockets in which I could carry maps, mini binoculars, and other items. I also carried a Pertex nylon windshirt (6.2 ounces—Karrimor Vector). A Polartec 100 Microfleece sweater (13.6 ounces—Craghoppers Airglow) and a Marmot down vest (14.6 ounces) sufficed for cold weather.

Rain gear was a Gore-Tex Paclite smock (15 ounces—Berghaus) and an old pair of polyurethane-coated pants (4 ounces). I never wore the pants, and I could have done with a lighter jacket, as I only needed it five or six times. The only time I wore it all day was when it rained while I was shopping in Tucson.

Other items were Patagonia Capilene briefs (1.5 ounces) and Marmot DriClime long-sleeved top (5 ounces). The latter was worn in camp on cool evenings when my shirt was sweat soaked. I also carried Helly-Hansen Lifa long johns (3 ounces) for camp and sleep wear in cold weather.

A good sun hat was essential, and I wore a cotton Tilley Hat (5.8 ounces) almost every day. A light fleece hat (2 ounces) kept my head warm in camp. I also had some thin polypropylene gloves (1 ounce) that I hardly ever wore.

Umbrella I'd never previously carried an umbrella on a hike, but having portable shade in the desert seemed a good idea. I used a GoLite Dome (9 ounces). It worked well but would have been better if I'd covered it with reflective silver foil. In open country it was easy to use, but the terrain was often too rugged to hike while holding an umbrella.

Hiking Poles

I like hiking poles, especially when carrying a big pack over rough terrain. My Brasher Guides (20.5 ounces) were excellent. The handle top unscrewed to reveal a camera thread so the pole could be used as a monopod. The poles doubled as supports for the tarp and for turning my pack into a backrest.

Miscellaneous Gear A host of small items always seem to end up in my pack, some of them essential, some for entertainment.

Petzl Micro Headlamp with spare AA batteries (9.5 ounces), candle (3 ounces), Silva Type 4 compass (1.4 ounces), safety whistle (0.5 ounces), first aid kit (2.5 ounces), gear repair kit (7.4 ounces), Suunto Altimax altimeter watch (2 ounces), Silva Alba Windwatch (1.8 ounces), Swiss Army knife (3 ounces), Sirius 8 x 21 binoculars (5.3 ounces), wash kit (toothbrush, toothpaste, bit of soap, 3 ounces), sunscreen (3 ounces), sunglasses (2.5 ounces), toilet trowel (2.3 ounces), toilet paper (1 ounce). I also carried a paperback to read in the evenings, various natural history guides, and a 144-page hardcover notebook with two pens (7.6 ounces) for recording the events of the day. I filled one and a half notebooks on this walk.

Total Weight The total weight of my gear without cameras was about thirty pounds. Of this about five pounds was worn or carried in-hand, (clothes, boots, trekking poles) giving a pack weight of twenty-five pounds. The camera gear weighed six and a quarter pounds, of which two and a half were carried in the pack.

I reckon the pack weighed about thirty pounds without food or water. At one point, when I carried three gallons of water and a six-day food supply, the total weight was about seventy pounds. The average was probably between thirty-five and forty pounds. Of course it could vary widely as I often picked up one or two gallons of water in the afternoon and then hiked on to a dry camp.

I could have carried four or five pounds less. The tarp, pack, and rain gear could all have been lighter, and I didn't really need a windshirt.

Photography

For the first time I used a digital camera, a Ricoh RDC-5000 (14.6 ounces), on a long walk, sending back Smartcards for uploading to a web site (www.bluedome.co.uk/arizonatrail/index.html). This worked well and enabled people back home to see the landscape that I was hiking through.

For slide shows, magazine articles, and this book I carried an SLR, the Canon Rebel 2000, the lightest one I know of that has a depth-of-field preview, which I regard as essential. To keep the weight down I took just one lens, a Sigma 24–70 zoom. The total weight was 23 ounces. I used Fuji Sensia II 100 transparency film and was very pleased with the results. I carried twenty rolls at any one time (20 ounces). I shot a total of fifty rolls.

As a backup and for use with print film I carried a tiny compact, the Ricoh GR1s (6.7 ounces), which has a superb 28 mm lens. I shot half a dozen print films (various Kodak 100 ISO types) and the results were excellent.

All three cameras were carried in a padded case, a Camera Care Systems Kangaroo (14.6 ounces), which was slung across one shoulder so I always had access to all my cameras.

I also carried a Cullman Backpack tripod (21.5 ounces), which was essential for low-light photographs as well as self-portraits.

Food

The Arizona Trail is not that remote and there are many places along the way where you can buy supplies. At times there is little choice, but it saves having to pack and mail supplies in advance, a particular problem when you're traveling from abroad.

Food for the trail needs to be nourishing and sustaining. Because weight and bulk is important high-calorie foods are best. I prefer organic, whole grain, unadulterated foods, and I bought these whenever I could. I must admit that when I ate more processed foods I didn't notice any effects on my energy level or well-being. I ate fresh fruit and vegetables at town stops, but carrying them any great distance without spoiling was impossible. Because of this I took vitamin C and vitamin B supplements every day (well, those days when I remembered anyway).

My trail diet, proven to work on previous long hikes, was to have four ounces of muesli or granola with powdered milk and sugar for breakfast; granola and energy bars (Bear Valley Mealpack especially recommended) plus trail mix for lunch and for snacking throughout the day; and dehydrated meals, usually pasta-based, for dinner. I often carried fresh garlic, dried herbs, a tube of pesto, and hard cheese to go with dinner. For hot drinks I had decaffeinated coffee; during the day I drank plain water. The total weight was two to two and a half pounds per day with a daily energy content around four thousand calories.

Maps

I used USGS topographic maps throughout the walk. These aren't current with regard to trails, but they do give excellent detail. I found them essential when traveling cross-country and for finding water. I also carried the national forest maps, which were useful for the whereabouts of roads and trails. Where hikers' maps existed—the Grand Canyon, Saguaro National Park, and popular wilderness areas—I carried these as well. I find maps essential to my understanding of an area and I often studied them in the evening and at rest stops.

The Arizona Trail Association

Without the dedication and hard work of the members of the Arizona Trail Association my walk would have been much more difficult. At the time of the walk roughly 70 percent of the Arizona Trail was built and signed.

Anyone hiking all or part of the Arizona Trail should consider joining the ATA. There is a newsletter, web site, and regular work parties. The ATA is the source for information about the trail. Contact them at Arizona Trail Association, P.O. Box 36736, Phoenix, AZ 85067; telephone: 602-252-4794; e-mail: ata@aztrail.org; website: www.aztrail.org.

SELECTED READING

Abbey, Edward. *Black Sun.* New York: Simon & Schuster, 1971.

———. *Desert Solitaire.* New York: McGraw-Hill, 1968.

———. *Good News.* New York: Dutton, 1980.

———. *The Journey Home.* New York: Dutton, 1975.

———. *The Monkey Wrench Gang.* New York: Lippincott, 1975.

Alden, Peter, and Peter Friederici. *National Audubon Society Field Guide to the Southwestern States.* New York: Knopf, 1999.

Annerino, John. *Adventuring in Arizona: The Sierra Club Travel Guide to the Grand Canyon State.* San Francisco: Sierra Club Books, 1991.

———. *Hiking the Grand Canyon.* San Francisco: Sierra Club Books, 1993.

———. *Running Wild: Through the Grand Canyon on the Ancient Path.* Tucson: Harbinger House, 1992.

Fayhee, M. John, and Jerry Sieve. *Along the Arizona Trail.* Englewood, Colo.: Westcliffe, 1998.

Fletcher, Colin. *The Man Who Walked through Time.* New York: Knopf, 1968.

———. *River: One Man's Journey Down the Colorado, Source to Sea.* New York: Knopf, 1997.

Ganci, Dave. *Hiking the Southwest.* San Francisco: Sierra Club Books, 1983.

Kutz, Jack. *Mysteries & Miracles of Arizona.* Corrales, N.M.: Rhombus, 1992.

Larson, Peggy. *A Sierra Club Naturalist's Guide to the Deserts of the Southwest.* San Francisco: Sierra Club Books, 1971.

McPhee, John. *Encounters with the Archdruid.* New York: Farrar, Straus and Giroux, 1971.

Muir, John. *Steep Trails, The Eight Wilderness-Discovery Books.* Seattle: The Mountaineers, 1992. (First published by Houghton Mifflin in 1918.)

Nash, Roderick. *Wilderness and the American Mind.* 3rd ed. New Haven, Conn.: Yale University Press, 1982.

Powell, J. W. *The Exploration of the Colorado River and Its Canyons.* New York: Dover, 1961. (First published as *Canyons of the Colorado* by Flood & Vincent in 1895.)

Sheridan, Thomas E. *Arizona: A History.* Tucson: University of Arizona, 1995.

Sikorsky, Robert. *Quest for the Dutchman's Gold.* Phoenix: Golden West, 1983.

Stegner, Wallace. *Beyond the Hundredth Meridian: John Wesley Powell and the Second Opening of the West.* New York: Houghton Mifflin, 1954.

Tighe, Kelly, and Susan Moran. *On the Arizona Trail: A Guide for Hikers, Cyclists & Equestrians.* Boulder, Colo.: Pruett, 1998.

Trimble, Marshall. *Arizona: A Cavalcade of History.* Tucson, Ariz.: Treasure Chest, 1989.

Watts, May Theilgaard, and Tom Watts. *Desert Tree Finder.* Berkeley, Calif.: Nature Study Guild, 1974.

Whitney, Stephen. *A Field Guide to the Grand Canyon.* New York: Quill, 1982.

INDEX

A

Abbey, Edward, 13, 52, 68–69, 82, 84, 128, 152, 195, 198, 219
Abbey's Road (Abbey), 219
A-Diamond Ranch, 87
Agassiz Peak, 164, 165
Agua Caliente Wash, 58
Ajax Peak, 93
Alamo Canyon, 92, 93, 95
Alder Saddle, 118
ALDHA-West (American Long Distance Hiking Association—West), 72
Alfalfa Well, 49
Aliens, illegal, 16–17
Anderson, Poul, 152
Anderson Mesa, 145, 146, 148
Anderson Tank, 173
Animal life, desert, 85
Animals. *See* specific animals
Annerino, John, 194
Antelope Peak, 75, 76, 83
Apache Indians, 100, 134
Apache Jump, 102
Arizona Snow Bowl, 165
Arizona Strip, 215
Arizona Trail, 14–15

Arizona Trail Association (ATA), 12, 15, 35, 69, 71, 92, 137, 169, 186, 243
Armored stink beetle, 86
Ash Creek, 53
Aspen Spring, 157, 165
Atlanta and Pacific Railroad, 156
AZ 87, 127
Aztec Mine, 33

B

Babbitt, Bruce, 169
Babbitt Ranches, 169
Babbitts General Store, 183
Backcountry Office, 178, 179, 204
Backpacker (magazine), 16
Barrel cactus, 59
Basho's, 152
Basin Region, 110
Bathtub Spring, 24, 27
Battle of Big Dry Wash, 134
Battleground Ridge, 135
Beale, Edward F., 156
Beale Wagon Road, 156
Bear Canyon, 61
Bear Spring, 122, 133
Bear Springs, 40

Benson, 51, 76
Beowulf, 159–162
Berger, Karen, 16
Bicknell, Pierpont Constable, 101
Big Casa Blanca Canyon, 40–41, 43
Big Mouth Billy Bass, 129
Black Sun (Abbey), 152, 219
Blair, Tony, 129
Bloodsucker Wash, 81
Blue Ridge, 135, 136
Book For All Seasons, A, 128
Bootlegger Well, 49
Boots, 236–237
Boulder Creek Trail, 119
Boulder Mountain, 107, 108, 109, 115
Box, The, 205, 206, 207
Box Canyon, 44
Boyce Thompson Arboretum, 102
Bradley Point, 203
Brasher, Chris, 186
Bray Creek, 133
Bright Angel Campground, 204
Bright Angel Canyon, 201, 204, 207,
    208, 209, 210, 211, 215
Bright Angel Creek, 200, 205, 209
Bright Angel Suspension Bridge, 198
Bright Angel Trail, 178, 187, 189, 190,
    191, 192, 206
Bright Angel Trail to the North Rim
    map, 188
    trail description, 187, 189–213
Brody Seep, 123
Brower, David, 195, 198
Brown's Peak, 117, 118
Brush Spring, 123
Brush Trail, 123
Brut (Layamon), 161
Buckhorn Creek, 115
Buckhorn Mountain, 116, 118
Buckhorn Ridge, 117, 118
Buckhout, Brad, 181–182

Buckhout, Karen, 182
Buckhout, Marc, 181–182
Buddha Temple, 194
Buffalo Park, 156
Bull Basin, 119
Bull Mountain, 119
Bullfrog Canyon, 124
Butterfield, John, 50
Butterfield Overland Stage,
    49–50

C

Cacti, 84
Café Espresso, 151
Camels, 156
Camp Grant Wash, 78
Canelo Hills, 28, 29, 30, 33, 74, 168
Canelo Pass, 30, 31, 33, 181
Cat Spring, 121
Catalina Camp, 66
Catalina Highway, 58, 60, 65–66
Cathedral Rock, 62
Central Highlands, 110
Chase Creek, 133
Cheops Pyramid, 194
Chinaman Trail, 42
Cholla, 31, 81–82, 83
Christmas Gift Mine, 33
Cienaga Creek, 45, 46, 48, 49, 77
Clear Creek, 201, 204
Clear Creek Trail, 199, 201, 204
Clinton, Bill, 129
Clothing, 239
CO Bar Ranch, 169, 170
Coconino Rim, 174
Collared peccaries, 28
Colorado Plateau, 110, 131
Colorado River, 178, 185, 189, 192,
    194, 195, 196, 198, 204, 218
Companions, hiking with, 97
Cooking equipment, 238

Cornwell, Patricia, 152

Coronado, Francisco Vasquez de, 18–19

Coronado National Forest, 44

Coronado National Memorial Visitor Center, 17, 19

Coronado to Patagonia
map, 20
trail description, 21–36

Cott Tank Enclosure, 32

Cottonwood Camp, 208, 210

Cottonwood Canyon, 109

Cottonwood Creek, 109–110

Cottonwood Spring, 109

Coyote Butte, 227, 229

Coyote Canyon, 228, 229, 230

Crane Lake, 219

Crest Trail, 22, 27, 181

Crook, George, 134

Crystal Spring, 218

D

Dan Saddle, 66, 122, 136

"Dead Skunk (in the Middle of the Road)," 133

Demaray Point, 203

Desert Solitaire (Abbey), 69, 82

Ditch Mountain, 43

Dog Lake, 219

Dominy, Floyd, 198

Dook'o'osliid, 158

Dragon Mountains, 30

Dry Lake Hills, 157

Duckett, Molly, 182

Dutch Woman's Butte, 110

Dutton, Clarence, 194

E

East Bray Creek, 133

East Canelo Hills, 31

East Cedar Tank, 169–170, 171

East Clear Creek, 135

East Rim Drive, 176

East Rim Trail, 183

East Rim View, 218, 219

East Verde River, 124–125, 134

Eating, 238, 241–242

Elden Mountain, 156

Elevation Mine, 33

Elk, 125–126

Elk Tank, 136

Empire Mountains, 49

Empire Ranch, 45

Empire-Cienaga Resource Conservation Area, 48

Encounters with the Archdruid (McPhee), 198

Equipment
clothing, 239
footwear, 236–237
key considerations, 235–236
kitchen gear, 238
miscellaneous gear, 240
packs, 238
for photography, 241
shelter, 237–238
sleeping bags, 238
umbrellas, 240
water containers, 238–239

F

Fears, dealing with, 39

Fire Lookout (Abbey), 219

Fires, forest, 138

Fish Canyon, 44

Fisher Point, 149

Flagstaff, 137, 140, 141, 147, 148, 149, 150, 151, 152, 153, 155, 163, 169, 172, 176, 181, 231, 232

Flagstaff, Pine to
map, 132
trail description, 131, 133–153

Flagstaff to the Grand Canyon
  map, 154
  trail description, 155–186
Flagstaff Urban Trail System, 149, 150
Fletcher, Colin, 13, 152, 194, 195, 198
Food, 241–242
Footwear, 236–237
Forest fires, 138
Four Peaks Mountain, 107–108, 109,
  115, 116, 117, 118, 122, 133
Four Peaks Trail, 115
Four Peaks Wilderness, 114, 117, 159
Francis of Assisi, Saint, 158
Freeman Road, 83
Fremont Peak, 163, 165
Fremont Saddle, 163, 164
Friedman, Kinky, 152

G
Garden Creek, 192
Garden Creek Canyon, 194
Gardner Canyon, 43
Gate Spring, 32
Gatlin, Will, 219
Gear. *See* Equipment
General Springs Cabin, 134
General Springs Canyon, 135
Gila River, 72, 73, 75, 83, 87, 88, 89,
  90, 91, 97
Glen Canyon, 194–196
Glen Canyon Action Network,
  195
Glen Canyon Institute, 195
Gold mining, 41–43, 99–101
Gonzales Tank, 138
Government Reservoir, 226
GPS (Global Positioning System), 137,
  142–143, 166
Grand Canyon, 14, 131, 135, 136, 172,
  173, 174, 175, 176, 177, 178, 179,
  180, 181, 182, 183, 184, 185, 186,

187, 189–194, 195, 196–198,
  200–201, 202, 203, 204, 207, 208,
  209, 210, 212, 213, 215, 216, 217,
  218, 219
Grand Canyon, Flagstaff to
  map, 154
  trail description, 155–186
Grand Canyon National Monument,
  160
Grand Canyon National Park, 217
Grand Canyon Village, 167, 171, 175,
  176, 184, 189, 202, 221
Grandview Entrance, Grand Canyon
  National Park, 175
Grandview Lookout, 175, 176, 218
Granite Spring, 115
Granite Springs Trail, 115
Grayback Hill, 87
Great American Desert, 84–85
"Great American Desert, The"
  (Abbey), 69
Great Unknown, The, 198
Grendel, 159–162
Gringo Gulch, 37
Guthrie, Woody, 52

H
Habitats, succession of, 26, 162–163
Hadji Ali, 156
Happy Valley, 54
Hardscrabble Mesa, 125
Harshaw Road, 33
Harts Butte, 44
Heaney, Seamus, 159
Heartbreak Ridge, 55
Hermit of the Superstitions, 104
High Country Inn, 126
Highline Trail, 131, 133, 134
Hogg, Frank, 71
Hopi Indians, 158
Hopi Spring, 123

Horse Camp, 123

Horse Lake, 146

Horse Ranch, 86

House Rock Valley, 218

Huachuca Mountains, 17, 19, 22, 26, 28, 29, 30, 35, 43, 182

Humphreys Peak, 158, 164, 166, 168

Hutch's Pool, 61, 62

I

I-10, 48, 49, 50, 51, 76

I-40, 149

Indian Gardens, 192, 193, 209

Indian Gardens Campground, 185

Inner Basin, 158, 163, 165

Inner Gorge, 193, 194, 196, 205

Isis Temple, 194

Italian Spring, 55, 57

Ives, Joseph, 184

J

Jacks Canyon, 137

Jacob Lake, 221, 223, 226

Jacob Lake Inn, 221

Javelinas, 28

Jimsonweed, 205

Joe's Canyon Trail, 21

Joe's Reservoir, 222, 226, 227

John Muir Trust, 130

Journey Home, The (Abbey), 69

K

Kachina Peaks Wilderness, 158

Kachina Trail, 165

Kaibab, definition of, 216

Kaibab National Forest, 172, 217

Kaibab Plateau, 215, 216, 217, 218, 219, 222, 226

Kanab, Utah, 221, 222, 223, 231

Kentucky Camp, 44, 45, 76

Kerouac, Jack, 52

Keyes, Alan, 128

Kitchen gear, 238

Klondike Spring, 108

Kollenborn, Tom, 100

Kunde Mountain, 33

L

Lake, The, 58

Lake Mary Road, 142, 145

Lake Powell, 194–196, 198, 231–232

Lawrence, Ed, 107

Layamon, 161

le Carre, John, 152

Leech, Paul, 72, 74, 93, 95, 112

Lemmon Creek, 65

Lew Tank, 166, 167

Lewis, C. S., 152

Life zones, 26, 162–163

Little Pine Flat, 119

Little Rincon Mountains, 53, 55

Lockwood Camp, 173

Lockwood Tank, 172

Lone Fire, 119

Lost Dutchman Gold Mine, 99–101, 102, 160

M

Man Who Walked through Time, The (Fletcher), 194

Manning Camp, 54, 55

Maps, 242

    Arizona, 6

    Bright Angel Trail to North Rim, 188

    Coronado to Patagonia, 20

    Flagstaff to the Grand Canyon, 154

    North Rim to Utah, 214

    Oracle to Superior, 70

    Patagonia to Oracle, 38

    Pine to Flagstaff, 132

    Superior to Pine, 98

Marble Canyon, 218

Mariposa Books, 34

Marshall Saddle, 65

Martin, Jim, 35, 69, 71, 72, 73, 74, 76, 83

Mather Campground, 176

Mazatzal, definition of, 122

Mazatzal Divide Trail, 121

Mazatzal Mountains, 66, 110, 114, 117, 121, 122, 125, 133, 232

Mazatzal Peak, 122, 123

Mazatzal Trail, 123

Mazatzal Wilderness, 120, 125, 159

McAneny, George, 44

McFarland Canyon, 121

McPhee, John, 198

Merriam, C. Hart, 162–163

Mescal, 49, 50, 51, 52

Mexican border, 18, 22, 23

Mexico, 22, 30

Mica Mountain, 55

Miller Creek Trail, 53

Miller Peak, 22, 54, 163, 181

Miller Peak Wilderness, 19, 22, 25, 28, 159

Miller Ranch, 53

Missouri Bill Hill, 169

Mistletoe Interpretation Trail, 175

Mogollon Plateau, 135

Mogollon Rim, 131, 133, 134, 135

Molino Basin, 58, 118

Molino Basin Campground, 58, 60

Monkey Wrench Gang, The (Abbey), 69, 128

Montana Mountain, 104, 106

Monte Vista Hotel, 150, 155

Montezuma Pass, 17–18, 22

Monument 102, 18, 22

Moqui Stage Station, 172

Mormon Lake, 136, 137, 139, 140, 141, 146, 169

Mount Humphreys, 139

Mount Lemmon, 60, 61, 62, 63, 67, 76

Mount Wrightson, 30, 37, 40, 43, 44

Mount Wrightson Wilderness, 40, 159

Muir, John, 42

Murray Trailhead, 220

N

Narrows, The, 47–48, 49

Nash, Roderick, 195

Native American Head Mountain, 33

Natural products, vs. synthetic, 143–144

Nature, seeing, 82–83

Navajo Indian Reservation, 232

Navajo Indians, 158

Navatekiaooi, 158

North American Desert, 84–85

North Canyon, 218

North Fork, 123

North Kaibab Trail, 101, 178, 204, 205, 209, 218

North Peak, 123

North Rim, 14, 136, 180, 183, 185–186, 189, 204, 208–209, 210, 212, 216, 223

North Rim, Bright Angel Trail to map, 188

trail description, 187, 189–213

North Rim Campground, 212

North Rim to Utah map, 214

trail description, 215–230

North Saddle Mountain, 33

North Sycamore Creek, 133

Northern Mystery, 19

O

Oak Tree Canyon, 44, 45

Old Florence Road, 86

On The Road (Kerouac), 52

Oracle, 35, 51, 52, 65, 66, 67–68, 71, 72, 73, 74, 75, 76, 87, 95, 96, 105, 127
Oracle, Patagonia to
  map, 38
  trail description, 37, 39–69
Oracle Ridge, 66
Oracle State Park, 69, 71
Oracle to Superior
  map, 70
  trail description, 71–97
Oza Butte, 215

P

Pack weight, 77, 240–241
Packs, 238
Page, 221, 222, 223, 231
Paria Canyon-Vermilion Cliffs Wilderness, 231
Parker Canyon, 29
Parker Canyon Lake, 28, 29, 113
Patagonia, 33–35, 40, 51, 74, 76, 96, 127
Patagonia, Coronado to
  map, 20
  trail description, 21–36
Patagonia Silver Mine, 34
Patagonia to Oracle
  map, 38
  trail description, 37, 39–69
Peralta family, 100
Phantom Ranch, 200, 201, 202, 204, 205, 208, 209, 210
Phoenix, 11–12, 87, 99, 113, 117, 119, 122, 231, 232
Photography equipment, 241
Picketpost Mountain, 93, 95, 102
Picketpost Trailhead, 99
Pigeon Spring, 114, 115, 118, 119, 128
Pima Indians, 100
Pine, 120, 124, 125, 126, 127, 128, 130, 131, 135, 136, 140, 141, 147, 150

Pine, Superior to
  map, 98
  trail description, 99–130
Pine Creek, 107, 108
Pine Grove Hill, 141
Pine Spring, 133, 139
Pine to Flagstaff
  map, 132
  trail description, 131, 133–153
Piñon Mountain, 115
Place of Snow on the Very Top, 158
Plant life, desert, 84, 102
Plants. *See* specific plants
Poison Creek, 133
Polles Mesa, 125
Powell, John Wesley, 198, 205
Prime Lake, 146
Pronghorn, 146
Pumice mining, 158
Pusch Ridge Wilderness, 61, 159

Q

Quests, 160–161

R

Range Region, 110
Ransome, Arthur, 80
Reading, love of, 152
Reavis, Elisha M., 104, 106
Red Bank Well, 32
Red Hills Trail, 123
Red Ridge, 66, 67
Red River, 196
Redington Pass, 57
Redington Pass Road, 57, 58
Redrock Canyon, 32
Redwall, 197, 210–211
Reef of Rocks, 66, 67
Reevis Canyon, 106
Reevis Creek, 104, 106
Reevis Gap, 104, 107

Reevis Grave, 104
Reevis Ranch, 104
Reevis Saddle, 104, 106
Reevis Trail Canyon, 104
Reevis Valley, 104, 106, 107
Ribbon Creek, 208
Ribbon Falls, 208
Rim Café and Motel, 126, 127, 128,
    129, 141
Rincon Mountain Wilderness, 53, 159
Rincon Mountains, 36, 44, 49, 52, 53,
    54, 55, 56, 57, 58, 62, 77
Rincon Peak, 55
Rio Colorado, 196
Ripsey Ranch, 86
Ripsey Wash, 86
Roads, problems of, 37, 39
Roaring Springs, 209, 217
Roaring Springs Canyon, 209, 210, 212
Roaring Springs Cliffs, 210
Rogers Canyon, 106
Rogers Creek, 106
Rogers Trough, 106
Rogers Trough Trailhead, 106
Romero Pass, 61, 62
Roosevelt, 109, 141
Roosevelt, Theodore, 160, 195
Roosevelt Dam, 112, 113
Roosevelt Lake, 109, 110, 112, 113,
    118, 120, 141
Route 66, 150, 155, 156
Running Wild (Annerino), 194
Russell Tank, 173, 174, 175
Russell Wash, 173, 174

S
Sabino Basin, 61
Sabino Creek, 61
Sacred datura, 205
Sacred Mountain of the West, 158
Saddle Mountain, 121

Saddle Mountain Trail, 121
Saddle Ridge, 125
Saguaro National Park, 54
Saguaro skeletons, 77
Salt River, 112, 113
Salt River Canyon, 115
Salt River Project, 112
Salt River Valley, 113
San Francisco Mountain, 158
San Francisco Peaks, 14, 26, 136,
    138–139, 141, 145, 151, 153, 155,
    156, 158, 162–163, 164, 165, 167,
    168, 169, 172, 215, 232
San Francisco Street, 155
San José Peak, 22
San Pedro River Valley, 19
San Rafael Valley, 30
Sandals, 236–237
Sansimon Mine, 33
Santa Catalina Mountains, 36, 56, 57,
    58, 60, 63–64, 66, 67, 118, 136, 156
Santa Cruz Mine, 33
Santa Fe Railroad, 150, 156, 184
Santa Rita Mountains, 30, 35–36, 40,
    41, 43, 44, 49, 62, 142
Santa Rita Water and Mining
    Company, 41–42, 44
Saway, Steve, 15, 32
Schas, Jake, 54, 72, 73, 74, 75, 76, 77,
    78, 79, 80, 81, 86, 87, 88, 89, 90, 92,
    95, 97, 109, 120, 128, 140, 141, 168,
    169, 170, 171, 173, 174, 176, 177,
    178, 179, 180, 212, 215, 218, 219,
    220, 221, 222, 223, 224, 225, 226,
    227, 229, 230, 231
Schultz Creek, 157
Schultz Pass, 157
Schultz Tank, 157
Schultz Trail, 157
Scotia Canyon, 28, 181
Service, Robert, 161

Seven Cities of Cibola, 19
Shakespeare, William, 97, 152
Sheep Creek Trail, 121
Shelter, 237–238
Shewalter, Dale, 15
Shoes, 236–237
Sierra Ancha Mountains, 109
Sierra Club, 195
Sky islands, 26, 189
Sleeping bags, 238
Sleeping pads, 237–238
Snead, Larry, 12, 15–16, 71
Socks, 237
Sonoran Desert, 26, 66, 72, 75, 79, 80, 84–85, 86, 99, 106, 110
South Kaibab Trail, 204
South Rim, 174, 180–181, 187, 189, 190, 192, 203, 204, 209, 215
Southern Pacific Railroad, 48
Stars, 80
Statistics, walk, 235
Stetson, James, 41, 44
Strawberry, 126
Summerhaven, 60, 65, 76
Summit Trick Tank, 225, 226
Sumner Butte, 201
Sumner Wash, 201, 204
Sunflower, 119, 120, 128
Sunnyside Canyon, 27–28, 181
Sunnyside Creek, 28
Supai Tunnel, 212
Superior, 95–97, 101, 102, 105, 124, 127, 169, 176
Superior, Oracle to
    map, 70
    trail description, 71–97
Superior to Pine
    map, 98
    trail description, 99–130
Superstition Mountain Historical Society, 100

Superstition Mountains, 66, 99, 100, 101, 102, 104, 105, 106, 109, 114, 115, 117, 232
Superstition Wilderness, 106, 159
Switzer Canyon Drive, 155
Sycamore Canyon, 61
Sycamore Canyon Reservoir, 61
Sycamore Reservoir Trail, 61
Synthetic products, *vs.* natural, 143–144

T

"Take Me To The River," 129
Tarps, 237
Tater Canyon, 219
Tecolote Ranch, 86
Teddy bears, 160
Telephone companies, 182–183
Tempest, The (Shakespeare), 97
Temporal Gulch, 39
Thicket Spring Trail, 121
Thomas, Julia, 101
Thompson Spring, 110
Thorn, Denise, 50–51, 69, 93, 97, 120, 127, 151, 174, 181, 182, 183, 186, 223, 233
Thorn, Hazel, 50–51, 151, 174, 223, 233
Thornapple, 205
Thorne, Abraham, 100
Time, 196–198
Tonto Creek, 113
Tonto National Forest, 93
Tonto Platform, 193, 194, 201, 203, 204
Tortilla Mountains, 86
Tower of Set, 194
Trail statistics, 235
Transept, The, 215
Transition Province, 110

Tub Ranch, 171, 172
Tucson, 13, 16, 43, 60, 61, 67
Tunnel Spring, 43
Two Bar Mountain, 109, 115
Two Bar Ridge, 109, 111

U

Umbrellas, 240
University of Northern Arizona,
    150
Upper North Canyon, 218
US 60, 96, 102
US 89, 232
Utah, 218, 220, 224, 226, 227, 229, 230
Utah, North Rim to
    map, 214
    trail description, 215–230

V

Vail Lake, 146
Vermilion Cliffs, 218
Vineyard Trail, 115
Vishnu schist, 196

W

Waddell, Bert, 45, 76
Wainwright, Loudon, III, 133
Walk statistics, 235
Walker Basin, 40
Walking, pleasures of, 13
Wall Creek, 208
Walnut Canyon, 88, 90, 147,
    149
Walnut Spring, 107, 108
Waltz, Jacob, 100–101, 160
Water, concern for, 12, 15–16
Water containers, 238–239
Watson, Bill, 15, 32, 93, 96, 108, 109,
119, 120, 124, 127, 128, 137, 174,
    175, 226, 227
Weatherford, John, 163
Weatherford Canyon, 157
Weatherford Trail, 163, 176
Weaver's Needle, 102
Weigles Butte, 44
Wells Fargo, 50
West Canelo Hills, 31, 32
West Chase Creek, 133
Whetstone Mountains, 30, 43, 49
White Canyon, 91, 92
White Canyon Wilderness, 91, 94, 97,
    99, 159, 179
White Horse Hills, 168
White Rock Spring, 125
Whiterock Mesa, 125
Whitford Canyon, 104
Wilderness
    defining, 161–162
    in literature, 159–161
    preservation of, 130, 144–145,
    194–196
Wilderness Act of 1964, 130, 159,
    161
Wilderness and the American Mind
    (Nash), 195
Wilderness of Rocks, 63–64, 156
Wildlife. *See* specific animals
Winter Holiday (Ransome), 80
World's Smallest Museum,
    101–102

Y

Yaqui Ridge, 21–22

Z

Zoroaster Temple, 193, 194, 198